D1242091

AMERICA FACES SOUTH

AMERICA
FACES SOUTH

By
T. R. YBARRA

DODD, MEAD & COMPANY
NEW YORK   1940

Spanish America

PRINTED IN THE U. S. A. BY
Quinn & Boden Company, Inc.
BOOK MANUFACTURERS
RAHWAY,   NEW JERSEY

To PENNY

The author acknowledges with thanks the permissions granted him by the editors of *The New York Times* and *Collier's Weekly* to use in this book material originally printed in those periodicals.

ONE MOMENT, PLEASE:

NEVER have I succeeded in visualizing the twenty republics of Latin America as something definitely this or that, to the exclusion of everything else.

Never, for instance, have they presented themselves to my consciousness as a business proposition pure and simple, just a mess of unadulterated economics, which is what they are to certain owlish friends of mine.

Never have they seemed merely a gorgeous blend of roses, revolutions and Ferdinand the Bull.

Never have they appeared before my mind's eye solely as something to be used for or against Franklin D. Roosevelt.

Never have they been to me a reason for sighing lugubriously at the thought that, when I was in college, I didn't prefer reading Prescott to cheering maniacally at football games.

Never!

Therefore, in this book economists are going to get only just so many statistics per chapter—not one iota more. Persons of incurably political appetites will be chucked, here and there, into a welter of volcanoes and cuisine and señoritas. Seekers after doubloons minted in Spain by Spanish kings will unearth "Aski" marks made in Germany by Hjalmar Schacht. Those who look for romance will find Cordell Hull.

"Your book about Latin America is just a hodgepodge!" will be the low growl leveled at me by one hundred per cent politicos and economicos and romanticos and historicos.

But I'll come right back at them with:

"So is Latin America!"

AUTHOR'S NOTE

This book was completed just before the outbreak of the war in Europe. Careful reading of its contents after hostilities there had started necessitated only a few unimportant changes and omissions. What will happen to Latin America in a number of fields on account of the war, notably in the relationship between the Latin American republics and overseas nations, is largely a matter of pure conjecture. For this reason the sections of this book which deal with this relationship as it existed early this year have been allowed to stand practically unaltered.

T. R. Y.

New York, September 25, 1939.

CONTENTS

ALONG Pennsylvania Avenue in Washington last March the trumpets of our new Good Neighbor Policy toward Latin America blared loudly; figuratively speaking, the Good Neighbor bass drums boomed; and the champions of Good Neighborliness-Pointed-South marched round and round, bursting with enthusiasm over a victory just won, and cheering madly in anticipation of more triumphs.

The victory already in the bag was this:

After a round of pleasant conversations between that very charming and suave gentleman, Senhor Oswaldo Aranha, Foreign Minister of big, pro-American Brazil—who had come up from Rio to Washington expressly to be conversed with by President Roosevelt and Secretary of State Hull—it was officially announced that the United States would extend to Brazil immediately a credit of $19,200,000 and, subsequently, create a reserve fund of $50,000,000 for establishing a Brazilian Central Bank. Furthermore, it was stated at the same time, the Export-Import Bank of Washington would take steps to facilitate payments to American exporters by Brazilian importers of American products.

"Boom!" went the Good Neighbor drums. "Tantantara!" went the Good Neighbor trumpets! But, into the midst of all this rejoicing, Argentina, least good of our Good Neighbors, suddenly dropped a big, bad bomb.

From Buenos Aires came an official report that the Argentine government had earmarked for exportation to our leading totalitarian rival in Latin America, Nazi Germany, 100,000 metric tons of wheat and 8,000 metric tons of wool, to be bartered—yes, *bartered*, right in the teeth of Anti-Barterist Number One, Cordell Hull!—for a big lot of German locomotives and steel freight cars and sleeping cars. Simultaneously, that same government, just for good measure, announced that it had concluded an additional barter deal, this time with our other totalitarian rival, Fascist Italy. It was as if the administration at Buenos Aires had said to the administration at Washington: "So you want to play ball with Brazil, do you? So the Brazilians are your favorite little white-haired boys, are they? All right. We don't like the Brazilians. We'll show you, Mr. Hull. Barter, barter, who wants to barter?"

A stinging blow for the idea of a Pan-American *Entente Cordiale*, which Secretary Hull is trying so hard to put over in Latin America. (Somebody of my acquaintance, by the way, calls it the Entente Cordell.)

And it was not the only blow.

Washington watch-dogs, including Senator Borah, promptly got busy. President Roosevelt, they barked, must not be given a free hand to pump taxpayers' money into Latin America. That Brazilian deal, they excitedly told the American public, was only the first instalment of a lot of contemplated loans to Latin American countries which, if not checked, might run into hundreds of millions of dollars. Congress, they insisted, must tie strings to any such generosity—especially since most of Latin America (including Senhor Aranha's Brazil) was in default to American investors on big bond issues, floated in golden pre-depression days.

Was Brazil going to resume payment on her slice of those bonds, now that Senhor Aranha had returned to his native land with such a gorgeous pocketful of American cash? That question, also others equally pertinent, were barked by the watch-dogs, while Good Neighborites indignantly barked back at them that, if we didn't buy ourselves into the Latin American market, we'd wake up some morning to find ourselves bought out of it by the Germans.

By gracefully announcing, early last summer, that payment would be resumed on her defaulted bonds, Brazil silenced the Washington Watch-dog Brigade. That is, she did for the time being. They are still keeping wide open eyes on the President, the Secretary of State, and other would-be lavish lenders of our money.

But, let us leave them, glowering and growling, and return to the purely foreign section of the Good Neighbor Policy's worries—a big enough headache in itself!—as exemplified by that bomb thrown by unneighborly Argentina. It taught overhasty Good Neighborites, busily celebrating in Washington, a brusque and bitter lesson, viz.:

You can't court a continent.

You most certainly cannot.

It was Comrade Maxim Litvinov, I think, when he was Soviet Russia's pudgy and pugnacious Commissar for Foreign Affairs a few years ago, who remarked, "Peace is indivisible." Today, there are Americans, particularly in administration circles at Washington, who feel much the same way about the sort of relationship that ought to exist between the United States and the twenty republics of Latin America.

"Our Good Neighbor Policy," they say in effect, "is indivisible."

Well, in the time that has elapsed since Comrade Litvinov bestowed his little aphorism on a peace-hungry world, events have not exactly borne him out. There would be difficulty, for instance, in eliciting enthusiasm about his dictum from, say, an Ethiopian, a Chinese, a Czech or an Albanian. Similarly, things have happened in our part of the universe tending to show that it is futile for us to try to win the friendship of Latin America by treating it as a whole, as an indivisible unit.

For it is nothing of the sort. Instead, it is highly divisible —divisible, in fact, into twenty parts, as many parts as it has republics. Each of these, if it is to be won by the Roosevelt-Hull Good Neighbor Policy, must be courted separately.

Latin America, like Europe, is almost entirely lacking in the elements making for continental solidarity. To suppose that any blanket formula of Good Neighborliness can win over all of its inhabitants to pro-Americanism is a fallacy.

Is there a single, comprehensive, honeyed formula of courtship which would be equally applicable to France and Germany? *There is not.* And that goes, on our side of the Atlantic, to cite only one of many examples, for those two glowering South American rivals, Brazil and Argentina, as we learned last March when Uncle Sam had that disagreeable experience of stretching out his good neighborly hand to feed cash and other financial comfort to Brazil and of having Argentina sneak up on him and bite the hand that was feeding the Brazilians.

There must be one approach for Brazil, another for the Argentine, eighteen others for the remaining Latin American republics. Argentina and Brazil are basically divergent. So are their Latin American sister nations. Our Brazilian and our Argentine relations stand on a different footing. So do our relations with our eighteen other Good (more or less) Neighbors.

For example, Brazil buys heavily from us and sells more heavily to us. On the other hand, we sell comparatively little to the Argentine and buy less from her.

Brazilians like us. Argentines don't.

Brazilians understand us. Argentines don't.

Racially speaking, Brazil and Argentina are poles apart.

Those are only a few of the many divergences between these two most important South American nations which doom a common formula of approach to almost certain defeat. And there are just as many divergences among the rest of the republics to the south of us.

They are not homogeneous. They have few points of contact. One doesn't often find them getting together in affectionate embraces and singing close harmony about brotherly love.

Latin America shows, in some ways, even less international cohesion than chaotic, disrupted Europe.

Almost all Europeans, for instance, though ready to fly at each others' throats at the mere mention of any one of a dozen ideological and political and territorial matters, feel in common the attraction of several venerable centers of European culture and focal points in European history. Practically every one of them who is able to travel at all wants to go to Paris—and usually does. Almost as many are drawn to London. And what native of Europe, despite Fascism and every other Ism, feels no urge to see Rome before he dies?

But there is nothing like that in Latin America.

Though it has an enormous and astounding metropolis— Buenos Aires—with a population, including outlying suburbs, of something like three million people, that metropolis is largely unknown to Latin Americans, with the exception of the Argentines themselves and a limited trickle of visitors from nearby countries—Uruguay, Paraguay, Chile, and (to some extent) Brazil. Barring these, it is safe to say that there is *hardly one Latin American acquainted with Buenos Aires to one hundred who know Paris.*

Ask a Venezuelan, a Guatemalan, a Peruvian, or a Mexican: "Do you want to go some day to Buenos Aires?" and in all likelihood he will answer, "Not especially."

And there is no other city in South or Central America, or in the lands bordering the Caribbean, possessing a drawing power remotely comparable with the power exercised over Europeans in general by Paris, London and Rome—not historic Lima, not beautiful Rio, not gay Havana. Nor is there, in the whole length and breadth of the twenty countries covering the southern part of our continent, any city which interests the natives of those countries as much as New York (and, to a lesser degree, Washington) interests Americans, even those living thousands of miles away from our metropolis and our capital.

That is one reason which keeps Latin America from feeling like a continent; that is one reason why courting it as a continent is out of the question. There are others. For instance:

Most Americans think of Latin America as *Spanish America.* They forget that, in two of its nations, Spanish is a foreign language. When reminded of this, they have a way of shrugging their shoulders and dismissing the subject with a careless "Well, if eighteen of the twenty republics down there speak Spanish, who cares if the other two don't?"

But there is good reason for caring.

The total area of the twenty republics of Latin America is, roughly, 8,000,000 square miles. In this vast expanse of territory Spanish is spoken in countries covering 4,600,000 square miles—*less than three-fifths of the whole.* Portuguese is used by the inhabitants of almost the entire remaining area, represented by gigantic Brazil, which, with its 3,285,000 square miles, is larger than the United States (not including Alaska). Besides Brazil, there is another republic south of the United States where Spanish is not spoken—Haiti—which has an area of 10,000 square miles and whose people speak French.

The total population of the twenty nations of Latin America, so often lumped together in our minds as Spanish America, is somewhat less than 125,000,000. Of these, *only 60 per cent, or three-fifths*, inhabiting eighteen of those nations, speak Spanish. Of the other two, the colossal republic of Brazil has a Portuguese-speaking population of something like 45,000,000, or 36 per cent of the total population of Latin America—*more than one-third*. Haiti is peopled by about 3,000,000 French-speaking inhabitants. Adding up Brazilians and Haitians, we get a solid mass of people in "Spanish America" who do *not* speak Spanish, of roughly, 48,000,000, as against a Spanish-speaking mass of about 77,000,000. In other words, those using Spanish as their native tongue comprise a total *only 60 per cent greater* than the total of those who do not use Spanish.

Yet some foreign business firms address all inhabitants of South America in the language of Spain—including Brazilians, who are intensely proud of their Portuguese descent. A Brazilian's interest in Spain and Spanish history has nothing personal about it. On the other hand, all that concerns Portugal hits him where he lives. Brazilians never forget that early last century the Portuguese royal family, driven from Lisbon by Napoleon, transferred itself across the ocean to Brazil, then a Portuguese colony, and reigned over Portugal (as best it could) from Rio de Janeiro, the Brazilian capital. Later, moreover, a scion of that same family erected Brazil into an empire, which his subjects always proudly considered an off-shoot of the mother-country, though that scion's first act was to declare the independence of Brazil from its Portuguese masters.

In the restaurants of Rio French, Italian and German wines are offered at prices showing plainly that their importers have been obliged to pay a high duty on them. But Portuguese wines—not only world-renowned Port, but brands such as Collares, Serradayres, etc., known, in Europe, only in Portugal—may be had at most reasonable rates. Which proves that the pro-Portuguese leanings of Brazilians have caused their government to scale down the duties on such wines to figures far below those assessed on other foreign vintages.

This helps to make understandable the anger of Brazilian merchants when they get letters from abroad in Spanish. Some of them, indeed, have been known to throw such missives, amid explosive and volcanic Portuguese comment, into the nearest waste-basket. It is much better to send to Brazil letters in English rather than in Spanish, for in that case they will be promptly translated into Portuguese as a matter of office routine, without rubbing any touchy Latins the wrong way.

The same, with modifications, applies to Haiti. Better, far better, to write a Haitian in English than in Spanish. For he is as proud of the connection of his country with France as a Brazilian is of the Portuguese past of Brazil. And he gets annoyed at being classed with Spanish Americans just because his native land is sandwiched in between the Spanish-speaking Dominican Republic and Cuba, and ringed around by Spanish-speaking Mexico, Central America, Colombia and Venezuela.

Then there is the racial angle:

You cannot use the same formula for impressing, say, Guatemala, whose people are overwhelmingly of Indian blood, and Costa Rica, where you can't find an Indian or near-Indian with a spy-glass.

You won't get very far if you use the same line of approach in the Argentine, where practically everybody is white, and in Haiti, where practically nobody isn't black.

The reactions of the millions of Mexico's Indians to siren songs from Washington will differ widely from those of Uruguayans of pure European stock, and from those of the varying blends of white, brown and black, from the Rio Grande to Cape Horn, with whom we want to do business. All these different racial elements present a tough problem. Only a policy combining caution and tact and flexibility and understanding and humanity can solve it. In this connection it is well to recall the recent remark of an Argentine statesman, apropos of the Roosevelt-Hull vision of continental solidarity in Latin America: "We Argentines feel more affinity with European nations than with some of the Indian republics of the American Continent."

And here is another snag in the path of courting a continent:

Every one of the twenty nations to the South of us is classed as a republic. "Ha!" exclaim unthinking advocates of the continental approach. "That means they're all democracies. Let's court them as such." Whereupon they rush blithely over the Caribbean, dreaming beautiful dreams of the great democracy of the north clasping the hands of the twenty democracies of the south, with the Southern Cross shining overhead and the Milky Way bathing the lovely picture in glamorous ghostly light, and run smack into a nasty dictator, who succeeded one just as nasty ten years ago, and is slated to be succeeded ten years hence by one even nastier, none of whom ever heard of democracy and thinks the national treasury of his country was expressly created for defraying his tremendous private expenses.

Of course, this won't always happen—and it won't happen half as often as in wicked pre-Good Neighbor Policy days.

Nevertheless, in Latin America, there is little democracy and much dictatorship. In fact, some of the republics there have had so little experience with the former that they wouldn't know it if they saw it. After years of seeing dictators marching in and out of their presidential palaces, they are inclined to accept dictatorship as the normal form of government.

In the majority of these countries several generations of intensive education will be needed before bodies of citizens can be created capable of giving their native lands genuinely democratic administrations.

Little Costa Rica is the most democratic of the lot. The people of that remarkable republic have actually succeeded to a considerable extent in making their government give them what they desire—and they desire, most emphatically, democracy. Costa Ricans have gone their own democratic way through decades of dictatorship in neighboring Central American countries. And they show no signs of changing.

In the other nineteen southern republics, democracy has had a rough time. Though in all of them politicians profess devotion to it, and the people really want it, the supply of democracy still lags woefully behind the demand. Even in progressive Argentina, even in little Uruguay with its advanced social legislation, even in Venezuela, which is just shaking off the memory of the Castro-Gomez dictatorships, which covered, consecutively, more than a third of a century, nobody can tell when a dictator will suddenly jump out of the bushes and blandly put the government in his pocket.

PATTIN' THE LATIN

Some foreign visitors to a Latin American country under a dictator (whom local conditions, probably, have imposed on that country far more than the dictator has imposed himself on it) are too much inclined to jump to erroneous conclusions. Being admirers of democracy, they naturally dislike the idea of dictatorship. Now, among the natives whom they meet, there will doubtless be some who hate the local dictator. These immediately pour into the ears of strangers tales of dictatorial iniquities, many of which are probably true, for Latin American dictators are not usually conspicuous for dovelike traits.

The visitor—unless he is very much from Missouri—tends to leap to the conclusion that, since his informants are opposed to the dictator, they must necessarily be opposed to dictatorship. The truth, however, in most cases, is that they are merely paying lip-service to democracy, with that flow of meaningless rhetoric which comes without effort to so many Latin Americans.

Such persons, as a rule, are simply the *outs* and the dictator and his pals the *ins,* those being the only political classifications with real meaning in the general run of Latin American lands. The foreign visitor becomes enthusiastic for the *outs* (of that particular moment) and prays for the speedy triumph of the revolution which (he has been told, sotto voce, in dim corners of cafés) is being concocted against the dictator. He fails to realize the sad truth that, if the revolutionists win, they will become the *ins,* and the dictator's entourage will become the *outs,* and will promptly start plotting to become the *ins* again, behind a façade of manifestoes and proclamations couched in language of such ultra-democratic grandiloquence as to enchant the heart of a Thomas Jefferson—provided he didn't look behind the façade.

Which reminds me of a story.

My father was a native of Venezuela. In his youth that republic was turbulent and revolution-ridden; and he, having chosen a military career, saw plenty of rough-and-tumble fighting and hard campaigning. Once, while he was leading a night march through a desolate region, in which an immense chorus of frogs was croaking a lugubrious accompaniment to the tramp of the soldiers, a private stepped out of the ranks, came to the side of my father's horse, saluted, and asked:

"General, do you know what the frogs say?"

"No."

"Well, you see, there are two big political parties in the Frog Republic. One of them is called *Tunga*, the other *Tungará*. Now, if you listen, you will hear the adherents of each of these parties alternately croaking its name."

My father listened: Sure enough:

"*Tunga!*"

"*Tungará!*"

"*Tungará—Tunga—Tunga—Tungará!*"

"And now listen carefully, general," continued the soldier, "and you will hear the frogs who have no political affiliations, and are fed up with the eternal pointless political noises of the rest, croak:

"*Tunga's the same as Tungará!*"

My father listened. From a hollow close to the road came, in a disgusted, bass croak:

"*Lo mismo Tunga que Tungará!*"

"Just like Venezuela, isn't it, general?" commented the soldier. And, with another salute, he dropped back into the ranks.

Tunga and Tungará still fight for supremacy in much of Latin America. And it would be well for visiting foreigners, who get all excited because the *outs* aren't in, and the *ins* aren't out, to calm themselves by repeating:

"*Lo mismo Tunga que Tungará!*"

And here is something else that may be useful to those threatened with an attack of snap judgments about Latin America:

Suppose a really decent, democratic, patriotic man becomes President of a Latin American country which has hardly ever known anything but dictatorship. Being decent and patriotic, he decides to govern democratically; to stage, at the end of his regular constitutional term, an absolutely fair and free election, to determine whether he is to have another term.

Taking advantage of the fairness of that election, his enemies —the president not having encircled the polling booths with bayonets and thus made voting against him a matter of high adventure—proceed to win the election. Down from his high office that decent, patriotic president must step, to be replaced by a regulation hey-hand-me-over-the-national-treasury dictator, who immediately lays plans to stay president just as long as the traffic will bear, without recourse to constitutionalism, congress, or anything whatsoever except sheer dictatorial nerve. And his cronies hold their sides with laughter at the thought of how stupid the previous president was in staging that free election and thus greasing the toboggan-slide for himself.

In other words: by using democratic methods that patriotic president cut short his stay in office and thus *furthered the cause of dictatorship* in his native land; whereas, had he remained president by dictatorial methods he would have *furthered the cause of democracy*. Latin America is full of such paradoxes.

[13]

Still another point of divergence among Latin Americans, which bars adopting the same approach to all of them, is the fact that some of them like us and some don't.

In Cuba there is not only a considerable liking for us but every year brings more genuine understanding of our ways of talking, thinking and acting. Indeed, we seem to have pierced through the outer shell of the Cuban and got at something resembling his real self more than we have in our dealings with any of the rest of our southern neighbors.

There is also distinct approval of Americans and comprehension of their ways in a growing number of the rest of our nearer neighbors, especially in four out of the five republics of Central America, and in Panama, Colombia and Venezuela. The fifth Central American nation, Nicaragua, still remembers the occupation of its territory by our marines, and still looks somewhat askance at us. But this feeling is waning.

Of our other immediate neighbors, Mexico is one of the least pro-American; and, in Haiti and the Dominican Republic, unpleasant memories of American occupation days (as in Nicaragua), still smoulder. But the Good Neighbor Policy of the last six years is helping to allay them.

Brazil has long been a good friend of ours, largely because of our great importance as a purchaser of Brazilian coffee. In a number of other South American nations—despite occasional outbursts of resentment, in which old terms such as "Yankee Imperialism" are bandied about in newspapers and conversations—the attitude toward the United States is growing every day, in every way, better and better.

But in Argentina, many of the natives definitely do not like us. And most of them carry a chip on their shoulders—in three shifts a day, of eight hours each.

For one thing, the Argentinos are jealous of the Brazilians

—so when we pat Brazilian backs, off goes the Argentine chip from the Argentine shoulder. Though there are 45,000,000 Brazilians against Argentina's total population of 13,000,000, the Argentines think that Brazil gets much more credit than she deserves as South America's greatest nation.

"We are the greatest," growl the Argentinos. *"We, only we,* among the inhabitants of the twenty countries down here, have achieved colossal success, and are really progressive, and have amassed wealth, and fought our way upward to the unstinted respect of the world's nations. Brazilians—bah!"

So, when we made that recent deal with Brazil (without thinking of possible repercussions in Argentina) those in the know were not in the least surprised when Argentina countered by bartering wheat and wool for German railway equipment—the surprise, for them, would have been if Argentina had *not* done so. *You can't court a continent.*

* * *

Diplomats and business men.

Those are the front line shock troops for the battle of winning Latin American good will. They ought to be hand-picked. If they are not, they can do us more harm in less time than any other American article of export.

Nobody has a better chance of helping along Washington's Good Neighbor Policy than an American ambassador or minister. Besides these, every Counselor of Embassy, every secretary and attaché, every consul and vice-consul in a Latin American republic, is an Ambassador-in-Miniature from the United States to that republic. If they show tact; if they work hard; if they study local problems; if they know how to become popular; if they are unprejudiced and adaptable; if they practice politeness and enjoy sociability, they will enhance, to an unbelievable degree, the status, in the country where they are stationed, of the "Great Republic of the North."

On the other hand, if they are the wrong sort, they can raise the devil with our prestige. It is folly, for example, to send to Latin America the sort of la-di-da diplomat, whom Hugh Gibson, our witty ex-ambassador in Rio, called "cookie pushers."

To help along Good Neighborliness, our diplomats should be conversant with a lot of things besides afternoon tea etiquette; and the proper sort of attire for every hour of the day or night; and who should sit next to whom at table; and who shouldn't sit there at all; and all that sort of social lore.

Latin America, fortunately, does not often play such havoc among budding American sprigs of diplomacy as do some European foreign lands; for south of the Rio Grande aren't any kings graciously responding to right-angled bows from our representatives, no haughty noble dames waiting for cookies to be pushed at them by the highly manicured hand of Percival Popinjay, Third Secretary of Legation.

Even in Latin America, however, Percival flourishes here and there—even in Latin America, far from the really nerve-racking points of etiquette and the truly brain-shaking questions of precedence, he simpers and smirks—even there, at times, he manages to arouse the profane wrath of hard-boiled visitors from the United States, like the one who, after meeting such a youth, bellowed: "The American Foreign Service is a finishing school for young Americans who have shown promise as snobs!"

But Percivals are few and far between—thank the Lord!

As to the proper way of doing business in Latin America, every head of an American concern desirous of selling its products down there should first base his campaign on a realization that business men in each of the twenty republics to the south of us have special characteristics, special commercial problems, special prejudices and sympathies, special ideas as to terms of payment, etc., etc., and should, therefore, be approached in a way implying a comprehension of all these special items. Too complicated? Maybe. But anyone who knows the game will tell you that if we Americans don't cultivate pattin' the Latin, the Germans will get the business.

Next, American exporters and would-be exporters should ask every man whom they intend to send southward two questions: "Do you like foreigners?" and "Do you get along with foreigners?" If the answer to one of these questions, or both, is in the negative, that man had better be kept at home. He may have plenty of business ability, plenty of capacity for applying it in his own country, but he won't do for Latin America. That may sound harsh. It's true, though—and the Germans know it's true.

In the Argentine, it's the English. . . .

The representative of a big American firm of machinery manufacturers entered the lounge of his hotel in Buenos Aires, threw himself tragically into a chair beside me, and just sat there—in black, indignant silence.

"What's the matter?"

"The nerve of those guys. . . ."

"What guys?"

"The colossal, unmitigated, unreasonable, hidebound nerve. . . ."

"Of whom?"

"The partners of that Argentine concern I visited this morning."

"Well?"

"The blasted, blank-blank-blankety—"

"What did they do?"

"Nothing!"

"What did they say?"

"Of all the pig-headed, double-distilled—"

"WHAT—DID—THEY—SAY?"

"Plenty."

"What?"

"This: We'll buy machinery from you on one condition."

"Well?"

"That it is made in England."

There's the kind of thing we are up against in Latin America. Just as the British are entrenched in Argentina, the Germans are elsewhere. And the Italians are entrenched in some places. Also the Japanese. And native prejudices and sympathies are entrenched all over the place. In order to beat the Latin American game, an American salesman must have a smile that would interest a bird in a tree and a mind that would shame a machine gun. He must be a combination of diplomat, go-getter, soft-soaper and field marshal. That's all.

* *

Diplomats and business men.

They are most assuredly the shock troops of our Good Neighbor Policy. But not only they. As I look back over years of residence in South America, and on several recent journeys through its republics, four men stand out as the right kind of emissaries from north to south.

* * *

First, in memory, I see a certain diplomat. He is tall and bright-eyed and handsome. He walks up to all who meet him, fellow-countrymen and foreigners, with outstretched hand and smiling face. He is able. He has charm. He has been stationed in many countries and likes them all. He has tackled the problems of each and mastered them. He has learned the language of each, and, what is more, he actually uses it in talking to natives, and isn't afraid of making mistakes, and laughs delightedly when they are brought to his attention. If I were asked to describe him in a single phrase, this would be it: "Portrait of a Gentleman, by an Old Master."

* * *

Second, I see a small, kindly, unimpressive, traveling representative of a big American bank. He and I are leaning over the rail of a steamship—rolling down to Rio, under the million stars of a tropical night.

He has been silent for some minutes. Then, in a quiet, hesitant voice:

"Gosh, I'm glad to be headed south again. For twenty-five years I've made trips to South America—I guess I've done it about fifteen times. I like the people down there. And, somehow, they really seem to like me. We don't just talk business. We sit around. We joke. We drink coffee together. They're a funny crowd, the South Americans, but then—so are we, aren't we?"

He looks long at the starry heavens.

"Gosh, I'm glad to be headed south again!"

Where is this man doing a better job as a hundred per cent American patriot—out in Ottumwa, Iowa, like a fish out of water? Or booking orders for his firm in Brazil by sheer ability to joke with a Brazilian over a cup of coffee?

* * *

Third, I see a man who is neither in diplomacy nor in business. But I guess he ought to have a place in the shock troops.

He is a doctor. His job is to help people fight malaria and other tropical terrors. He goes into dense jungles, crosses deadly swamps, braves snake-bite and pestilence. His work takes him far away from all comfort, close to all sorts of peril.

He could do his work keeping himself to himself, thinking in long scientific terms, looking on natives as mere robot-sources of information. Instead, there is not a native whom he meets who does not love him. The president of each republic which he visits delights to honor him. The humblest Indians, in the remotest villages, come to him with their troubles and go away with some little bottle or package of medicine: "I don't know that it will do them any good," he says modestly, "but they think it will—and they're an awfully good sort."

Can't the Good Neighbor Policy include the mobilization of several hundred Americans like this one?

* * *

Fourth, I see an oil prospector.

He, too, goes into dense jungle and pestilential regions filled with cruel wild beasts. He, too, stays away from civilization for weeks on end, and he is lucky to get back to it without some tale of disease or injury or narrow escape. He, too, lives among humble natives, and learns their secrets, and gives them advice, orders them around with a grin, and bawls them out when they won't work, and likes them whether they will or not.

But he won't talk about it.

If you meet him in Buenos Aires, or Santiago de Chile, or

Lima, he is full of conversation about some new night club, which, after diligent search, he has located. But, just as you begin to think that he is a playboy, he disappears. Having missed him for a couple of days, you ask his associate at the big, shiny local office of the big American oil company:

"Where's Bill?"

"Gone to the headwaters of the Ucayali—out in the jungle —hundreds of miles away. He simply couldn't stand it in Lima any longer. The last time I saw him he bawled out everything in this city—especially the night clubs."

"How long will he be gone?"

"Three months—unless he manages to stretch it into six."

"Does he like it?"

"Loves it."

"Do the Ucayali Indians like *him?*"

Bill's associate looks at me in pitying wonder.

"Say, boy," he replies, "don't you know that every damned one of them eats out of his hand?"

* * *

With ambassadors like those four, President Roosevelt and Secretary Hull won't have to worry. That sort of man will find the right approach wherever he goes, and, if given sufficient leeway, he is capable of courting a whole continent and seeing that it stays courted.

But the general run of our Good Neighbor Policy fishermen in Washington, now angling in the troubled seas of United States-Latin American relations, should always remember that Latin America cannot be landed in any one net, but only with twenty different hooks, on twenty different lines, each with a different kind of bait.

WHAT do the Latin Americans in general think of us?

That question took on special importance last winter as a result of the Pan-American Conference at Lima. Its importance has now been heightened by onslaughts of totalitarian nations against weaker nations on the European, African and Asiatic continents, which may conceivably lead to similar acts of aggression on the American Continent, unless we and our southern neighbors make it perfectly clear that such acts will be attended with serious consequences to aggressors.

Early this year I made a long tour through a dozen of the Latin American republics—a valuable cross-section of the lot of them. It brought opportunity for numerous talks with well-informed native and foreign residents of those countries, as well as for steady and careful perusal of local newspaper comment and close study of local conditions. All this has confirmed me in the belief that *the anti-Americanism prevalent among Latin Americans some years ago is definitely decreasing.*

Exceptions must be made, of course, to this sweeping statement. In some lands, latent hostility toward the United States, nurtured over a long period of time, still stubbornly persists. And even in countries where it had tended to become quiescent, there is no telling when it may leap suddenly into flame.

But, on the whole, dislike of this country, that flourished so luxuriantly around the beginning of this century, is on the wane. It is becoming reduced more and more to a feeling of mere alien-ness—to the expression, without admixture of active aversion, of the fact that there always has been, now is, and probably always will be a gulf between Americans of the north and those of the southern republics of this hemisphere which no amount of international cooperation on paper, no amount of solemn burials of hatchets at official functions, can effectually bridge.

This, however, is a very different thing from the old conception of Uncle Sam, among people living south of the Rio Grande, as a swaggering, arrogant, uncouth barbarian; as a ruthless collector, at the point of the pistol, of money unscrupulously amassed, through shady deals, by Americans in Latin America; as a brandisher of the "Big Stick," who, scorning the polite circumlocutions so dear to Latins, thinks only of exploiting others for his own selfish ends. That sort of picture is growing increasingly rarer in the minds of Latin Americans. They tend to find more and more dissimilarity between the Uncle Sam of Theodore Roosevelt and the Uncle Sam of Franklin Roosevelt.

Proximity to the United States has had much to do with our influence on Cuba; and it may be said, in a general way, that—with a few exceptions—proximity has also favorably influenced our relations with outer parts of Latin America. All the Caribbean republics, nearer to us than the rest of their Latin American brethren, tend, as a rule, to become more and more pro-American as the years go by, to sink old grievances and foster new and binding ties.

In all of them we occupy a predominant commercial position, and trade is a great enemy of preconceived prejudices. American oil men, increasingly familiar to Venezuelans, are active propagandists for more cordial American-Venezuelan relations. Costa Rica, basically and stubbornly democratic,

[23]

feels a growing affinity with us in these days of dictatorial unscrupulousness. Colombia, Guatemala, El Salvador and Honduras, viewing the rising tide of their business with us, think less and less of the anti-American bogeys of yesteryear. Geographical proximity, plus commercial intercourse, is proving a good cement for friendship.

And it is not alone in nearby Latin America that our popularity is gaining.

Once, in a certain European country which was going through one of those spasms of acute unfriendliness toward Americans so common in Europe, I met a fellow-countryman who had worked himself up into a grand rage.

"I don't mind being disliked because of something I have said or done," he spluttered, "but I'm hanged if I can see why I should be disliked because of something I *am!* Here they dislike me, before I open my mouth or stir a finger, simply because I am an American! It's not right. I'm going home."

And he did—by the next boat.

So, with his rage still fresh in my memory, it was pleasant, within a few hours of my first setting foot on the soil of Brazil, at Rio de Janeiro, the Brazilian capital, to encounter an American who had lived there for years, and to be told by him, with a beaming smile all over his face:

"It isn't what you say or do that will make people here like you. It's what you *are.* If you tell Brazilians 'I'm an American' they'll begin liking you. Afterward, of course, you may say or do something to queer yourself, and they'll dislike you —in spite of your being an American. But take it from me, you'll start right." Everything I found during my stay in Rio confirmed his words.

Friendliness toward Americans is characteristic of the place. One reason for this is our lively trade with the Brazilians.

In 1938 we exported goods to Brazil to a total value, in round figures, of $71,500,000. The aggregate value of our imports from that country for that same year was about $101,000,000. Both these figures show a decrease from the corresponding totals for the preceding year, during which the aggregate value of our exports to Brazil was somewhat over $76,000,000 and that of our imports from that country more than $126,000,000.

As will be noted from these figures, we buy from the Brazilians much more than they buy from us—in other words, they enjoy, and have enjoyed for years a favorable balance of trade in their dealing with us. This may be an important contributing reason for our popularity in their land. The principal factor in this state of affairs is, of course, Brazilian coffee, which finds its biggest market in the United States.

In 1938 we bought 34 per cent of the total exports from Brazil. The Germans, our most formidable competitors there, took 19 per cent, while the British purchased less than 9 per cent, a serious decrease from earlier years.

But, regarding *exports to Brazil*, the Germans in 1938 won out in their neck-and-neck race with us. Of the total of all goods imported by Brazil from foreign countries, 25 per cent were from Germany and only 23.9 per cent from the United States. The British, with 10 per cent, were a poor third. The aggregate value of German exports to Brazil in 1938 was $73,817,000, as against $71,518,000 for American, and $30,-661,000 for British exports.

The Brazilians, on the whole, have seldom if ever succumbed to Yankeephobia as acutely as other Latin Americans, even at periods of history when that disease was most rampant; nor have they let fear of "Yankee Imperialism" rob them of their night's sleep. They admire our democratic institutions and ideals. And they have proved how highly they have esteemed, in the past, the doctrine which binds us most closely to Latin America, by calling the ornate building in Rio de Janeiro, where their Senate meets, the Monroe Palace.

One reason for our popularity in Brazil is that the Brazilians, being of Portuguese and not of Spanish descent, are, like the Portuguese, conciliatory and tolerant, inclined to see the good points in all foreigners, including North Americans—whereas, on the other hand, people in other parts of Latin America are fiery and short-tempered, like their Spanish forefathers, and, like the Spaniards, easily offended and prone to misunderstand foreigners—especially those who, like ourselves, are of a different temperament, entirely alien in thought, speech, manners and customs.

This clash between Spanish Americans and those of Anglo-Saxon heritage is a source of much amusement to easy-going Brazilians. When they read of another sudden flare-up of bad feeling between *el tío Samuel* (Uncle Sam's name in Spanish America) and one of his touchy southern neighbors—another case of "the Wolf of the North" allegedly preparing to gobble up some helpless Spanish American lamb—they simply smile, shrug their shoulders, chuckle "The Yankee Peril again!" and go on sipping that blend of midnight and dynamite known in Brazil as after-dinner coffee.

They flatly refuse to get excited any more about such things. And this Brazilian attitude is becoming increasingly common in the Spanish-speaking, Spanish-thinking American republics. The disagreeable impression made by landings of Uncle Sam's marines in various parts of Latin America has been largely dispelled. People in those parts are coming more and more to believe that what Uncle Sam is carrying in his hand is not a big stick at all.

Another reason why Brazilians like us is because they have a desire to like everybody and be liked in exchange. Still another, of more recent growth, is fear of possible aggression from overseas. The Brazilian coast, it must be remembered, is the nearest part of the entire American Continent to Africa —where Nazi Germany covets colonies—and to Europe, whence she and her totalitarian ally, Italy, glower savagely at the international status quo. In view of this, the prospect of prompt and powerful assistance from Washington, in case of aggressive action from across the ocean, against the present or a future Brazilian government, is extremely comforting to the average Brazilian.

In Brazil, people grasp our hands in sincere pleasure and explain to us what a high opinion they have of our democracy and our machines and our faces. And, in playful patriotism, they repeat again and again, "Brazil is bigger than the United States." (It is. Brazil's area is greater than that of the United States *without* Alaska. And when Brazilians think about the United States they never think of it *with* Alaska. Patriotism forbids.)

In Peru, on the opposite coast of South America from Brazil, we occupy an important position commercially and stand high in the esteem of the natives.

In Chile, despite active competition from Germany, we are holding our own in business. As for Chilean feelings toward us, these are conditioned, as in Mexico, largely by the status of relations with big American business interests. Individually, the average Chilean has little or nothing against the average American; and, what with American moving pictures and other weapons of penetration, his friendliness toward us tends to increase with the years. But with many Chileans, friendliness is dependent on the situation with regard to

American copper and nitrate companies—which, in turn, is dependent on the local political situation.

Despite reluctance in Argentina and Uruguay to act in accordance with Roosevelt-Hull ideas and of the stubborn refusal of anti-American feeling to die out completely in certain other parts of Latin America, one cannot repeat too often that this feeling is not what it used to be.

In addition to the influence of the screen, there is that of the growing army of Latin American students sent from all over Latin America to the United States, to be educated at our schools and colleges. These youths, receiving the full impact of American ideals and outlook on life during their most impressionable years—and usually enjoying themselves to the full while doing so—return southward transformed, consciously or unconsciously, into zealous champions of Americanism among stay-at-home friends and relatives.

Another factor working for Uncle Sam in Latin America is the dissemination there of news from American sources. Two big American news agencies supply material in increasing volume to newspapers in most of the twenty Latin American republics. This accustoms readers to the American "slant" in reporting world affairs and helps offset the steady stream of news offered to those papers by agencies in the totalitarian nations overseas.

The factors enumerated above, taken together, foreshadow a heightening, at a more rapid tempo, of American penetration of Latin America—economically, culturally, and, in an indirect and purely non-aggressive sense, even politically.

Some veteran students of Latin American affairs with whom I had talks, both formal and informal, were convinced that last winter's Pan-American Conference at Lima was sure to usher in an era of unprecedented friendliness between the

Latin American countries and the United States.

Others, though, were frankly pessimistic as to the chances, in our lifetime, of appreciably greater international cordiality between the northern and southern parts of the American Continent.

"You must always remember that relations between the United States and the twenty other American republics are both complicated and unpredictable," warned a particularly well-informed analyst of conditions down there. "They are subject to abrupt variations of temperature in governments and individuals. They show a regular alternation of violent squalls with stretches of agreeable international sunshine. Of late, thanks to the steady development of the Roosevelt-Hull Good Neighbor Policy, the sunny spells have been longer and sunnier. They will probably stay that way. All of us, North and South, hope so. But—look out for squalls!"

* * *

Whenever pessimists nowadays shake their heads in doubt as to the prospects of a better understanding between the United States and the Latin American countries, the optimists rush to the attack. Anti-Americanism in many parts of Latin America, according to them, is dead, for two reasons, viz.:

1. Our Good Neighbor Policy, on its own merits, quite aside from any menace to Latin America from totalitarian States overseas.

2. The lively foreboding aroused throughout Latin America by the surrender at Munich in the autumn of 1938 of the two leading European democracies to the two leading European dictatorships, which set Latin Americans to wondering how long it would be before the dictators turned covetous eyes on this part of the world.

"It won't be long now!" croak believers in the Good Neighbor Policy, "unless drastic steps are taken to prevent it." And having got that off their chests, they continue somewhat like this:

"What drastic steps can Latin America possibly take without the guidance and effective cooperation of the United States? What Latin American voice, addressing warnings to Europe, can possibly carry the weight of the voice of the 'Colossus of the North'?

"What thinking Latin American can doubt for a moment the answer to those questions? Every aggression by dictators across the water stresses the necessity for solidarity—solidarity with a genuine significance and without the slightest trace of Big-Stick-ism, of North American domineering—between the United States and the twenty Latin American republics."

With such words they fight the battle for a better relationship between the countries on this continent. If their exhortations bear fruit, history may yet show that genuine Pan-Americanism was born in the autumn of 1938 at Munich.

In Latin America a big international poker game is being played. The stakes are trade and prestige. The best hands are held by the United States and Germany. Great Britain is also sitting in. So is Fascist Italy. So is Japan.

On the face of Nazi Germany is a confident smile. Britain seems a bit worried. Italy tries to look aggressive. Japan is glum. Uncle Sam's expression, as becomes a star poker player, is inscrutable.

Chips worth millions of dollars are in the pot. Who will win it? Who will come out big winner at the end of the game?

Nazi Germany holds excellent cards. John Bull, too, though he has been dropping a lot of money, thinks he can stage a comeback. But both of them will have to play all the poker they know.

In the trio of overseas totalitarian Powers now striving to increase their economic, political and cultural influence in Latin America, Germany is by far the most dangerous. Neither Italy nor Japan can hold a candle to her there as a rival of the United States. Both of them, to be sure, merit vigilant attention on our part, especially now that, in Rome and Tokio, lust of expansion, grimly exemplified by recent happenings in Ethiopia, Albania and China, responds ever more threateningly to the restless dynamic urge of Fascist imperialistic leaders.

But the German is the man to watch.

There is nothing new about that. He always was. People in this country readily forget that for several decades German business men of a most enterprising stamp have been active in every one of the twenty republics in the southern part of this continent. Long before Adolf Hitler and National Socialism were born Teutonic influence was strong among Latin Americans. And ever since Nazism unfurled its banners of aggression, that influence has grown steadily stronger. It may attain a dominating position unless effective measures are taken to check its impact on our commerce, our ways of thought, our democratic ideals of government, and our concept of what sort of future our twenty sister-republics ought to have.

Firm believers in the bright future in store for trade relations between the United States and Latin America contend that though Europe, in the past, has been of greater importance in our foreign trade than Latin America, it is becoming increasingly apparent that, in a general way, *Latin America has what we want most to import, and needs what we want most to export, whereas Europe doesn't need what we want most to export and hasn't got what we want most to import.* This should mean a growing value to us of Latin American markets. Not long ago official investigators in Washington reported that, broadly speaking, the countries whose purchases seemed likely to increase most rapidly were those which wanted our manufactured products, especially our mechanical devices, and that countries whose purchases seemed likely to increase less rapidly were those which imported a larger proportion of our food, materials and oil products.

Now, our exports to Latin America are mostly manufactured products in great variety, such as machinery, electrical appliances, tools and gadgets of many sorts. Our imports from there consist mainly of a few extremely important foodstuffs and raw materials. Nearly all the *coffee* we drink comes from Brazil and other southern lands; nearly all the *sugar* we consume comes from Cuba; nearly all the *bananas* we eat are from Central America and northern South America; nearly all the *petroleum* we get from abroad is shipped from Venezuela, Colombia, Mexico, Ecuador and Peru; nearly all the *nitrate* we buy abroad comes from Chile.

Our investments, direct and indirect, in the twenty Latin American republics, total around five billion dollars—a recent authoritative estimate put them at $4,600,000,000. This enormous stake includes money poured by American investors, during the pre-depression era, into Cuban sugar and Central American bananas; into mines and oil fields; into public utilities; into bonds (still largely in default) of States, provinces and cities; into many other fields which seemed promising.

Our best year was 1920, when, in addition to huge permanent investments, we exported goods to the value of nearly $1,500,000,000 to Latin America, and imported from there products worth over $1,700,000,000. In 1921 and 1922 there was a slump; but between 1922 and the depression the record was one of steady improvement, except for a slight drop in 1927. In 1929, the year that saw the beginning of the depression, our imports from Latin America were worth about $1,000,000,000, our exports $900,000,000.

After that, the depression played havoc with our trade, as it did with international business all over the world. But later, improvement again became noticeable.

Our total trade with the twenty southern republics for 1933 amounted to just short of $532,000,000 in value, as against $517,000,000 for 1932. Exports to all the South American countries showed an increase (except in the case of Ecuador), the gains ranging from 4 per cent for Brazil to 49 per cent for Chile.

In 1937 the aggregate value of United States trade with Latin America reached more than one billion dollars, and in 1938, somewhat less than that—a total most emphatically not to be sneezed at. The actual totals, according to figures compiled by the Department of Commerce and the Pan-American Union at Washington were $1,250,814,000 for 1937 and 948,515,000 for 1938. This represents, for the latter year, a falling off from the previous year's record of $302,000,000, or slightly more than 24 per cent.

In the 1938 total *imports into this country* from our twenty southern neighbors reached a value, in round figures, of $453,645,000, as compared with $672,611,000 during the preceding twelvemonth—a decrease just short of $219,000,000, or 32½ per cent. *Exports from the United States* to all of Latin America, in 1938, aggregated in value nearly $494,870,-000 as against $578,203,000 in 1937, a decrease of $83,333,000 or about 14½ per cent.

There was nothing remarkable in the decline in our business dealings with the Latin American nations during 1938, for it was merely part of a general recession in the whole field of world trade.

That year brought no continuation of the general improvement registered during 1937, thus dashing to pieces the fond hopes of international traders throughout the universe that the worst was over for them and that brighter days of bigger profits were just around the corner. The 24 per cent decline in our trade with Latin America, as compared with the 1937 record, went hand in hand with a corresponding decline of nearly 21½ per cent in trade between the United States and the rest of the world.

In seeking to find reasons for this recession, the analysts and statisticians in the handsome marble headquarters of the Pan-American Union, just behind the White House, poring with frowning brows over serried masses of figures, hit upon this one—which, in varying forms, permeates the whole structure of our trade relations with Latin America, and partly explains the obstinate tendency of nations down there to hook up with Nazi Germany in barter deals which outrage American principles of multilateral trading:

"Perhaps the best explanation of this decline is the fact that there was not sufficient dollar exchange during the year with which Latin American countries could buy in United States markets; the drop in United States purchases of Latin American raw materials was largely responsible for this condition."

That is a polite statistician's way of saying that Latin Americans wouldn't buy from us because we wouldn't buy from them. And since the Germans, as usual, were quite willing to buy whatever Latin America had to sell—even if they had to resell it, sub rosa, in other markets—Latin Americans, last year, got inveigled into an increased number of barter transactions with Germany, though these involved complications with "Aski" or compensation marks, and acceptance of big shipments of German goods, whether wanted or not.

Though the total value of our trade with Latin America has declined of late, this decline is as yet by no means serious. In 1929, that trade represented 20 per cent of the total volume of our business dealings with the rest of the world; in 1937 this percentage dropped to 19.4 and, in 1938, to 18.8—which, when all is said and done, means a decrease of only slightly more than 1 per cent, which is not so bad, no matter how one looks at it.

But it is a drop, all the same.

And something ought to be done about it, if we really mean to show the Germans and other overseas competitors of ours that we intend to be top dog in Latin America's foreign trade. The agreement made with Brazil at Washington last Spring was a good beginning. More of the same sort of thing, carefully tempered to the needs and idiosyncrasies of each Latin American country, ought to have a salutary effect on United States-Latin American trade statistics.

In 1938, the total value of the trade of the United States with the rest of the world reached five billion dollars. In this total, imports into this country represented about two billion dollars and exports from the United States to foreign countries about three billion dollars. Our Latin American neighbors provided us with 23 per cent of our imports that year and absorbed 16 per cent of our exports.

During the preceding year, 1937, we did business with all of the rest of the world to the tune of nearly six and one-half billion dollars, with imports aggregating slightly less, and exports slightly more, than one-half. During that year almost 22 per cent of our imports came from Latin America and we sent to Latin American countries 17 per cent of our exports.

Imports into the United States from Latin America during 1938 showed, in general, a decrease from the totals for the preceding year. This decrease ranged all the way from less than 1 per cent from Guatemala to *over 70 per cent* from Argentina—an eloquent reflection of the unsatisfactory status of American-Argentine trade relations.

For that same year, our total exports registered an increase in the case of only five Latin American countries—Honduras, Costa Rica, Chile, Colombia, Venezuela. Decreases in our exports to the remaining fifteen ranged from around 2 per cent in the case of Panama, to *nearly 62 per cent* in that of Uruguay. There, too, American trade is in the doldrums, with German Aski marks and barter deals doing a triumphant march over our (for the time being) prostrate form.

Statistics going back nearly one-third of a century show that Uncle Sam has maintained an unbroken lead on all other nations as an importer of Latin American products—a record which certainly ought to entitle him, in the commercial field anyway, to expressions of affection from Latin Americans. These statistics also make clear that, having wrested the lead from John Bull a quarter of a century ago, as an exporter to Latin America, Uncle Sam has likewise kept in first place, as such, ever since. Indeed, export and import figures, covering the business dealings of all twenty of the Latin American republics with the six leading foreign nations with which they do business—the United States, Great Britain, Germany, Italy, France and Japan—disclose the interesting fact that, except for temporary setbacks, *only the United States and Germany* have registered substantial gains in the Latin American market since 1910, both as exporters and importers. The other four, especially Great Britain and Japan, despite transitory spurts, have been slipping.

In 1910, 34½ per cent of all Latin America's exports went to the United States, and 23½ per cent of all its imports came from there. In that same year, Great Britain took a little less than 21 per cent of all these exports, much less than our percentage. But the British sent to the Latin American nations 26 per cent of everything imported by them, somewhat more than our corresponding total.

By 1913, however, we were not only holding our lead as an importer, but had nosed out the British as the banner exporters to Latin American countries, having imported from them nearly 31 per cent of all the goods they had shipped abroad and sent to them 25 per cent of the total of goods purchased by them from foreign lands. Britain's percentages that year were, respectively, 21 and 24. What is more, we have not only kept this double jump on Britain ever since but have improved on it.

Here are American and British percentages, during the past few years, of the total imports and exports of the twenty countries of Latin America:

	UNITED STATES		GREAT BRITAIN	
	Imports	*Exports*	*Imports*	*Exports*
1932	32.3	32.1	16.3	19.4
1933	29.2	29.4	18.1	22.1
1934	30.1	29.4	17.3	20.2
1935	31.7	32.8	14.7	18.6
1936	31.5	32.8	14.3	19.2
1937	34.	31.	13.2	17.7
1938	36.1	31.7	12.2	16.3

During the period between 1910 and the present the Germans have forged ahead in the Latin American market to such an extent that—though still far behind the United States both as exporters and importers—they have actually passed their old rivals, the British, in the former capacity, and are getting dangerously close to them in the latter.

Between 1910 and the outbreak of the World War, the Germans supplied, roughly, 16 per cent of Latin America's total imports and took 12 per cent of her exports. The war, of course, hit them hard—even as late as 1932, fourteen years after its close, they were shipping to Latin America less than 10 per cent of its total imports and absorbing only 7 per cent of its total exports.

Since then, however, they have been getting down to work with a vengeance. In 1937 they supplied 15½ per cent of everything imported into Latin America (just under their pre-war average) and took nearly 9 per cent of everything exported from there.

In 1938 they supplied 17 per cent of all goods imported by the Latin American countries and absorbed 10.6 per cent of all exports from those countries.

Meanwhile, our Italian, Japanese and French competitors, in the southern republics of this hemisphere, have not been doing any business worth writing home about.

In 1910, Italy exported to those republics nearly 5 per cent of everything they purchased abroad and imported a little over 1 per cent of all they sold in foreign parts. In 1937, the former percentage fell to 2½ per cent (one-half of the 1910 figure) and the latter had risen to only 3 per cent. In 1938, Italy accounted for 3.1 per cent of all Latin America's imports and for 1.5 per cent of all exports from there.

As for Japan, she caused serious alarm between 1933 and 1935 by her spectacular dumping of Japanese products, especially cheap textiles. She poured these into Latin America in such unprecedented quantities that her percentage of the total imported there rose from a humble 1 per cent in 1932 to more than three times that figure in 1935. Since then, however, exports of Japanese merchandise to most of the Latin American nations have dropped.

As for France, the sixth member of the Big Six in Latin America's trade, her volume of business there, both as importer and exporter, has been cut down to less than one-half what it was just before the World War.

In the past, endeavors to flatten down tariff barriers have

been wrecked all too often by lack of cooperation between our government and the governments of Latin America. And many attempts to do business in defiance of those barriers have been hampered, or even entirely frustrated, by the prohibitive nature of the duties levied.

President Roosevelt and Secretary Hull have set themselves the difficult task of doing away with this state of affairs. They are certainly up against a tough situation! Their position, as they valiantly advance to the attack, with the banner of the Good Neighbor Policy proudly flapping over their heads, reminds one of that of another crusader, Martin Luther—and of the words spoken to him at the Diet of Worms by that hard-boiled Teutonic general, Frundsberg, as Luther rose to confront his judges:

"Little monk, little monk, thou goest upon a hard road!"

From the moment that our ship had begun to slip along the steep, green coast of Brazil, we passengers had become as restless as a lot of caged jungle beasts. We simply could not wait patiently for our first glimpse of the harbor of Rio de Janeiro, enthusiastically acclaimed by those of us aboard who had seen it as the most marvelous in the whole world.

We had taken to pacing the decks, up and down, for miles. We had developed a habit of suddenly rushing to the rail and gazing expectantly shoreward, as if in hope that such tactics might persuade Rio to move a bit northward and put us out of our suspense. We had stopped playing the strange new dice game taught us by South American fellow-travelers, which, having raged without intermission ever since the beginning of the voyage, had earned the enthusiastic approval of the smoking room steward, a canny Britisher, because "it lasts just long enough, sir, for you gentlemen to want another drink."

But there was one exception to the general rule of restlessness. The man whom we had nicknamed Me-for-Naples remained aloof and skeptical about the reputed wonders of Rio. Buttonholing each of us in turn, as we vainly tried to control our impatience, he would intone once more the litany which we had first heard from him when the Statue of Liberty was scarcely out of sight astern:

"Me for Naples! I tell you, there's nothing in all the universe like Naples. Oh, boy—that glorious bay, and Vesuvius, with the curling wisp of smoke over it, filling up the whole background. Ever seen Naples at sunrise? Ever seen Naples by moonlight? Ever listened to the chatter of the fishermen on the Neapolitan water front and bargained for coral ornaments in a Neapolitan shop? Me for Naples!"

And ignoring the green strip of Brazilian coast line, heedless of excited exclamations such as "By gosh, there's the entrance to the harbor right ahead!" and "Why, of course that big mountain over there is the Sugar Loaf!" he calmly sat down to a solitaire version of the strange South American dice game, with nobody to look at the hands he threw except that travel-hardened Britisher, the smoking room steward.

I did not have any more conversation with Me-for-Naples that day. I had no time for him. Like innumerable travelers of all nationalities who had preceded me, I was overwhelmed, left gasping, struck breathless, knocked speechless, by what I saw as our ship entered the bay of Rio de Janeiro.

On all sides were islands of fantastic shapes, headlands of weird contour, silvery inlets cutting deeply into the land, to the very foot of enormous mountains, towering, rocky and sullen, over verdant shore and sunlit water. Straight ahead was the Sugar Loaf, most striking and famous of Rio's peaks, a bald rock as forbidding as Gibraltar; and in the background loomed Corcovado, "the Hunchback," mounting guard behind Brazil's metropolis, as the Sugar Loaf mounts guard in front of it. Ahead lay the city, crowded in between mountain wall and sparkling bay, its docks lined with ships, its tiled roofs flashing in the tropical sunlight—with ferryboats darting toward the opposite shore, and church bells pealing joyously.

Several hours after landing and getting my first idea of Brazil's capital, my mind was still a jumble of bewildering first impressions.

[42]

CITY OF ENCHANTMENT

Is any other city in the world so mixed up with nature, so intertwined and interwoven with natural beauty?

In Rio, the hills, clothed from base to apex with tropical verdure, seem to be pushing themselves into the very streets. A visitor emerges from a business call, glances casually to right or left, and there, apparently a few yards away, is a green-draped peak, with palm trees studded all over it.

He strolls along the Avenida Rio Branco—Main Street— looks over his shoulder, and, seemingly near enough to serve as the target for a stone, is a regular chunk of forest primeval. He walks a block or two further, and, poised on the pinnacle of a high, steep crag, the magnificent statue of Christ the Redeemer bursts suddenly upon his vision, with such overpowering effect that it seems an apparition from another world.

Seldom, in Rio, is one out of sight of the hill range behind the city—luxuriant Tijuca, jagged Corcovado, massive Pico de Gavea. Seldom is one without a glimpse of the entrancing bay —that fantastic fugitive from fairyland—with its serrated islets and gloriously curving shore line. And there is seldom a moment when you cannot contemplate the superb Sugar Loaf Mountain. Never does the sight pall of that upthrust of rock, with the little basket-car that takes visitors to the summit, dangling precariously from a swaying cable.

Even after sundown, electric lamps trace the outline of the Sugar Loaf in golden brightness against the black velvet of the night; and the tiny, slowly moving basket-thing, now just a speck of light, its cable invisible in the darkness, seems like a little lost star trying to find its way across the heavens.

Rio! What other city is encased in such a glorious natural setting? What metropolis on earth is encircled by such an aureole of natural beauty?

In the midst of all this bewilderment I ran across Me-for-

[43]

Naples. Obviously, he, too, was bewildered; and it was equally obvious that he was enjoying himself.

"Well?" I asked. "How does it compare with Naples?" But he became cautious and evasive.

"A good town, this," he finally admitted, with a judicial air. "I like the surroundings. I like the uniforms of the police, and their high boots. I like the coffee. I'm strong for the eyes of the women. And—say!—did you ever see such a mixture of races? Coal black, black, light black, dark brown, brown, light brown, dark yellow, yellow, light yellow, touch-of-the-sun, white—you meet every one of the shades every time you walk a block. And they're all friendly. Have you noticed it?"

I had.

In Rio, everybody smiles. Everybody is polite. In the elevators of business buildings (one of them is twenty-two stories high!) every man whips off his hat when a woman enters—unlike New York, where we draw a careful distinction between a hotel elevator, in which we have agreed to be courteous to the opposite sex, and an elevator down around Wall Street, where we haven't.

I got into a pay-as-you-leave Rio omnibus, and, on getting off, dropped a coin into the box. "Not enough," objected the driver. "One cent more." I fumbled in my pocket, could not find the required coin. "Oh, no matter," he said, smiled all over his face, and drove away.

Out of the city proper, with sharp peaks and green-clad islands framed at the ends of narrow streets, you emerge upon the superb bay shore drive, the proudest possession of Brazil's fairest city. The drive, with its strips of lovely gardens, and mosaic pavements laid out in fantastic, many-colored designs, and grand statues of national heroes, and rows of pretty villas, fringes the waterfront for miles, presenting, in unbroken suc-

cession, gorgeous vistas of mountain and sea. Scattered along
this driveway are several beaches of smooth sand, transform-
ing the Brazilian capital into a seashore resort; and the natives,
unimpressed by the fact that their principal business and resi-
dential streets are just around the corner, wander along the
shore drive clad in bathing toggery of a scantiness just within
the law, and plunge into the salt water, with the tumultuous
motor traffic of Rio surging past only a few yards away.

Says one of many helpful Brazilian acquaintances: "You
simply *must* drive to—" Follows a string of strange, exotic
names.

So, obediently, you hire yourself a motor car with a smiling brown chauffeur, and off you speed, straight upward,
around innumerable hairpin turns, into the natural park which
fringes the heights overlooking Rio Bay. No need of manufacturing a park here—all that the municipal authorities had to
do was to build a road (some job that, though; the grades and
the sharpness and steepness of the curves are appalling) and
keep the forest primeval from gobbling up the road when nobody was looking.

The vegetation—rich, dark, exuberant, tropical jungle—
comes down to the very edge of the driveway. Mysterious
birds, deep in the somber glades, utter mysterious noises. Butterflies, blue and red and golden yellow, flutter in front of
your car. Palm trees soar upward from the midst of dense
underbrush. Banana trees wave their enormous, low-hanging
leaves as you pass. And scattered about in the woods, you
glimpse a strange tree, a mass of silvery foliage, which the
chauffeur, appealed to by excited passengers in awful Portuguese, introduces as the "imba-ooba," or something to that
effect.

"Imba-ooba!" Isn't that a grand tropical word? An American in the party is immediately inspired with an idea for a popular song—to be written out as soon as the automobile stops joggling him—which is to have the refrain: "Come with me far south of Cuba, be my little imba-ooba."

And then out you come from the forest to the edge of a precipice; and there, thousands of feet below, is the bay of Rio, with dozens of jagged peaks lining its shores, and bizarre islands all over it, glistening in tropical sunshine.

The chauffeur swells with patriotic elation as you and all the rest of the party gasp in delight.

"Is that not beautiful, senhor? Have you such a view at home, senhora? But—now I will show you still more beauty."

And he shepherds you into the car and whirls you again into the forest, with its brilliant colors and fragrant odors and grim depths, its loquacious birds and dazzling butterflies. Along the sides of the road are native vendors, of varying hues of brown and black, displaying for sale, on little stands, various kinds of native fruit—one, with an artist's fine eye for the picturesque, has chosen a steep, foaming forest cataract as a background for his business establishment. "Bananas! Raspberries!" they shout, as your car rushes past—"Bananas!" in a quite hopeful tone of voice, when you whiz into sight around one curve, and—rather less hopefully, as you whiz out of sight around the next curve: "Raspberries!"

Surely there cannot be much of a turnover in this roadside trade. But the vendors wear pleasant grins, and they look very comfortable as they squat beneath the cool trees, and they are all part of the friendly scene.

And then you are whirled to the edge of another precipice, and below you once more is Rio Bay, in a new and glorious setting, and your chauffeur points to some stone seats around a table made of stone slabs, and tells you: "This is the Emperor's Seat. Here the Emperor Dom Pedro II used to have lunch and gaze at the view. Is it not marvelous?" And a dusky native business man, cheerfully using the Emperor's Seat as a counter for his stock of stubbly little bananas, wild raspberries, bottled fizzy drinks and tired-looking ham sandwiches, suddenly plunges into the forest primeval and emerges just as suddenly, with a lovely tropical flower in his hand, which he presents to one of the ladies of the visiting party, with a bow and flourish worthy of the Emperor Dom Pedro himself.

And one of our party, his eyes glued to the incredibly beautiful panorama below him, suddenly blurts out: "God did too much for this place!" And I wonder why more Americans don't come to Rio.

And then I suddenly notice Me-for-Naples, with another party, gazing at the view with an absorption almost reverential.

"How does it compare with Naples?" I ask. But he eyes me askance, as if I had interrupted him in prayer, and moves away from me.

A few minutes later our car bumps down the mountain road again, and lands us inside the city, and I am back at the job of wandering around Rio's pleasant streets.

Opinions differ as to just why it is that Brazilians are so friendly toward the "Colossus of the North," that formidable monster which arouses among other Latin Americans such distrust and apprehension.

"You see, it is this way," explained one inhabitant of Rio, after emptying a cup of coffee—probably his fifth or sixth that morning—outside one of the city's pleasant sidewalk cafés: "We Brazilians have no inferiority complex. We are fully aware that Brazil, like the United States, is a great nation—are

[47]

there not 45,000,000 of us?

"We know that our natural resources are unlimited, that our country is destined some day to have a population of 200,000,000, and an importance second to that of no nation in the world. We fully agree with what your famous Theodore Roosevelt said when he was here: 'The eighteenth century belonged to Europe, the nineteenth belonged to the United States, the twentieth will belong to Brazil.' So, in our relations with you, we do not feel overwhelmed by your size and power and wealth and importance.

"That is not true of other Latin American countries. They feel themselves so completely outclassed by you that they are filled with envy. They have an inferiority complex."

*   *   *

Rio is full of memories of Brazil's colorful history. That history included something very rare indeed on the American Continent—an Emperor. Brazil had two in fact.

She did not slip from monarchy to republicanism but from monarchy to monarchy. She drove away a king to give herself an emperor. In 1822, Brazilian independence was declared under Emperor Dom Pedro I, who superseded his father João VI, king of Portugal. This monarch-to-monarch transition exerted a unifying influence on Brazil which was largely absent elsewhere in Latin America.

In 1824, when João VI died, Pedro, who thereby became automatically king of Portugal, proved himself more of a Brazilian than a Portuguese by promptly abdicating in favor of his little daughter Maria, thus keeping Brazil an independent empire, instead of making her again a dependency of Portugal.

After a series of chaotic complications, Pedro again abdicated. This time it was the Brazilian imperial throne that he gave up, in favor of his son, who became Emperor Dom Pedro II. The latter reigned nearly sixty years, kept the peace in Brazil, and—with his fine flowing beard, democratic ways and neat wit—endeared himself alike to fellow-countrymen and foreigners. In 1876, he visited the United States, where he made a great hit. Toward the end of his reign slavery was abolished.

Eventually, the amiable Dom Pedro found himself powerless to cope with rising republican sentiment, though he used to point out to his opponents that he was the best republican in all Brazil. Finally, in 1899, General Deodoro Fonseca and *1889* General Floriano Peixotto—familiarly called, in Brazil, after the cheerful Brazilian fashion, just Deodoro and Floriano—proclaimed Brazil a republic. Poor old Dom Pedro was exiled from his beloved Rio to Europe, where he died two years later. On the occasion of his dethronement, somebody said: "The only republic in South America, the empire of Brazil, has come to an end."

After some turbulent years, there was an era of comparative quiet, though by no stretch of the imagination can Brazil be said to have become a real democracy, then or at any time since then. In 1930, Getulio Vargas became President after the forcible removal from office of his predecessor. Vargas soon made himself dictator. He still is.

* * *

As a result of the friendly feeling of Brazilians for Americans, they are quick to imitate us. Being enthusiastic attendants at motion picture theaters, whose programs consist mainly of American films, they are prone to introduce into their everyday speech Americanisms such as are used by actors and actresses of the screen. A young blood of Rio will meet a crony on the Avenida Rio Branco, or the Largo da Carioca, ask him, in Portuguese, how he is feeling, and, as likely as not, be answered, in perfectly good American: "All right!"

"Let's lunch together," continues Young Blood Number One—still in Portuguese.

"O.K.," agrees Young Blood Number Two, quite as if he were on Broadway.

In the busy downtown quarter there is a large shop called "New York." And there is a café which proudly advertises "American drinks," among which particular attention is called to a specialty of the house labeled "milk shack."

At the magnificent gambling casino, one of the features of night life in the Brazilian metropolis, American money is cheerfully accepted from northern visitors keen to try their luck at roulette and other dangerous pastimes. And the croupiers wrinkle their brows in polite endeavors to understand English, and reply, when asked whether this or that play is permitted: "Oh, yes. Very well. All right."

Study of American methods by up-to-date Brazilians has resulted, within the last few years, in a cleaning up of Rio worthy of ranking with the best efforts in that line of our own Gorgas in Panama or Waring in Havana.

Not so long ago Brazil's capital was a pest-hole. Disease was rampant, especially yellow fever. There were times when whole clusters of foreign vessels lay at anchor in Rio Bay, enveloped in tragic silence, with every member of their crews dead from "yellow jack" and no signs of life on their decks except from the native watchman set to guard them.

But since the late Dr. Oswaldo Cruz and his helpers started to clean up the city, yellow fever and malaria have been practically wiped out. There is a statue to Dr. Cruz in Rio today, also a street named after him. And there ought to be. He did a splendid job.

*   *   *

It was the hour of nightfall. I was on top of the Sugar Loaf, whither I had been whisked by the little cage-like car, hanging from its narrow cable. It had landed me on the mountain top after dangling me for some minutes hundreds of feet over the city and making me feel about as important in the scheme of the universe as a new-born flea.

By my side was the man whom we had dubbed Me-for-Naples. Neither of us had spoken a word for some minutes—with that enchanting panorama of rock and water before us, talk seemed sacrilege.

Suddenly he exclaimed—and there was real concentrated feeling in his voice:

"Why don't more Americans come here? They see far too much of Paris. And of London. And of the Rhine. And of the Riviera."

"And of Naples?"

He looked me squarely in the eye.

"Yes, sir, *and of Naples!* This place gives me a much bigger kick than Naples ever did. Look. By golly, look!"

He seized my arm, and breathless from excitement, pointed downward toward the city.

All along the wonderful bay shore drive, the street lights had suddenly been lighted. The line between bay and shore was now picked out in clear iridescence, as if by a well-disciplined army of gigantic fireflies. Other fireflies, tapering off from the main body along the water front, had set themselves to lighting the slopes toward the mountain tops, outlining the course of other thoroughfares with parallel lines of white flame.

Me-for-Naples gazed in silence for a while. Then he drew a deep sigh of admiration.

"Me for Rio!" he said.

AN American in South America, idly turning the pages of a trade magazine in the reading room of his hotel, just to pass the time, decided to count the advertisements according to the nationalities of the advertisers. There were two ads of American firms—and *sixty-four* of German firms.

That is typical.

All over Latin America the Germans are on the job morning, noon and night as competitors of ours. Germany may be counted on to play every hand she holds, in the great international poker game there, both shrewdly and effectively, as long as she has any chips in front of her.

Through radio broadcasts from Berlin, Latin Americans are subtly made acquainted with the Nazi point of view on world affairs. Many of these broadcasts are innocent enough—they confine themselves to musical programmes (all-German, however), travelogues and the like. To others, though, dealing with international news of the moment, a Nazi "slant" is imparted by the broadcasters. Some Latin Americans, of course, are well aware of this and take what they hear with plenty of salt; others, though, either already pro-Nazi or unversed in the wiles of propaganda, hearing this sort of thing day after day, tend to absorb, consciously or unconsciously, the Nazi point of view.

Equally zealous are the agents of Berlin who supply "boiler plate" news features to newspapers. Some of this material, like some of the radio features, is comparatively straight news, but much of it is strongly impregnated with propaganda. As it is supplied free of charge, it is a temptation even to anti-Nazi editors. I saw one of these Berlin-born "boiler plate" features which was a good sample of the sort of thing now being offered. It was a review of the first six years of the Hitler régime. Beginning harmlessly enough, as if it were nothing but an objective chronicle, it soon slipped into mellifluous propaganda—all that Hitler had done, readers were craftily led to believe, was an outstanding achievement for the welfare not only of Germany but of the whole world.

Space available for news in the paper where this feature was printed was very limited. Therefore, one could not escape the conclusion that it had been paid for by Nazi propagandists.

But despite the seriousness of German efforts at penetration through the radio and the press, they pale before Berlin's direct campaign.

Obedient to the Fuehrer's slogan of "export or die," those behind Nazi Germany's tremendous struggle for increased business drive it forward with relentless power and efficiency. Their most formidable weapon is the system of barter deals based on Germany's now famous "Aski" marks. These are put through as follows:

Germany approaches a Latin American republic with an offer to take off its hands a big quantity of some one of its staple articles of export—say, coffee in Brazil, chilled meat in Uruguay, wheat in the Argentine. But there is a catch: instead of receiving real money in exchange, the purchasers must accept payment in "Aski" marks, credited to them by Germany, which are good only for purchases of German articles of export. This method is diametrically opposed to the system of multilateral trade at the root of the Roosevelt-Hull Good Neighbor Policy which Washington is now so earnestly championing.

Despite natural reluctance to tie themselves so firmly to Berlin, Latin American nations enter into this sort of barter transaction with Germans, because the latter offer "Aski" marks at most seductively low rates, accompanied with other inducements which, at first sight, seem most advantageous to those before whom they are dangled. But on closer scrutiny, these sometimes resemble shackles more than advantages.

Closer scrutiny, however, often comes too late. Of recent years, the Nazi spider has been increasingly successful in luring foreign flies into the web of its barter system of trade. Indeed, this method has attained such momentum that the most strenuous endeavors of Americans and other competitors will be needed to keep the banner of successful anti-Nazi competition flying over Latin America.

Thanks to the varied methods already touched upon—to which must be added cultural penetration through lectures by many a Teutonic Herr Professor to students at Latin American institutions of learning—Nazi Germany has pushed her influence forward of late in a number of lands, notably Brazil, Argentina, Chile and Uruguay.

In Brazil, Germany has found an excellent groundwork for her campaign.

In the southern part of that vast country Nazi agents are able to pursue their aims in the midst of a compact mass of inhabitants of Germanic stock. These, though mostly more Brazilian in sentiment than Teutonic, have, nevertheless, kept alive a strong attachment to the land of their ancestors. Among them, too, are many recent immigrants, who left Germany after the World War—including headstrong youths all too prone to assimilate Nazi ideas. These often meet half-way the efforts of Hitlerite propagandists and tend to counteract pro-Brazilian, anti-foreign admonitions of older and less impressionable inhabitants of the region.

In Chile, also, there is a big body of people of German blood. Most of them are descendants of settlers who left home half a century or more ago. The Chilean Germanic community is mostly composed of thrifty farmers, or members of the "white collar" class in certain towns of South Central Chile—Valdivia, Osorno, Concepción, etc. It is much less numerous than its counterpart in Brazil, less influential in the politics of its adopted country, and rather more Chilean in outlook than the Germanic element in southern Brazil is Brazilian. But its excellence as a foundation for propaganda is self-evident.

Besides Brazil and Chile—the countries where inhabitants of Germanic stock are present in the largest numbers and concentrated in the compactest form—the spread of Nazi influence is helped in other southern republics by smaller Teutonic nuclei. On these the Berlin government brings pressure through a whole series of effective measures.

All over Latin America there are powerful German business firms. Through these, also through German clubs, the Nazis work subtly and relentlessly. Now it is a hint from Berlin about the undesirability of an employee of some firm that causes him to be fired; now it is a similar hint to the heads of a "Deutscher Verein" in some Latin American city that means the disappearance of somebody's name from the list of membership. There are cases, of course, where business executives or club committees, hotly resenting such dictation from Berlin, have opposed it. But that may easily mean dire trouble for relatives in Germany. So, when it comes to a showdown, Berlin usually wins.

Yet, strong as are the Germans in the southern part of the American Continent, they are up against a number of factors which may combine to beat them in the long run.

First among these is the new American determination to fight back. This was forcibly displayed last March in that loan of ours to Brazil and the promise of a new liberality toward Brazilian importers of our products which went with it. This determined action on our part must have been a sour morsel to Berlin. It also made many Latin Americans realize that we were prepared to fight with acts not words, with concrete businesslike bids for their patronage instead of hymns praising democracy and damning dictators. As a keen commentator on Latin America said: "When a Latin American goes into a shop he forgets politics and remembers only prices." That is a good thing for American competitors of Germany to bear in mind.

Another factor militating against further German penetration is the highly developed nationalism of the republics to the south of us. Teutonic tactlessness is constantly wounding the nationalistic sensibilities of their inhabitants.

This has been shown most clearly of late in Brazil. There the government headed by President Getulio Vargas, suddenly cracking down on Nazi activities in the states where inhabitants of Germanic stock predominated, dissolved Nazi organizations, forbade pro-Nazi teaching in schools, and began to build, in the midst of an especially Teutonic community, a big barracks to be garrisoned by a big force of Brazilian soldiers.

Another instance of the alertness of Latin Americans, when confronted with over-zealous Nazi activities, was the prompt action some months ago of the Argentine authorities against alleged German plans to take over parts of Patagonia for the Reich.

To offset Nazi and Fascist influencing of Latin Americans

over the radio it was reported recently that American radio engineers were about to install a short wave one hundred per cent American "Big Bertha," as a front-line fighter in the ideological war now being waged between democracy and dictatorship for the soul and cash of Latin America. They had been spurred on to do this by the fact that the Nazi German government's radio station had increased its power so greatly that it was "blanketing" some of our stations. American experts had noticed at times, when our stations were broadcasting German news, that a strange roar arose that completely smothered our broadcasts. The new "Big Bertha," it is expected, will make such interference impossible.

This move is part of a burst of increased activity among our radio agencies in their aim to compete against the dissemination of Nazi-Fascist news to the Latin American republics. Already American efforts in this direction are meeting with flattering success. Latin Americans have sent in hundreds of letters praising our improved radio service. Items in this service are broadcast by expert announcers, born in Latin America, after translation into Spanish or Portuguese by translators thoroughly versed in these languages, who work in shifts, all around the clock. This news, according to its sponsors, is perfectly impartial.

"We tell the truth even if it hurts," remarked one of them solemnly.

Experts at the Department of Commerce in Washington, who keep a most watchful eye on our trade rivals, said a short time ago, that in the early part of 1939, Germany was not getting along so well in Latin America as during the preceding year. Her trade with our twenty southern neighbors, according to their figures, fell off 27.2 per cent during January and February 1939, as compared with the same period in

1938. On the other hand, United States trade with Latin America, for those same two months in 1939, declined only 18.7 per cent in comparison with January-February 1938.

One reason for this German slump was that the Germans were no longer able to offer to Latin American customers barter transactions as alluring as those of earlier years, when barter trade and "Aski" marks were in the first bloom of their youth. Moreover, Latin American countries entering into such transactions now obtain no free exchange as a result of them; and they complain, in addition, that German manufacturers, on account of the preponderant attention now being given in Germany to rearmament, impose most vexatious delays upon Latin Americans who order German goods before delivery is made. All of which works out to the credit side of the trade methods advocated by Washington's Good Neighborites and helps to put "Aski" marks and barter tricks in general more and more into the "red."

Pursuing their investigations into the great Trade War now being waged in Latin America—in which Secretary of State Hull is intrepidly leading forward the cohorts of Multilateralism against hot enfilading volleys of "Aski" marks pouring from the Bilateral trenches—Department of Commerce wiseacres came out some weeks ago with the following significant announcement:

"During the three years 1936, 1937 and 1938 imports into sixteen countries with which trade agreements have been concluded *showed a much larger average rate of increase from the United States over the two pre-agreement years* [*1934-1935*] *than imports from Germany, the chief exponent of barter, clearing, compensation or similar trade programs.*"

These sixteen countries, at the time the above announcement was made, included the following in Latin America:

Brazil, Colombia, Costa Rica, El Salvador, Guatemala, Haiti, Honduras and Nicaragua.

It was found furthermore by Washington analysts of the trade situation in Latin America that, since the penalties of large scale barter or compensation deals (i.e., those involving "Aski" marks) more than offset the advantages, many countries which have tried them have taken definite steps to decrease such transactions in future. Investigation also showed that the very features of barter deals which have tended in the past to make them seem so attractive to Latin America, militate, in the long run, against the expansion of business based on barter.

For example, take coffee. Only a certain maximum quantity of coffee can be exchanged or sold by Germany to third countries. Consequently, when the Germans, by means of a barter deal, get this maximum quantity from one coffee-producing country, they are unable to contract for further shipments of coffee from other coffee-producing countries. This was clearly shown in the early period of German barter transactions with Latin American republics, when Germany made barter agreements with the Central American countries and Colombia. At first, imports of German goods into those countries (in compensation for the coffee exported by them) jumped gaily upward.

But soon afterward, when Germany also committed herself to take big lots of coffee from Brazil, she had to curtail her purchases of coffee from Central America and Colombia. Therefore, trade between Germany and those countries went into a decline, except in cases where the Germans managed to buy considerable quantities of other Central American and Colombian products to take the place of coffee.

In addition, the adoption by Nazi Germany of the barter

system has brought about a steady shifting of her import and export trade to countries which can supply her with much-needed raw materials. As a consequence, a growing proportion of German exports of manufactured goods has been going to such countries, whereas there has been a steady decline in German exports of such goods to nations not in a position to send to Germany raw materials in exchange.

In the catalogue of snags found in their path by countries doing barter business with Germany Department of Commerce analysts include the gradual creation of large blocked balances of "Aski" marks, which can only be liquidated by further purchases of German goods. As a result of this, barter agreements sometimes fail to work satisfactorily; in fact, some of them get absolutely deadlocked until such blocked balances can be liquidated.

Analyzing still further the disadvantages to Latin Americans who have embarked on barter business with the Nazis, the Department of Commerce states:

"In some countries the greatest difficulty encountered in the barter or compensation trade is that Germany has purchased practically the entire output or production of certain principal crops of raw materials, *effecting virtual economic domination of the country in question*. In many cases Germany has resold these goods to third countries at a discount." (When I was in South America last Spring there was a great hubbub on account of alleged sales by Germany, in the open market, of Brazilian and Colombian coffee obtained in barter deals wherein the Germans had expressly promised honest-to-goodness-cross-my-heart that they would consume every bit of such coffee themselves and not try to sell a single bag of it to anybody else.)

"Thus, the country with which Germany had the barter

arrangement lost these former customers, together with the
foreign exchange that was usually paid for such transactions.
The surplus above its own consumption, which Germany has
sold to third countries at a discount, has tended to lower
world prices on these commodities, and again this has ad-
versely affected the countries producing them."

The Department of Commerce also took care recently to
point out that economic subservience to Germany, engen-
dered by over-indulgence, on the part of some Latin American countries, in barter deals with the Nazis, *might eventually
lead to political control from Berlin.*

As if stung by these "naughty-naughty" admonitions from
Washington, Dr. Walther Funk, Fuehrer Hitler's Minister of
Economics—the Nazi big shot who recently toured the
Balkan States hoping to scoop them up in the barter nets
already craftily spread for them by Nazidom's Financial
Wizard-in-Chief, Dr. Hjalmar Schacht (now temporarily so-
journing under a cloud)—sent recently a most eloquent defense of barter trade to an influential newspaper in Brazil, a
country which the Nazis would dearly love to lead around on
a nice strong chain with "Aski" marks as its links. Dr. Funk's
remarks, condensed, boil down to this:

Having been robbed of her colonies, her investments
abroad, and other assets, Germany was forced to find new
ways to do foreign business. Among these, the "Aski"-barter
system seemed, to her experts, the most promising.

Though negligible in importance in 1932, barter trade had
gained so phenomenally that in 1938, five years after Hitler's
advent, it equaled Germany's entire trade for the banner year
1929. Through barter transactions, Brazil's trade situation had
been enormously improved—for instance, it was the main
reason for the development, at an unprecedented rate, of

Brazilian cotton planting. Moreover, it had benefited Brazilian coffee planters and producers of other staples, while, at the same time, enabling Brazil to import all sorts of good cheap German products without depleting her gold reserves.

"Germany is a decisive factor in Brazil's economic life," concluded Dr. Funk, "and she is ready to collaborate with Brazilians in every way."

Fresh evidence that the German export situation is becoming increasingly serious came recently from a city whose experts certainly don't enjoy painting it in gloomy colors and assuredly would get enthusiastic about it if they could—Berlin.

Since the second half of 1937, investigation by Berlin delvers into statistics shows, German exports have been on the toboggan. The quota of the Reich's total industrial output which is exported dropped recently to just under 11 per cent, an alarming state of affairs for the Nazis, since even their most optimistic analysts believe that at least 20 per cent of that total must be exported if the Nazi government is to escape the disagreeable alternative of lowering the standard of living of Germany's population.

And here is a bit of good news for the champions of our Good Neighbor Policy:

As a result of the increased economic pressure on Nazi Germany, her export markets nearer home, especially in Southeastern Europe, are being developed to the detriment of her exports to Latin America. Owing to this change in the route taken by German exports, Berlin statisticians report that they dropped, during the first quarter of 1939, as compared with the corresponding period in 1938, as follows: to Mexico, 20.7 per cent; to Brazil, 25.1 per cent; to Argentina, 28.5 per cent; and to Peru, 37.5 per cent.

But American traders with Latin America must not get over-confident after study of this sort of thing. Their German competitors are far too resourceful to be discomfited by setbacks which may prove to be merely temporary. They're a resilient lot—if pushed back in one place they are quite likely to bob up triumphantly in another. The proper number of hours for their competitors to allot every day to fighting them is twenty-four.

When people in Latin America start trying to figure out what may happen to them if totalitarian aggressors get on their trail in earnest, their apprehension is almost entirely centered on Germany. They have little fear of Italy, less of Japan.

Italian influence in Latin America is still largely cultural. It is most marked in Argentina. Immigration from Italy began in that country many years ago and has continued through several decades at such a rate that it has left a definite impress on the population. In Buenos Aires there are several hundred thousand Italians or Argentine-Italians. So much are they a part of metropolitan life that the brand of Spanish spoken there is plentifully sprinkled with Italian turns of phrase and semi-Italian words—to the intense disgust of Argentine sticklers for the purity of their Castilian mother-tongue.

In the Brazilian state of São Paulo there is also a strong Italian element. Like the Germans elsewhere in southern Brazil it presents a certain danger for the future.

This is because southern Brazilians, when they get angry with the central government at Rio—they often do—talk darkly of secession. In view of this, there is always a possibility that Italy's Fascists, in alliance with Germany's Nazis, may take advantage of such separatist talk to foment secession movements in Italianate São Paulo, and that similar plotting may some day stir up trouble in Teutonic Rio Grande do Sul and Santa Catharina, with Nazi-Fascist agents using as pawns the masses of inhabitants there who have German blood. But the present Brazilian government, as has been pointed out already, is fully aware of this peril and apparently quite capable of coping with it.

Italians are also influential in Peru, especially in banking. A number of other Latin American countries likewise have colonies of Italian or partly Italian residents. The members of these, ever since the advent of Fascism in Rome, are often reminded of their duties as champions (no matter how far they may be living from Mussolini) of one hundred per cent Mussolini-ism.

But at the present writing, they are not even formidable commercially, much less politically. Some day this may be no longer true; just now, however, Italian pro-Fascist elements to the south of us (both the genuine article and the band-wagon brand) don't get much beyond cheering, flag-saluting, "Giovinezza"-singing, and aggressive stretching out of the right arm.

As for Japan, she started such a big drive for trade in Latin America a few years ago that it looked for a while as if she would make a serious dent in the business of all her competitors. Soon, though, the drive weakened; it was shown to have been largely due to expert juggling of exchange. Today, in most of Latin America, she is far behind British, American, German and Italian competitors.

São Paulo, in southern Brazil, where Italians are so numerous, also has quite a colony of Japanese; in fact, one runs across villages there entirely populated by them. And along the Peruvian coast, there are towns and rural districts where thrifty little brown men from the Nipponese islands make up the bulk of the shopkeeping class and are branching out into ownership of plantations and other lines. But—as yet—there is little need for apprehension concerning them. They have a long way to go before qualifying as a Yellow Peril of even the palest sort.

*   *   *

At the present time, only the Germans, among our totalitarian rivals, are a real peril in Latin America. And even they are dangerous only in the economic field. Later on, they may raise their heads as a political or military menace; in view of Hitler's overweening ambitions, such an eventuality cannot be ruled out altogether.

But despite their strength and resourcefulness, Uncle Sam apparently holds the strongest position in Latin America. He is nearer to it; he is richer than any totalitarian competitor. And then there is that tremendous industrial investment of his in the southern republics of this hemisphere, which seems sure to add enormously, in the long run, to the volume of his trade and the degree of his prestige. That is, if he plays his hand skilfully.

IF you would see Old King Coffee in all his glory, go to southern Brazil, into the land of the renowned "red earth," where coffee shrubs blossom sometimes for a full hundred years; where they spread themselves before you in countless thousands until they vanish over the edge of the horizon, flanked by banana trees, their faithful henchmen, and guarded by palm trees, their slender sentinels. Enjoy the hospitality of a *fazenda*—as they call a plantation in Brazil—where you will find modernity going hand in hand with an old-fashioned welcome to casual visitors which is like a fragrant breeze from a past of leisure and courtliness. Yes, go to the land of the "red earth"—and I guarantee you will never again look upon your morning cup of coffee as something to be gulped down indifferently, with one eye on the paper and the other on your watch, lest you arrive late downtown. Never again!

Old King Coffee's realm is centered in the Brazilian state of São Paulo, and the place where he holds court is in the city of São Paulo, southern Brazil's metropolis, and the port whence he sends out yearly billions of coffee berries for brewing the world's favorite beverage is Santos—sweltering below the mountain wall separating the Brazilian interior from the sea—where, from the moment of your arrival to that of your departure, you breathe coffee, taste coffee, feel coffee and smell coffee.

There is a hot street in Santos where merchants and brokers and carters and carriers, Brazilian and Portuguese, Spanish,

Italian and German, move about in shirt sleeves, and mop wet foreheads with dripping handkerchiefs, while they transact a major part of the world's coffee business—for Brazil grows one-half of all the coffee in the world, and about two-thirds of the colossal Brazilian crop comes from São Paulo State and is shipped through São Paulo City to Santos and thence to all parts of the world, especially the United States.

A rough idea of the significance of this may be gained if you consider that recent bumper crop years in Brazil have yielded as much as 29,000,000 sacks. And here is another little item: In Brazil there are *nearly three billion* coffee plants, of which something like *two billion* are in the state of São Paulo. These figures may sound dull to those who read them in North America; but, should you ever get to Santos, and dodge freight cars and motor trucks and mule carts on its waterfront, all loaded with coffee, and tread on coffee berries wherever you go, those millions of sacks will seem to be right on the spot and those billions of coffee plants just around the corner!

Because you and enormous numbers of human beings like you simply must have coffee for breakfast, São Paulo lives and prospers. In boom times São Paulo's wealth runs up into fabulous totals, and her magnates rush off to spend accumulated profits in New York and Paris, and Old King Coffee smiles. When times are hard, down tumble São Paulo's fortunes, her magnates mope at home, there is melancholy along that hot street in Santos, and Old King Coffee mournfully shakes his grizzled head!

Then—presto!—times improve. The *fazendas* of São Paulo State, the clubs of São Paulo City, the counting-houses of Santos, all buzz with elation. Acres of new coffee trees are planted by the *fazendeiros*. Trains of coffee cars roll seaward. Myriads of bags, chock-full of little green berries, are dumped into hundreds of ships, transported over thousands of miles of water and land, brewed into millions of gallons of dark, steaming, savory fluid—all because you and countless other human beings, reaching out a hand with an empty cup in it, have chanted in clamorous chorus: "Another, please!"

Of late years, Old King Coffee has felt glum. For some time the magnates of São Paulo, in alliance with the Brazilian government, have been fighting hard to overcome the coffee crisis by means of artificial control of prices. More than once the government has saved the magnates from serious loss by taking off their hands big quantities of their output and holding it in expectation of a brisker demand.

A few years ago the stocks thus accumulated increased so alarmingly that the government, faced with the necessity of providing space for more millions of sacks from new crops, was compelled to destroy huge lots of coffee for which it could find no remunerative sale. Travelers from Santos to São Paulo suddenly became aware of an overpowering odor, saw thick clouds of smoke rising from fields by the roadside, and realized that tons of berries, which should have brought stimulation to the world, were crackling to destruction because the world could not afford to buy them.

Between 1931 and the summer of 1939, the colossal total of 67,000,000 *bags of coffee*, it is reliably estimated, each containing 132 pounds, went up in smoke—*nearly nine billion pounds of coffee!* But, despite this wholesale destruction, there were times when it failed to keep down the stocks on hand, owing to the enormous size of the new crop. Of late, since annual crops have been smaller, the stocks have dwindled, and the situation has become less serious. For instance, in 1938, the Brazilian coffee crop totaled only 21,000,000 sacks, as against the 29,000,000 of bumper years. Last summer it was estimated by experts that Brazil would have an output, for the whole of 1939, of around 21,000,000 sacks of coffee, the same as in 1938.

In the boom years, many coffee planters in São Paulo and elsewhere in Brazil, relying on indefinite continuation of the days of golden profits—"permanent prosperity"—planted many thousands of acres with additional coffee plants. So enormous was the crop, as a result of this, that, by the end of 1930, the number of bags of coffee piled up in readiness for shipment through Santos was estimated at more than 26,500,000—more than 1,000,000 bags above the world's total consumption of coffee during 1929, the first year of the world depression.

Since then, large tracts of this additional coffee land have been turned over to cotton planting, to meet the increasing demand (particularly from Nazi Germany) for Brazilian cotton, and, at the same time, afford relief from over-production of coffee.

Some years ago, an organization known as the Coffee Institute was formed in Brazil to cope with increasingly serious conditions in the coffee market. It tried to reduce the total amount of coffee available for export, and at the same time, keep prices high. But by 1930, the black year, the poor Institute was overwhelmed with trouble. Unable to continue borrowing money abroad for its manipulation of the market, it threw up the sponge, whereupon prices slid to appallingly low levels and many coffee planters, instead of seeing their optimistic dreams of wealth come true, went broke.

After the clouds of smoke from millions of pounds of burning coffee had hung like a pall over São Paulo for six years, the Brazilian government, presided over by Dr. Getulio

Vargas, realized that something else had to be tried to end the cataclysmal state of affairs. Abandoning its former policy of seeking to control the coffee market it left Brazilian planters to fight their battle alone, as best they could, against competition from the rest of the world. At first the consequences were again appalling. There were more bankrupt coffee planters, more wails, more anti-government demonstrations. So government control was restored. Of late, the situation has improved somewhat. It is still, however, some distance from satisfactory.

But Old King Coffee refuses to despair. Like that other royal non-worrier, Old King Cole, he settles himself on his throne, and smiles confidently, and calls for his pipe, and calls for his bowl, and calls for his fiddlers three—the bowl, in his case, being filled not with punch but with that luscious beverage, black as yet and strong enough to lift the top off your skull, which is the favorite tipple throughout his Brazilian domain.

It is to the United States that Old King Coffee's eyes turn most hopefully. Of all his foreign customers, Uncle Sam is the best.

For many years now we have been buying about half of Brazil's exports of coffee; and since São Paulo supplies the biggest share of the whole Brazilian crop, we are well thought of in the land of the Paulistas, and São Paulo City has reared skyscrapers with a real American look to them, and filled its streets with American din and bustle, and affectionately named a big store "Yankee Bazar."

Westward and northward from the metropolis roll the coffee lands which have brought the Paulistas prestige and wealth—those lands of the "terra roxa," the "red earth," whose soil really does show as ruddy as dried blood whenever a gash is made in it by pick or shovel. Over its undulating surface, amid ridges so red that they seemed artificially stained, I was taken in a motor car by a Brazilian friend, a retired coffee planter, to whom every bit of this fertile territory had been familiar since birth.

Coffee shrubs began to appear when we were about twenty-five miles from town; and, after that, we were hardly ever out of sight of them. "Old plantations," my guide informed me; "some of them were laid out a century ago." The shrubs, some as much as ten feet high, stretched in long, straight rows into the far distance—with here and there tracts which had been allowed to go to waste—sad signs of the depression.

As we sped along the winding road we constantly met groups of the *colonos*, who pick the state's huge coffee crop, help in the cleaning and drying of the berries, and, out of the harvest season, tend the plants, weed them at regular intervals, and do the other multifarious chores needed to keep a *fazenda* going. Among them were many Portuguese and Spaniards, also individuals of Italian or Teutonic blood.

Originally, the *fazendas* were worked by slaves, but the abolition of slavery in Brazil in 1888 necessitated the introduction of the "colono" system. Each "colono" gets a small house, built on the estate where he works, together with a patch of ground for raising necessaries for himself and his family. Some of these dwellings along the route of my trip were dirty and ramshackle; others, though, were neat, trim little bungalows—"with electric light," proudly remarked my Brazilian guide.

At one *fazenda* we surprised the family taking a dip in a private swimming pool worthy of a millionaire's place on Long Island. But—again that touch of the exotic!—while they conversed with us about Paris and grand opera, a collection of strange pets eyed us curiously—solemn monkeys, herons with long, looped necks, pink flamingoes, beautiful blue and yellow parakeets—the latter called, locally, "politicians," because (I was told with a grin) "they chatter so!"

At Campinas, the principal town of the neighborhood, we found, at one turn, an Agronomical Institute of the most modern sort—where coffee and other plants are tested and studied, and the resultant scientific data supplied gratis to *fazendeiros*—and, at another, donkey carts, horsemen with broad-brimmed felt hats, bestriding wiry little horses, and one-story shops painted in bright hues, wide open to narrow streets—all the characteristics, in short, of a typical Brazilian country town, hardly changed since the days when it acknowledged the King of Portugal as its overlord.

Beyond Campinas begins the domain of the really big coffee estates. Hereabouts are some twenty enormous *fazendas* with more than one million coffee shrubs each. In the Riberão Preto district, in the heart of the best tracts of the "terra roxa," lie the huge coffee lands once held together in a vast feudal unit by the celebrated Colonel Francisco Schmidt, greatest of all Brazilian coffee potentates.

He came to São Paulo in the '80s of the last century, as a poor German immigrant, with nothing but ambition and the determination to gratify it. When he died, a few years ago, he was the owner of a string of plantations on which grew something like *sixteen million* coffee plants—a record probably never equaled before or since in Brazil. His plantations constituted a veritable principality. On them were palatial residences for their owner; private railway lines; a private telephone system connecting outlying parts with the central administration headquarters; and an army of thousands of "colonos," employed exclusively in tending and harvesting the colonel's immense crops.

Already he is a legendary character in the "terra roxa." They still tell strangers there of his uncanny sense of direction, which kept him from ever losing himself amid the monotonous, landmarkless vastness of his domain; and of his marvelous memory, which enabled him, after whole weeks spent in cattle purchasing and horse trading and bargainings involving immense lots of coffee, to remember, without the aid of a single written note, how much of each he had bought or sold, and what profit or loss each transaction had represented.

And they recall also that he had an extraordinary fondness for that squashy, exotic fruit, the "jabuticaba"—so much so that he called for it almost to the moment of his death—showing that his long reign as the greatest of the São Paulo coffee lords had made him more of a Brazilian than a German.

We motored back cityward through glorious sunset which streaked the sky with fantastic coloring and brought out, with weird emphasis, the reddish hue of the soil. With the people of the countryside my Brazilian host stood on terms of charming familiarity. When he stopped for directions he would call those whom he addressed by the unvarying appellation of "chief."

"Chief, is this the right road to São Paulo?" The "chief"— a youth with blue eyes and yellow hair, whose ancestors undoubtedly drank much beer and sang many songs about the Bavarian Mountains—replied: "Yes, senhor, just keep on going."

"Obrigado!" (That means "thanks.") And off we buzzed. After a few miles my host would halt again.

"Chief, this isn't the road to São Paulo, is it?"

"No, senhor. Go back and take the first turning to the left."

"Obrigado."

And the "chief"—in this case a "colono" with shining black skin and ivory white teeth—acknowledged our thanks with a grin stretching right across his face.

All the way my guide raised loud lament about the coffee crisis. If only some means could be found to stimulate the world's appetite for coffee! If only Americans would drink more coffee!

"And why only for breakfast?" he exclaimed—one hand idly toying with the wheel, the other waving in emphatic gestures, and the car going at fifty miles an hour! "Why, I say, only for breakfast? What is the matter with coffee all day?—at lunch, in the afternoon, in the evening, as we Brazilians drink it? Good coffee is good at any hour of the day or night."

As we sped toward town in the twilight he told me what I had already heard on every hand—that Brazil's coffee crisis was largely a matter of over-production. When the country was turning out its record annual crop of around 29,000,000 sacks, prudent observers promptly got alarmed. "Too much of a good thing," they croaked. "Look out!" But the optimists didn't care. The orgy of planting continued.

My host recalled how, when coffee was pouring into ports like Santos and causing a serious break in prices, the government established its so-called "regulating warehouses"—he obligingly took his hand off the wheel to point one out to me—along railways in the coffee-growing regions. In these, São Paulo's surplus stocks were stored, which were later released in quantities too small to force prices down. At first, also, the government made loans to the producers of these stocks, reimbursing itself out of the proceeds of sales.

But soon the stored coffee reached a total of *20,000,000 sacks*—and no remunerative sale in sight! Obviously, something more drastic had to be done! So the wholesale coffee holocaust began. My host sniffed the air. "Ah, now one can breathe again!" he said. "There was a time not long ago when breathing around here was almost exactly like drinking coffee!"

In addition to the huge quantities of coffee destroyed in those days by fire, other millions of pounds were loaded into big scows and dumped into the sea.

The main reason for all this wholesale annihilation was that those responsible for it considered it better than to allow the vast new acreage, so lavishly added before the depression to Brazil's coffee-producing area, to go to waste. Enormous numbers of new coffee shrubs in this acreage were just reaching maturity.

Now coffee shrubs continue to bear during 10, 20, 30 or 40 years, on an average—sometimes up to 100 years. One can easily understand, therefore, the reluctance of Brazilians to doom to destruction hundreds of thousands of these valuable plants, because of what most of them viewed as merely a temporary crisis.

Depression or no depression, heavy trains loaded with coffee converge every day on São Paulo City from the "terra roxa." These converging lines, aggregating some 7,000 miles in all, may be likened to the ribs of a gigantic fan, with the city as the top of the fan's handle, and, at the bottom of the handle, the port of Santos. The handle itself is formed by one of the most extraordinary railways in the world—the renowned line from São Paulo City to Santos, over which practically every single sack of the millions produced yearly in São Paulo State has been hauled for over half a century.

Only forty miles long, this road is one of the world's marvels of engineering. Its stockholders (mostly English, for the road is English-built) received regularly, over a long period of years, a dividend of *fourteen per cent*. When the World War and the subsequent coffee crisis cut into the earnings of the "Coffee Railway," the stockholders howled in anguish because their dividends were reduced to a puny, beggarly ten per cent!

If you take this railway from Santos to São Paulo, your train runs for some miles over perfectly ordinary flat country. Soon, however, you get to the foot of the steep mountain barrier, and the train is broken up into short sections of three or four cars each, which, gripping a cable operated on the endless-chain system, are hauled up a grade that is simply wicked (you rise 2,000 feet in 6 miles!) to the top of the mountain range. There the various sections are coupled together again, placed in charge of an ordinary locomotive, and hauled over more flat country in a perfectly conventional manner, into the city of São Paulo.

To negotiate the cable section of the journey takes about half an hour. There are five cables in all—as soon as you get loose from one, you are hooked onto the next, and sent up another stretch of terrific steepness. Precipices yawn below; crags scowl above; your life, apparently, hangs by a hair. But the Coffee Railway is doubtless the safest in the world, despite the fact that the huge quantities of coffee which it transports are a serious strain on its capacity.

Its roadbed is banked and buttressed with solid walls of masonry and stone. The cable is minutely scrutinized at short intervals by track-walkers. Every little mountain torrent, foaming down from the heights, is taken in hand early in its career, and tamed within an inch of its life, and forced to run prettily in solid cement beds. It is steered under the rail line; and, finally, when no longer in a position to make trouble, it is allowed to continue its natural course from some point far down the mountain slope. As a climax to all these precautions, the rocks on each side of the right-of-way are daubed with a special paint to keep them from disintegrating and thus causing the roadbed to shift.

All in all, the Coffee Railway is the most petted, scrubbed, brushed, manicured, shampooed, dry-cleaned-and-pressed stretch of track in the universe. An American engineer who traveled over it, when asked by his English hosts for suggestions as to how it might be improved, dryly remarked:

"Well, you might carve all the ties into artistic designs and set the ends of every rail with diamonds!"

Hard times during recent years have made some Paulistas realize the disadvantage of living in a one-crop state. Now and then they show a certain sensitiveness about their dependence on coffee. Heroic attempts are being made to diversify activities and thus avoid the perils arising from putting all one's eggs in a single basket.

They like to tell foreigners how promising is their cotton industry, how encouraging the progress of the silk industry, how well the textile mills, scattered through the "red earth" region, are doing. And they resolutely substitute for coffee discussions tales of the wonders which immigration has wrought—interwoven with impressive statistics of the great masses of Italians and Portuguese, Spaniards and Germans who have settled in the state and who influenced local character and customs and speech. And they will talk about the Japanese, now immigrating in growing numbers—to the elation of some Paulistas, believers in the doctrine of "the more foreigners the merrier"; and to the alarm of others, who do not relish the idea of these Orientals getting a foothold in Brazil, and living mysterious lives of their own in hundred per cent Japanese communities, where only Japanese is spoken and the very street signs are in Japanese.

Also, Paulista apostles of "get-away-from-coffee" will talk politics at great length and damn the latest move of the Rio de Janeiro authorities with fervid profanity.

And, of course, they will ask the foreigner for his impressions of the "Snake Farm." "Surely, you have seen our famous Snake Farm?"—and then comes much lore about that remarkable institution, unrivaled in the world, at which scores of venomous snakes fix cold eyes on visitors, while they bask before the little rounded cement cells in which they live. From these cells they are fetched by white-clad experts and forced to spit out their poison, which is then made into serums and sent into the interior, for combating the snake bites which are nearly as common there as head colds are with us.

On all these matters, the Paulista will discourse freely and intelligently, until, little by little, coffee fades from your thoughts. You emerge from such general discourse and head for your hotel. After the manner of tourists, you allow your eyes to roam carelessly to the trolley cars clanging along the streets, in order to learn, by perusal of what is printed on them, where they are bound or what company owns them.

But in São Paulo, trolley cars don't tell you such idle trifles—except as an afterthought! To your astonishment, you read, printed on the side of one of them, in big, bold lettering:

"To plant fine coffee is a patriotic duty!"

And, on another:

"Planters! Grow good coffee always, bad coffee never!"
And, on a third:

"High-grade coffee is gold and gold is worth what it weighs!"

The one-track mind at work. The efficiency shark on the job. A cheerful potentate, but at the same time, one with a lively sense of his importance, and of the undivided loyalty due him from his subjects, is Old King Coffee!

BRAZIL, with an area larger than that of the United States, a population of almost 45,000,000, and a wealth of raw materials to be found in scarcely any other land, would be a particularly valuable plum for the have-not nations—especially Germany.

The French and British surrender to Hitler at Munich was looked upon in Rio de Janeiro and throughout the Brazilian republic as a dire threat to the weaker nations of the world, particularly to those which, like Brazil, are basically democratic and peace-loving.

Many Brazilians felt instinctively that the dictator of Nazi Germany, unless checked, might take steps to obtain a firm foothold in their country—even by forceful intervention.

Not that they scented any immediate danger of German naval demonstrations in South American waters or landings by German troops on Brazilian soil. But they refused then, and still refuse to relegate such possibilities entirely to the realm of sheer fantasy.

Underestimating one's rivals—as Americans living in Brazil, who have had occasion to test German efficiency at close quarters, constantly point out—is both foolish and dangerous. And it will not do Uncle Sam the slightest good in fighting the gigantic drive for supremacy that the Nazis have launched in the biggest, most populous and potentially richest of all the Latin American republics.

Residents of German extraction in Brazil are prominent in

the most variegated walks of life—as planters of coffee, cotton and other products; in banking, manufacturing, exporting and importing; as owners or employees of some of the best shops in the capital and in other cities, where they sell hardware, jewelry, dry goods, optical instruments, tools, toys, books and stationery; as brokers, insurance agents, hotel-keepers.

The activities of some of the German concerns and families in Brazil began several generations ago; and so successful have some of them been that quite a body of German-Brazilian millionaires and near-millionaires has sprung up.

All that an American visitor, doubtful of the solidity of the Germans in Brazil, needs to do is to take a stroll along the Avenida Rio Branco, Rio's busiest thoroughfare, and cast an eye on the luxurious headquarters of wealthy German concerns that line it, or to turn into the Rua da Alfandega, the local Wall Street, where he will see most impressive marble and granite buildings occupied by banks whose home offices are in Berlin.

German experience, garnered from long years of dealings with Brazilians, is analogous to the record of the sons of the fatherland in many other Latin American countries. Instead of being mere birds of passage, like most Americans, Germans emigrating to Brazil have frequently married Portuguese-Brazilians and reared children who have sometimes turned out more Brazilian than German.

Many German families in Brazil have been living there for three or four generations. Their members may answer to names like Schmidt or Mueller or Schultz, yet they often speak better Portuguese than German. And they display, in their dealings, a mentality that is as much Latin American as Teutonic.

This duality is of incalculable value to its possessors. One hundred per cent Portuguese-Brazilians who do business with them scarcely think of them at all as foreigners—a sharp contrast to the average Brazilian attitude toward Americans, who usually remain aliens to the natives from start to finish of every business transaction.

Germany's influence in Brazil would be serious enough even if no special efforts were being made from Berlin to further it. But when one considers that, under the Hitler régime, not a single day is wasted nor a single trick forgotten, in pushing the Nazi cause in Brazil, the unprecedentedly favorable position occupied there by the Germans becomes instantly apparent.

In addition to the methods of penetration already enumerated, the German Nazis have introduced some new "wrinkles" which, as the British would say, are simply "not cricket."

Pressure, for instance, is exerted through young German-Brazilians, who, forced upon old-established business concerns by Berlin propagandist departments, soon make it quite clear to employers that reluctance to climb on the Nazi "bandwagon" may have dire consequences to profits.

Included in the Germanic element are a number of Jewish merchants, naturally anti-Nazi to a man, whose positions are becoming increasingly disagreeable. Against them Berlin is conducting a campaign of intimidation and discrimination that in some cases has made their continuance in business well-nigh impossible.

Efficient work was also being done by Berlin a few months ago, when I was in Rio, to replenish the Reich's depleted coffers with money amassed by traders of German extraction in Brazil.

A Nazi agent, for example, would go to a local business

man and hint that, as a patriotic German, he ought to live in Germany. Sometimes such "hints" were of a nature that only the most courageous and untrammeled could ignore. So the man would sell his holdings at what looked like a liberal figure, have the proceeds credited to him in Germany, and sail away.

Scarcely was he out of sight of the Brazilian coast before the agent would resell the holdings that he had just acquired and credit the sum thus obtained in foreign exchange—desperately needed by Germany—to his Berlin employers.

Upon arriving in his native country, the returning patriot (if his case resembled that of many others in like circumstances) soon felt uncomfortable in the undemocratic atmosphere that he had exchanged for the free air of Brazil. Moreover, he found that heavy taxes were eating big holes in his patrimony. So he decided to go back to Brazil.

"Go ahead," the Nazis would tell him, "but all you can take away with you is ten marks." So the chances are that the disillusioned patriot stayed where he was, watching his capital disappear, while the Berlin government not only retained the precious foreign exchange derived from the sale of his Brazilian holdings, but also had a good prospect of scooping up the whole, or most of the sum credited to him in Germany.

On the occasion of my last visit to Brazil the Nazis seemed to be lying low, following the recall of Karl Ritter, German ambassador to Brazil, who had displayed a remarkable talent for antagonizing officials and others whom he encountered. The violent wave of unfriendliness toward Berlin's methods of infiltration that had suddenly swept over Brazil seemed to have sobered them. Meanwhile, influential local newspapers were denouncing Nazism. Bland assumptions, in the Berlin press, that remarks by President Vargas about foreigners guilty of aggressive tactics were obviously meant as a warning to the United States, were arousing shrieks of derision in the Brazilian press. As one leading Rio daily sarcastically put it:

"Hitler annexed Austria because of the Germans there. He crushed Czecho-Slovakia because of the Germans there. Yet we are asked to believe that it is the United States that covets southern Brazil because of the Germans there!"

Officials in the Brazilian capital, correctly gauging popular sentiment, were quietly but firmly defiant in their dealings with Nazi Germany, in spite of the risk of bringing upon themselves retaliation from an angered Berlin. Brazilian defiance was renewed proof that Hitler's aggression against Austria and Czecho-Slovakia with all its implications, had made a deep impression in South America.

On the showing made by the United States in Brazil will largely depend our ultimate position in the bitter economic warfare being waged between the great American democracy and the Nazi Third Reich, for supremacy in the Latin American market. In that war Germany's new and ruthless methods, intensified to an unprecedented degree since her victory at the Munich Conference, have placed her in an excellent strategic position.

These methods, superimposed on the coordinated activities of German diplomats, banks and business firms, working in a harmony based on generations of experience with Latin Americans, combine to make a system of economic penetration possessing an efficiency beyond anything that can be shown by any competitor, including the United States.

Take, for instance, Germany's "Aski" mark campaign in Brazil.

Before December, 1937, most transactions in "Aski" marks between Brazilians and Germans were handled by German banks in Brazil, a great advantage to the Germans. In that month, however, the Brazilian government introduced a system of foreign exchange control, covering all foreign countries, and later the Bank of Brazil took over the exclusive control of all operations in foreign exchange, including those in "Aski" marks.

This greatly annoyed the Nazi government, because it lost control over these marks, which had made possible juggling them to its own advantage, and because German banks in Brazil could no longer make profits through manipulation of "Aski" marks.

German policy at that time was aimed at keeping the Bank of Brazil "long" on "Aski" marks, a convenient method for exerting pressure advantageous to Nazi Germany. For instance, by increasing purchases of certain Brazilian products to a point beyond the quotas specified in agreements with the Brazilian government, Germany, on one occasion, forced the Bank of Brazil to stop accepting any more "Aski" marks, because of the large total which the bank already had on hand. The bank's position was modified later in favor of certain exports of coffee, cotton and other products.

Soon the situation was again complicated by the German purchase of 300,000 bags of Brazilian cocoa, obviously intended for storage in Germany as possible war rations for the German army. This completely upset conditions in the cocoa market and again flooded the long-suffering Bank of Brazil with "Aski" marks.

As a result, the bank once more suspended all transactions involving these marks, nor did it for some time loosen its restrictions except to authorize the export of 10,000 tons of

Brazilian cotton and 200,000 bags of Brazilian coffee, which exhausted the 1938 quota of 1,600,000 bags agreed upon with the Brazilian government.

The Bank of Brazil's policy proved eloquently how worried it was because of its "long" position. It also supplied convincing evidence of the cleverness and unscrupulousness of German methods in Brazil.

Despite exasperation in Brazil at German trading methods, some Brazilians favor the continuance of barter transactions with Germany. But many others are against it.

The latter hailed our recent deal at Washington with Brazil's Foreign Minister, Senhor Oswaldo Aranha, as the harbinger of a concerted American campaign to undermine the ascendancy of German traders in the Brazilian market.

Those favoring more barter with the Germans contend that Germany must be humored because she offers an excellent outlet for Brazilian products in general and the best outlet for Brazilian cotton. Those against it are keen to have their native country wriggle out of economic subservience to Nazi Germany.

Most Brazilians agree that many of our products are the best—among them our railroad equipment, machinery, office and electrical equipment, tools, motor vehicles, chemicals, drugs, pharmaceutical preparations, paper and toys. For these they are willing to pay a slight premium if necessary, but they shy at the 25, 30 and even 50 per cent extra price in relation to similar goods from Germany, which has at times been asked in the past by American exporters.

In addition to the excellent quality of our merchandise and Brazilian preference for it, we have two other outstanding assets which, if duly emphasized in a sales campaign, might bring about a sensational alteration of the situation in our favor, according to American business men with whom I talked in Rio. These are:

1. Our prompt deliveries, in contrast to vexatious delays recently in the deliveries of German merchandise ordered by Brazilian firms, because of Germany's intensive armament campaign.
2. Special inducements now being offered to American exporters to Brazil, in the way of lower carrying charges, longer terms of credit, etc.

In any event, we must gird ourselves for a desperate struggle. We must realize that we are up against a solid front of German opposition to our economic penetration of Latin America, in which only united efforts on the part of our exporters, backed by effective governmental aid from Washington, can make any appreciable dent.

Americans in business in Brazil suggest various ways for helping the American cause there. One is to meet the urgent local need for capital—"most of the nations down here are flat broke," remarked one American in Rio—by using some of our enormous resources in capital to make possible credits in Brazil and other Latin American countries, thus tiding them over bad times. Already we have taken steps in this direction.

Another suggestion is that we might counter German and other competition by establishing a two-price system on some of our products—one price for export, another for the domestic market—which would not only favor exporters but increase employment in the United States.

The Brazilians, it cannot be repeated too often, like to do business with the United States. But they complain that we have not been conspicuous in the past in meeting them half-way. Accustomed to the most liberal concessions, especially from Germans who bid for their orders, they resent grudging credit concessions from American firms, and—most particularly—demands for cash payment made by our exporters.

They also dislike, in common with their Spanish American cousins, our tendency to look on the Latin American market as something secondary, not to be mentioned in the same breath with our domestic market.

The Germans never act that way. For them the harvesting of orders for their products in Latin America is a matter of supreme importance.

Their home market is limited. The average German will make one pair of shoes, for instance, last twice as long as will an American. He will still be wearing the same suit of clothes long after an American has bought a new one. He is quite content to drive, year in year out, an automobile which an American would soon look upon as antediluvian.

The sort of home market resulting from such thriftiness explains in part the desperate drive of German manufacturers to dominate foreign markets, especially the South American.

These Germans never give prospective purchasers there the feeling that they play second fiddle to customers at home. They are not like a certain American firm which I heard about in Rio.

This firm used to pester its Brazilian agent for orders during the first post-depression period. It accused him of shirking and refused to listen to his pleas that Brazil also was suffering from bad times. At last the situation improved and the agent managed to book some excellent orders.

Filled with elation, he hastened to transmit them to his principals—only to receive a curt note to the effect that the domestic market in the United States having taken a decided turn for the better *they could not be bothered with foreign orders!*

In a Latin fury, the Brazilian severed relations with that American concern. Ever since he has refused to represent any other. No exporter in Germany would ever act like that.

Far too many Americans, out to sell the products of their native country in Rio, surrender to the easy, cheerful life of the place. They put up at expensive hotels, get to know the night life, visit too freely the renowned gambling rooms out on Capacabana Beach, draw too heavily on the stock of expense money supplied by their bosses back in the United States. Soon the non-business interests of some of them take up many more hours than their business interests. Their day begins at dusk.

But most of their German rivals start business early in the morning, are still at it late in the afternoon, stay up well into the night trying to figure out the problems which it presents. Usually they live at cheap boarding-houses. They learn Portuguese. They read up on Brazilian history—which very few Americans ever deign to do. These Germans avoid heavy drinking, steer clear of the gambling rooms, fight shy of the company of the pretty ladies of Rio. And in their business dealings, they and their employers back in Germany try to give customers what they want, instead of what they think they ought to want—as, unfortunately, many of our salesmen and manufacturers persist in doing.

"And do those Germans book the orders?" exclaimed an American rival ruefully. *"I'll say they do."*

Naturally easy-going, tolerant and prone to like all foreigners, Brazilians nowadays are showing unmistakable signs of growing disapproval of Hitler's Germany. This was especially noticeable at movie theaters a little while ago.

BRAZIL AND THE SWASTIKA

Whereas, Brazilian movie audiences there and in other Brazilian cities used to betray little or no excitement when newsreels of world events were shown, they had taken to stamping and whistling and hissing loudly when pictures of Hitler or Goering or Goebbels appeared on the screen. Mussolini also got his quota of this sort of thing. But he was not in the same class with the Nazi Big Three.

But in combating German penetration, Brazil is in a difficult position. She resents Nazi aggression, but is afraid, for the time being, to antagonize Germany definitely, since German purchases of her products, especially cotton and coffee, are vital to her prosperity.

In her embarrassment, she scans the horizon eagerly for potential aid. How far, she wonders, would her old friends, Great Britain and the United States, go in her behalf if Hitler should really get her cornered?

The British, many Brazilians fear, would concentrate on protecting the British Empire, letting Brazil (also other countries under the Nazi menace) go the tragic way of Czecho-Slovakia.

When these uneasy Brazilians turn their eyes toward the United States they are somewhat encouraged, but not as much as they would like to be. They are inclined to take at their face value assurances of friendship from Washington. They feel reasonably sure that the United States would protect Brazil effectively in case of foreign attack.

But "reasonably sure" is not sure enough. The margin between certainty and uncertainty keeps these Brazilians (and other Latin Americans) in a constant state of worry.

Opposition is developing, both among the older Germanic element in Brazil and the Brazilians themselves, against the tactlessness and high-handedness of Berlin's methods. But the

Nazis plunge blindly ahead, confident that they are men of destiny, before whom all resistance must crumble. It has not yet crumbled in Brazil, however. Side by side with Brazilian determination to protect the country's dignity and sovereignty, there is a marked feeling of apprehension for the future. In Rio, I learned, from an absolutely truthworthy source, that in high governmental circles it was feared persistence by the Germans in their present course might easily result in some serious international incident.

TAKE the average man of a cosmopolitan turn of mind, suddenly drop him at one of a score of spots in America's biggest
city—Forty-Second Street, the East or North River waterfront, Park Avenue, Bowling Green, the Lower East Side,
Chinatown, Little Italy—ask him "What city is this?" and
he will answer, without an instant's hesitation, "New York."

And it would be the same in the capital of France, or the
metropolis of Britain, or the Eternal City. Drop that man
at one of many seemingly different yet essentially similar
spots in those cities, ask him the same question, and he will
instantly reply "Paris" or "London" or "Rome." There is
something you can't get away from in those places; they are
so saturated with their own exclusive personalities that they
are unmistakable. Which is also true (to a somewhat lesser
degree) of a dozen other big cities of this world.

But I have found a metropolis, one of the biggest of all,
where that average cosmopolitan's experience would betray
him sadly.

There I would like to set him down on a fine, wide, tree-
lined avenue, its sidewalks sprinkled with little tables at each
of which men-of-the-world, amid a whirlpool of traffic and
a tornado of noise, sit sipping drinks and reading newspapers.

"Where are you?" I would ask him.

"Paris," he would answer.

"Wrong," I would retort.

And I would whisk him away—a mere two or three blocks,

[93]

mind you—to a magnificent, marble-encrusted bank, where alert executives, clean-shaven and clear-eyed, work at desks labeled with their names, right out in the open, in plain sight of customer, sightseer or bomb-thrower.

"What city?" I would query.

"New York."

"Wrong!"

And I would rush him a few hundred yards, to an eating-house paneled in dark wood, and shove under his nose a bill of fare featuring haddock and Guinness and kippers and ale.

"London."

"Wrong."

And I would transport him around a couple of corners, to a street fringed with big arcades, thronged with swarthy folk, fragrant with the smell of spaghetti and of good red wine.

"Name it," I would challenge.

"Rome."

"Wrong again!"

And finally, I would spirit him away—not more than four blocks away—to a narrow thoroughfare, free from wheeled traffic, where pedestrians crowd the roadway from curb to curb, where supercilious young bloods, leaning against the portal of a clubhouse of incredible luxuriousness, boldly stare at every pretty female passer-by, and the policemen who direct traffic at every cross-street wear pieces of white cloth, sticking out from the rims of their hats, over their eyes, and down the backs of their necks, to keep off the heat.

"Where are you?" I would ask.

And my cosmopolitan would reply in bewilderment:

"I haven't the faintest idea. I give it up!"

And then I would announce triumphantly:

"You are—and you have been all along, when you thought yourself in Paris and New York and London and Rome—in the metropolis of South America, in the capital of Argentina, in Buenos Aires!"

For Buenos Aires is a city fighting to express its true nature—a city battling, today, for its own tomorrow, against the alien leveling forces of yesterday.

Constantly, as you wander over its colossal, vital, pulsating surface, you sense that unknown quantity, the Buenos Aires of tomorrow, busily chipping away at foreign influences, like a prisoner tunneling his way toward freedom. Buenos Aires is the spearhead of a mighty attack, now under full swing down in Argentina, through which the Argentines are asserting their country's right to rank among the great nations of the world, by proving that it possesses a national character and a national soul. New York is power. Paris is beauty. London is substance. Chicago is force. Berlin is starkness. Rome is splendor. Buenos Aires, now eighth among the world's greatest cities, and in some ways the most vital and astounding of the whole lot, is clash.

Clash of European culture against something youthful and unexpectedly obdurate. Clash of American business genius and financial daring against something new and suddenly defiant. Clash of a dying South America, filled with guitars, cowboys, mantillas, Indians, rhetoric and revolution, against a rising South America of—what? That is the question. Of what? Nobody as yet knows the answer. Clash—impact—conflict. That is Argentina. That is Buenos Aires.

Buenos Aires hits you like a fist.

Oil tanks, very ugly ones, like gigantic white mushrooms, are the dominating feature of the first glimpse of it.

The foreign visitor, approaching by sea from Brazil, has

exchanged the glories of Rio's bay and harbor for the low-lying monotonous shores of the River Plate. That broad stream, tinged to muddy brown by its shallowness, has taken the place of variegated islets and gracefully curving water-front.

Gaunt grain elevators, instead of friendly green hills, jut upward. Colossal buildings, fifteen or twenty stories high, seem to bestow on the newcomer looks as hard and cold as the stone of which they are made. No outposts of the tropical jungle behind it—no alluring beaches in front of it—no towering figure of Christ the Redeemer pronouncing a benediction on it—this is Buenos Aires, not Rio.

Your ship ties up at the unsmiling landing place. You go ashore.

And suddenly the clenched fist of the Argentine metropolis opens into a hand stretched out in greeting—not exactly a friendly greeting, such as Rio instantaneously gives, but a greeting, nevertheless.

"I'm different, that's all," it seems to say. "Not smooth—rough. Not soft—hard. But a good fellow. Glad to see you. Step right in." The next moment Buenos Aires grabs you by the scruff of the neck and ducks you in its maelstrom of speeding traffic and pushing business and throbbing vitality and mad money-making.

Buenos Aires! Courage and daring and power. The thrill of action, the breath of the future, the chink of innumerable gold coins.

According to the most recent statistics, it is now the largest Latin city in the world, with Paris second. On the whole American continent, there are only two cities that are bigger —New York and Chicago. In addition to those two, the only ones in the whole world which rank ahead of it in population are London, Tokio, Berlin, Moscow and Shanghai.

It fronts on the broad estuary of the Rio de la Plata, or River Plate, which is lined for miles with gigantic docks at which you may see ships flying the flags of practically every nation possessing a seagoing merchant marine. There they unload machinery and barbed wire, plows and hydraulic pumps for Argentine earners; and costly motor cars and all sorts of articles of luxury for Argentine spenders. And before they steam away, they load up with thousands upon thousands of tons of wheat and meat, which, rolling into Buenos Aires from the huge ranches and vast grain lands stretching behind the city, northward and westward and southward, make Argentina one of the most bountiful feeders of the hungry human race.

Yet three hundred years ago, Argentina was wild and almost unpeopled, and Buenos Aires was a cluster of miserable huts huddled around a puny fort. A little over a century ago it was a dirty, smelly, Spanish colonial town, boasting only one paved street, which straggled from the waterfront to a ramshackle bull ring; a place where shaggy "gauchos," the cowboys of the pampas, galloped and boozed and brawled; where rough oxcarts floundered through lakes of mud. In the 60's of last century it had reached a population of only 150,000. In 1880 it could muster only 350,000. Today, it has over 3,000,000, nearly one-fourth of the population of the entire Argentine Republic.

You sense the clash that is typical of it in that tree-fringed avenue which seems so much like Paris. Look twice at its men-of-the-world, reading newspapers in front of its cafés, and you will notice that those newspapers, though they resemble superficially the ones which Parisians read along their boulevards, bear strange, un-Parisian names, such as *La Prensa* and

La Nación, Buenos Aires Herald and *Deutsche La Plata Zeitung.*

You sense clash in that eating-house so typical of London when you read, beside an invitation to partake of beefsteak-and-kidney pie, announcements that you may also consume *salpicón* and *humitas* and *pejerrey.* And, along that arcaded street so redolent of spaghetti and Italy, you will find, hob-nobbing with straw-covered Chianto flasks, bottles filled with native wines of which you never heard before and probably won't again—*Barón de Rio Negro* and *Pinot* and *Trapiche.* All of which is Argentina, and Buenos Aires, its metropolis, fighting their way toward individual expression.

Every day, from four in the afternoon until eight in the evening, the policemen with the pieces of stiff cloth sticking out from under their caps sternly warn away every kind of vehicle from the Calle Florida, and permit pedestrians to reign supreme. At the height of the afternoon rush during the season (December to March, the Argentine summer) if you stand somewhere a bit above the street level, the Calle Florida looks like a solid stream of straw hats, so dense is the crowd of shoppers and saunterers packed on its narrow roadway and narrower sidewalks.

There you will see Argentinian beauties in all their glory. Black-eyed señoritas and golden-haired ones, with tripping gait and flashing eyes; matrons of proud poise and leisurely locomotion; singly, in twos and threes, in loquacious bevies—thread the Calle Florida every afternoon, many among them flawlessly turned out in clothes which have just been launched on the rue de la Paix.

And on the Calle Florida, you will see, in its perfection, the favorite Argentine pastime of ogling pretty women. Men are proficient at this in most Latin cities, but in Buenos Aires they are world champions. They don't merely stare—they give a conquering, comprehensive glance which, one often fears, must necessarily go in one side of a girl and out the other.

And they don't confine themselves to staring. If a young woman is really attractive, many Argentine swains contrive, by hook or by crook, to elbow her, jostle her, brush up alongside her, push against her, pinch her, bump into her, with a concentrated efficiency which would take them far on a football field.

One day I followed for several blocks on the Calle Florida a man who was obviously a star player. His technique was superb. Not once did he miss a pretty damsel, no matter how many other persons might be acting as interference when he first caught sight of her. At one point, in trying to execute a jostle from placement, he jammed himself right through a narrow opening between two lovely ladies, sending one staggering to the left and the other tottering to the right. The colors of the Argentine Republic are blue and white; those of the Argentine woman must be black and blue!

Women, by the way, play second fiddle in the Argentine. They occupy the thoughts of the men there to an amazing extent, but they have not as yet achieved anything like the degree of equality to which their sisters have struggled in other lands. Up-to-date though the Argentines are in many ways, they have still, toward their women-folk, what an American in Buenos Aires described to me as "the Mediterranean point of view." Argentina remains a man's country.

In Buenos Aires you can find, if you look hard enough, a few women doctors. There is also said to be a woman lawyer, but I cannot vouch for this, my time in South America having been too limited for toilsome, patient exploration.

What I *can* vouch for, though, is the fact that a pair of socially prominent young señoritas, resolutely throwing overboard generations of repressive tradition, recently opened an arts-and-crafts shop in an exclusive part of the Argentinian capital. There were very pretty things in that shop, and a whole squad of assistants, and an appalling overhead. But one day, when one of my Buenos Aires acquaintances went there to buy a beautiful bowl which she had admired in the show-window a week or so before, she found nobody but an elderly caretaker, who told her that the whole stock was locked up, and that he hadn't the keys, and that she would have to come back some other time, when the proprietresses were there.

"Where are they?" she asked in astonishment.

"At Mar del Plata." (Mar del Plata is the most fashionable seashore resort in Argentina.)

"When will they be back?"

"In two months."

"Two months!" gasped the horrified would-be purchaser. "Impossible!"

The caretaker was shocked by all this unseemly excitement.

"Didn't you know," he asked coldly, "that the two señoritas *always* spend the entire summer season at Mar del Plata?"

*   *   *

I have stood open-mouthed before the mansions around London's Park Lane. I have hovered diffidently outside the private palaces about the Place de l'Étoile and the Parc Monceau. I remember when, in my youth, on Fifth Avenue, the red chateau of one Vanderbilt frowned at the white chateau of another, while both glanced from the corners of supercilious eyes at the twin "chocolate ice cream" mansions of an

older and less lavish Vanderbilt generation. Nor have I forgotten how, in the same haughty neighborhood, the social
citadel of Mrs. William Astor, autocrat of New York's Four
Hundred, overawed, with its expensive splendor, every one
of us pedestrians who plodded humbly past it.

But none of these was a whit more gorgeous than the
present-day residences of Buenos Aires multimillionaires.

Just across from one of the prettiest of the city's squares,
the one with the equestrian status of San Martin, the nation's
hero—well-known to American cocktail-bibbers emerging
from the nearby Plaza bar—is the mammoth château of the
Paz family, owners of *La Prensa*, that very rich and renowned
Buenos Aires newspaper. Before the insolent grandeur of the
Paz home, memories of Mrs. Astor and the Vanderbilt clan,
likewise visions of most of what their successors of today are
doing in the way of marble and granite and onyx and lapis
lazuli and brocade and tapestries and assorted flunkeys, grow
dim and pale.

Incidentally, on the occasion of my first visit to Buenos
Aires, I was told that Señor Paz was accustomed to occupy
the place *only one month every year!* And close by I was
shown another sumptuous palace whose owner, I was gravely
told, *didn't occupy it at all!* Its shutters were never flung
open, so my informant said; its iron doors remained always
locked. Its owner, flitting from Paris to Biarritz, from Biarritz to the Riviera, must have chuckled with superior glee, in
those halcyon days of Argentine spending, whenever he
picked up a copy of *La Prensa*, and read: "Señor Paz and
his family have opened their Buenos Aires mansion, as usual,
for the month of—"

The affections of the residents of this section are largely
concentrated on French culture. They flock to Paris, to stay

there as long as possible. They are foremost in bringing across the ocean eminent Frenchmen, who give lectures on French literature and French art, to Argentine audiences who try to look as French as they can.

Some of these eminent Frenchmen, when they get back home, do not always please the Argentines, who have paid for their transatlantic trips, by what they say and write about their South American adventures. Recently, one of them, commenting on the tendency among the aristocracy of Buenos Aires to ape Europe, called the Argentine "a European colony without a flag." That didn't make a hit in Buenos Aires.

Buenos Aires has fine night clubs in its swell Palermo section. They rejoice in sophisticated names such as are to be found in New York and London and Paris. These, one decides, after a cursory glimpse, might be exported, without alteration, for use in Manhattan's Upper Fifties, or on Montmartre, or off Bond Street.

But suddenly, outside one of the swellest of the lot, I came upon a big charcoal fire, right alongside the driveway used by motor cars of patrons, at which an individual of most exotic aspect was roasting a whole lamb, just as the "gauchos" used to do it out on the pampas a century ago—and still do it, for that matter, to this day, in parts of the Argentine to which not even the most modest brand of night club has ever penetrated.

Aside from that charcoal fire, though, and the roasting lamb, and the exotic individual presiding over them, there was only one other striking thing about that night club when I first visited it: the way the tango was danced. Argentines, men and women, were dancing it to perfection, with a grace and sureness and beauty such as imitators of other nations cannot hope to achieve.

But when I went back a few years later—last winter, in fact—swing music was pushing the tango into the background. It was the same all over Buenos Aires. Only conservative dancers, it seemed, were still enamored of the old step so characteristic of their country; the young ones, many of whom had been to New York, had brought back swing with them and were clamorously demanding it from musicians. At one metropolitan resort not a single tango was played. "At this rate, it soon will be forgotten here," sighed an old-timer sadly.

Most things in Buenos Aires remind you of something somewhere else. Not so, however, the Recoleta Cemetery. That is unique.

I am sure that no country elsewhere in the whole world can show anything at all comparable with the sheer profusion and sumptuousness and costliness of the monuments to the aristocratic dead of Buenos Aires which crowd the Recoleta to the last square inch of available space.

It is one silent street after another of white and black and gray mortuary shrines, often adorned with sculpture of extraordinary beauty. Into these shrines visitors can peer through half-opened portals and see the jeweled caskets of the dead placed on shelves, sometimes one above the other—instead of being buried out of sight, as in other countries. And they can catch glimpses of mourning relatives, in funeral black, who have come to heap flowers on the coffins, or to sit beside them on chairs kept there for that purpose, while they think of the departed and pray for their souls.

The name of practically every aristocratic family that has figured in the history of Argentina may be found carved on the monuments of the Recoleta. Some families acquired plots in it more than a century ago and have been reverently laying their kin to rest there for generation after generation. Presidents of the Argentine Republic repose there; warriors who distinguished themselves in the country's early battles; eminent jurists and writers and men of science. Of all the things that must be seen in Buenos Aires, the Recoleta stands foremost; of all the possessions of that great metropolis it is only of the Recoleta that the Argentines can say: "This is our own. No city in another land has anything like this."

Close to the Recoleta, the foreigner stumbles again on the contrast which is everywhere in Buenos Aires.

Right across the street from the cemetery's superb shrines of marble from Carrara, its monuments carved by eminent European sculptors, or by native sculptors saturated in the traditions of European art, there is a restaurant which serves nothing but typically Argentine, primitive, provincial dishes, cooked just as they are cooked for the "gauchos" in the "cow towns" of the interior.

You sit in a patio, close to a kitchen such as they used to have in Argentina when it was a Spanish colony, and eat a mixed grill that seems to include selections from every single part of the steer or cow from which it came. And they also give you *humitas*—corn pounded to a pulp, mixed with tomato, onion, sugar and pepper, served piping hot, in corn leaves; and there is wine from vineyards in the remote province of Salta, which few people even in Argentina ever drank or heard of.

And after you have put all this down, you walk out the front door and find yourself face to face with a French château!

Behind the façade of that château, for all its Frenchiness, and behind dozens of façades resembling it, you may be sure that the owners, despite long sojourns in France, will drink "yerba maté," the favorite native beverage. It is brewed from leaves, gathered, thousands of tons of them, in faraway Brazilian forests; it tastes somewhat like the strongest and greenest of green tea. It is sucked up by its hosts of Argentine admirers through a silver tube known as a "bombilla," stuck into a funny little gourd. And it is about as French as an alligator!

Uptown Buenos Aires, where the private palaces and big night clubs are, is the old Argentina almost dominated by Paris; downtown Buenos Aires, with its fine banks and deafening turmoil, is New York trying to dominate the new rising Argentina. And if you would sense still another sort of clash, go out to Tigre. There you will see the Argentina of today and the Argentina of tomorrow at grips, not with Europe or the United States, but with an old South America of jungle and mystery and vastness.

Tigre is a pretty resort about fifteen miles from the center of the Argentine metropolis. It nestles amid a network of waterways, branches of the great Paraná river—whose mouth is the River Plate—which cut up the region round about into numerous little islands. At first glance, Tigre reminds one vividly of the Thames region above London. It has the same attractive villas; the same yachts with bright rails and rippling pennants; the same lawns, so neatly manicured that they might be fitted, almost without change, into the landscape around Marlow or Henley.

But—your launch rounds a bend, and you come upon a swarthy man in shirtsleeves, bedraggled hat, and trousers precariously held up by a badly frayed belt, rowing a boat from which he peddles vegetables, or fruit, or meat, to the owners of the villas lining the bank. Not much like the Thames! Then, dropping down the waterway a short distance, you see, peeping out of the woods, mud huts so primitive that they might be the abodes of aboriginal tribesmen untamed by civilization.

Then, with extraordinary suddenness, your launch emerges from a quiet backwater onto a wide, turbulent, dark brown stream, all angry white caps and swirling eddies and gloom and malevolence—the mighty Paraná itself!

Out of the very heart of South America the Paraná comes; it bears to the sea the waters of rivers scarcely explored; dipping on the breast of its perilous current is débris from forests into which the sun never penetrates, through which naked Indians crawl and savage animals prowl. As your launch is tossed about on its grim waters, you seem actually to hear the stealthy footsteps of those Indians and smell the hot breath of those animals.

*　　*　　*

Many Argentinos, especially those who love Europe, do not love us. They find the United States a big, bad wolf of a land. To them, Americans are uncouth of manner and materialistic of soul.

"We're just gringos down here," an American banker in Buenos Aires told me. To the criticisms leveled at America and Americans, which sometimes get quite acid, the more peppery among the American colony retort by calling Argentina a "cow country," and its cities, even its lordly capital, "cow towns." This is altogether too sweeping to be just. Yet there is more than a little truth in it.

The millions of cattle which roam the vast Argentine pampas have been, for decades, the backbone of the country's wealth; only within comparatively recent years has wheat challenged the supremacy of meat among Argentina's articles of export. And those millions of steers and cows are the foundation of most of the great fortunes which have made possible the parks and palaces of magnificent Buenos Aires.

Argentines with a sense of realities—and a sense of humor—are quite willing to recognize this. One of them, an aristocrat noted for his wit, was showing an American over the splendid Jockey Club of his metropolis. The American paused in admiration before a fine painting by a famous French artist.

"That must be very valuable," he commented.

"It is," said the Argentine. "It cost at least two thousand cows!"

On that broad thoroughfare of swirling dust and yelling news-boys and honking, speeding, dangerously careening motor traffic, the Avenida de Mayo, center and focus and heart of the throbbing life of Buenos Aires, metropolis of Argentina and Latin America, the visitor from the United States, strolling along past leisurely coffee-sippers lounging at tables in front of cafés, and past hurrying pedestrians who impolitely elbow him out of their path, halts suddenly, his eye caught by a big poster—pasted up beside a furious denunciation of Nazi Germany—with the following printed on it, in enormous letters:

"Down with Yankee Imperialism! The United States has already stolen one-half of the territory of Mexico! It has grabbed Panama from Colombia! It has assassinated Sandino, defender of Nicaraguan independence! It has enslaved our sister-republics of Central America and the Caribbean! It has fomented the Chaco war on behalf of American oil interests! He who forgets all this cannot claim to love liberty!"

This terrific outburst is signed "Alliance of Nationalist Youth." Across it somebody with far-different sentiments has affixed a placard reading, "Propaganda paid for with German money!"

No special importance need be attached to the occasional presence just now of such anti-American posters on the Avenida de Mayo. But the fact remains that they keep bobbing up there. They serve to remind visitors from the North that, despite some genuine friendliness, despite many cases of individual popularity of Americans, active dislike of the United States still exists in South America. There is no getting around it—Latin Americans, in general, don't "get" us. And we don't "get" them. Our man in the street has classed them far too often in the past as "greasers"; their man in the street has been only too prone to lump all of us North Americans together as "gringos."

In our attitude the main ingredient has been indifference; in theirs it has been antipathy. This has remained true despite the spilling of oceans of eloquence about "the ties that bind us," "the mutual esteem that unites us" and similar oratorical flubdub.

In Latin America, the average Frenchman or Italian is accepted as a good fellow until he proves himself otherwise; the North American, on the other hand, is often held to be an "outsider" until he proves himself a good fellow. Even our cousin, the Britisher, also frequently kept beyond the pale of popularity, is, as a rule, better liked than we are.

For one thing, he is supposed to make less noise. The average Englishman, even when he is so full that his right leg doesn't know what his left leg is doing, usually manages to preserve shreds of his lofty British calm—and that goes big with Latin Americans. We, on the other hand—sober or drunk—are accused of being too boisterous.

In Argentina they still talk about the occasion when a shipload of American tourists, on a cruise around South America, was invited to enter the sacred precincts of that most renowned, luxurious and exclusive social organization, the Buenos Aires Jockey Club. The tourists availed themselves of the invitation in large numbers, but some of them drank so deeply and yelled so enthusiastically that the officers of the club, shocked beyond words, refused to issue similar blanket invitations to Americans.

"Englishmen wouldn't do that!" the Argentines insist reprovingly. As for the French and Italians—well, first, says your Latin American, they don't drink much, and, second, when they do, their Latin dignity somehow remains with them.

This attitude of misunderstanding between the inhabitants of the two Americas is especially unfortunate when it comes to trade relations. Antipathy toward us inclines people in the southern republics to do business with Europeans unless the advantage of doing it with us is overwhelming; and our indifference toward them frequently makes us shut our eyes to potential profits.

In Washington nowadays there is elation at the changing sentiment toward us which is becoming noticeable in Latin America. This is especially apparent in newspaper comments. Even in journals hitherto hostile, nice editorials about Uncle Sam are appearing—all the more remarkable when it is borne in mind that, just as twisting the British lion's tail has been a popular political pastime with our journalists, so, in Latin America, a favorite amusement has been tweaking the American eagle's tail feathers. *Yankee plots for expansion southward!* are still a bugaboo with many alarmists down there— likewise *Yankee Imperialism* and *Yankee dollar diplomacy!*

We have remained indifferent, as a rule, to what our marines might be doing in Nicaragua; the average Latin American, though, got quite rampant on this subject. The late General Augusto Sandino was, to most of us—according to the degree and character of our interest in Nicaraguan affairs—a rebel, a bandit or a nobody. But south of us, he was acclaimed loudly, while he was bucking the United States Marine Corps, as a heroic patriot, a champion of the Latin race against the menace of the "gringo."

It was the same with regard to our actions in Haiti and Santo Domingo. The average American, in the period of our occupation of those countries, noticing something about them in his morning paper, used to read the headlines and then turn to items which really interested him. The Latin American, on the other hand, frothed at the mouth and clenched his fists.

As for Mexico and Panama and Cuba, we show for them, on occasion, signs of intense interest. But this is usually because they bulk large as issues in our internal politics. To many of our southern neighbors, though, Mexico is a courageous outpost of Latinism against scheming Anglo-Saxonism, Panama an illegitimate child of Yankee aggression, trying hard to stay Latin, Cuba a fly struggling not to be strangled in the web of the North American spider.

Fear of the North American devil-fish, supposedly stretching out its tentacles to crush weaker neighbors, has been largely fostered by literary men of Latin America. The books of our principal foes there, Manuel Ugarte, Rufino Blanco Fombona, José Enrique Rodó, to cite only a few—are still in demand at bookstores, along with those of younger and equally unfriendly writers—though by no means as much as some years ago.

Latin Americans still read—and agree with—this estimate made of us by Ugarte, a brilliant and most venomously anti-American Argentine, on the occasion of a visit to the United States:

"A supreme contempt for everything foreign, especially for all that proclaims its Latin origin, and a lively self-satisfaction, rather parvenu in aspect but based on palpable success, give the North American a certain rough, brutal tendency to outdo other races, a certain diabolical exclusiveness, which crushes and humiliates the newcomer. . . . To the popular mind, we Latin Americans are savages, ridiculous phenomena, degenerates. . . . Nobody concealed his Olympian disdain for 'the little republics of adventure' which swarmed to the south of the North American Union."

Our leading Venezuelan enemy, Rufino Blanco Fombona, an able and prolific writer, is even harsher toward us. Once he called the people of the United States "a nation of hypocrites, who, with the Bible on their lips, have in their hearts greed and lies."

Equally zealous as a defender of Latinism against the Yankee Peril, yet essentially different from certain other writers in that he remains always the courtly Spanish cavalier, was the late José Enrique Rodó, of Uruguay. His works were on sale in his native Montevideo six years ago, while Secretary Hull was laboring to change the feeling of Rodó's countrymen toward Americans—indeed, the park beside which stands the hotel where Secretary Hull stayed during the Montevideo Conference, is named after Rodó.

The knightly caliber of the man is finely shown by the introduction to his best-known attack upon us:

"Any severe judgment on the North Americans must needs be preceded, as in a duel with a noble adversary, by the chivalrous tribute of a salute."

Then he gives an analysis of the United States and its inhabitants which—though couched throughout in urbane language—is a sizzler. Here is a translation of a small part of it:

"North American civilization produces, as a whole, a strange impression of insufficiency and emptiness. The American nation lives for the reality of the present, subordinating all its actions to selfish search for individual and collective welfare. It is a pile of wood to which nobody has been able to apply a match. Genuine art lives in North America only in the guise of individual rebellion. Emerson and Poe, in their North American environment, seem like forms of life hurled from their proper surroundings by some geological upheaval.

"Neither the ideal of beauty nor that of truth arouses enthusiasm in the descendant of the austere Puritans. He despises all thought which does not lead to some immediate finality, no matter how futile it may be. Research is, to him, merely a preliminary to utilitarian application. The very nature of the North American precludes the possibility of his ever exercising domination over other peoples."

* * *

Argentina is the most progressive, most business-like, most self-confident and most aggressive of all the nations in Latin America. Yet the average Argentino discloses constantly an essential kinship with leisurely, reflective, philosophical Europe. His Europeanism reaches its climax when he is confronted with things North American.

In spite of the record of his country, which is undeniably similar to that of the United States, and of its development, which, in the economic field, is unquestionably analogous to our own, he insists, in a sort of paradoxical perversity, on looking for inspiration toward countries which have never worshipped commercial gods as he has, nor bowed so reverently to the gods of materialism.

Aside from this Europeanism of outlook, he feels antagonism toward us for several specific reasons, among which the feeling that his country and not ours should exert predominant influence on Latin Americans is often apparent. Argen-

[113]

tinos, scornfully ignoring the fact that Brazil is much larger than their own country and that it has more than three times the population of the Argentine, pour derision on the Brazilians, branding them as lazy and incompetent.

Prejudice—which seldom becomes actual hostility individually but often develops into suspicion of "North" Americans collectively—is to be found, in some form or other, all over Latin America, even in essentially pro-American Brazil. But nowhere does the visitor from the United States find it so frankly, frequently and forcibly expressed as in Buenos Aires.

In view of this, American residents of Buenos Aires are convinced that it is the logical base from which to press whatever advantages—and combat whatever disadvantages—the Lima Conference may prove to have brought to our interests in Latin America. The Argentine republic, they keep reminding us, although it has only 13,000,000 inhabitants, of whom some 3,000,000 live in and around the capital, is the one that carries most weight among its fellow-republics. And in accordance with the course taken during the next few years by American-Argentine relations, our influence in the whole of Latin America is sure to rise or fall.

Anti-Americanism in Argentina elicits biting gibes at our expense. For instance, our endeavors to persuade Argentines to turn away from Europe, in favor of an orientation based primarily on the Americas, inspired one leading Argentine statesman recently to point out that our arguments were inconsistent, in view of our record in the Philippines and Hawaii, which could hardly be adduced as proof that we had always confined our attention exclusively to this hemisphere.

Another commentator inquired:

"Suppose we Latin Americans lined up with the United States against the peril of aggression from Europe, presumably from the totalitarian States. What guarantee would we have that if you Americans suddenly fell out with the British, you would not expect us to follow suit, though the British are not totalitarians at all?"

And a journalist of the River Plate region wrote recently, in allusion to Rooseveltian appeals for solidarity between North and Latin America:

"No matter how noble and fine President Roosevelt's intentions may be, we must not forget that, in every international union between a strong and a weak nation, the protection of the latter tends to become transformed into pressure by the former . . .

"Moreover, with regard to foreign protection in general, what happened to Czecho-Slovakia provides food for thought. That country was offered defense of its frontiers, the most ample and surest protection, and it was made to incur enormous expense in order to perfect its defensive system within a general scheme of cooperation with its allies, only to have the latter tell it to hand over that defensive system to the very nation against which it was to have been protected."

One of the commonest beliefs in Argentina about Americans is that they are mere bluffers. This attitude has been fostered partially by past performances of shady promoters from the north, whose unsavory memory is so persistent that, according to one American business man in Buenos Aires, the ill effects thereof—together with those due to other causes—will not be entirely eradicated for two generations.

Americans in Buenos Aires do not take this sort of thing lying down. They come back good and hard with telling arguments to prove that they are a most valuable asset to the metropolis. They point, for example, to the fact that whereas local British banks and other big concerns tend to employ a large proportion of Britons, imported for the purpose from Europe, American business houses employ a majority of Argentines, thus opening to the latter a future of prosperity and importance denied to them by our British competitors.

To say that the Argentine is the focus of anti-American prejudice does not mean at all that this prejudice is unanimous there; on the contrary, some Argentines are distinctly partial to us. The following three causes have contributed, of late, to strengthening this partiality:

First, the belief that British influence has been allowed to get too powerful in Argentina.

("If only you Americans would build just one railroad down here!" an important local personage exclaimed to me in Buenos Aires. "All our big railroads are British—which is too many for our good!")

Second, the general improvement in American-Argentine relations caused by the Roosevelt-Hull Good Neighbor Policy. In Argentina, as well as elsewhere in Latin America, it has made a favorable impression—though one must acknowledge that President Roosevelt and Secretary of State Cordell Hull have made more of a hit with the average Argentino as individuals than as exponents of political and economic theories.

Third, the apprehension aroused all over Latin America by the surrender of democracy to totalitarianism at Munich a year ago. This greatly strengthened the arguments of friends of ours in the Argentine who have been insisting, ever since Nazism and Fascism began to show their claws, that Latin America may fall an easy prey to totalitarian invasion unless protected by the full armed power of the United States.

Yet in spite of the gains accruing to pro-Americanism in Argentina from these three causes, the fact remains that it comes more easily to the average inhabitant of that republic to be against the United States than for it.

"If the German Nazis continue to act as aggressively as they are now acting," said the same important local personage who had sighed because there was no American-owned railroad in Argentina, "those of my fellow-countrymen who now refuse to see the necessity of American protection for their native land will undoubtedly be cured of their blindness. And since, in my opinion, the Nazis will plunge right ahead with their aggressiveness, the relations between this country and yours, as well as those of the United States with Latin America in general, are bound to improve."

* * *

Suspicion of our motives has never died in Argentina. Even the minimum of personal observation, even the most casual conversations with residents, native and foreign, will suffice to make that clear.

When the Argentine delegation to the Pan-American Conference at Lima left Buenos Aires last winter (I was there at the time) emphasis was carefully laid on the fact that the delegates must stick close to traditional Argentine policy—a prominent ingredient of which, in the past, had been opposition to anything even remotely resembling North American hegemony over the American Continent. And Dr. Saavedra Lamas, who was Argentine Foreign Minister and played an important rôle in the two previous Pan-American get-together parties at Montevideo and Buenos Aires (where he and Secretary Hull did not hit it off over-well) chose the eve of the Lima meeting to publish a book reviewing the record of those meetings and reminding readers that Argentina's traditional policy had been maintained at both of them and should be maintained at Lima.

North is North and South is South, and never the twain shall meet. Latin Americans are essentially different from North Americans. They just don't have the same mentality.

The Argentinos are nice enough to those of us who visit their country. But though Buenos Aires, their metropolis, resembles an American city more than it does Paris, the average native of Buenos Aires is a Parisian—a Parisian, to be sure, who has received a terrific injection of businessitis—but a Parisian, just the same.

"Why don't you like Americans?" I asked an Argentino.

"You patronize us."

"Anything else?"

"You don't speak our language."

There! He had said it. Not only in the literal sense, but in the figurative we and the Argentines *don't speak the same language*.

And apparently there is nothing to be done about it. Some day Americans, instead of French and Italians and English and Spaniards, may hold top place in the affections of the Argentine. But we of this generation will hardly live to see that day. Our sons, maybe. But it would be more prudent to bet on the chances of our grandsons.

* * *

Buenos Aires is Chicago in body and Paris in soul. Its inhabitants can vie with anybody in the United States as business men; they think in terms of business, leap gladly to meet problems presented by big business projects and bold business ventures. Yet, deep down, they preserve, through thick and thin, unshakable sensitiveness to the culture and elegance and basic modes of thought of Continental Europe. Some of them, accustomed to seeing Englishmen in their midst, often indeed with an English strain in their blood, like England; but, almost without exception, every Argentino loves France.

France is his spiritual home, Paris his earthly Paradise. And, almost everywhere else on the European Continent—in Rome and Madrid, Vienna and Budapest and Stockholm—he finds something that appeals to his congenital Europeanism. Even in present-day Germany, though it shocks him with the blatancy of its Nazism and the cruelty of its anti-Semitism, he does not feel entirely alien. After all, Berlin is in Europe.

Therefore, it is difficult for us to persuade the average Argentino that he should turn his inmost thoughts away from Europe. Even when we use the most persuasive arguments, harping on the enormous advantages to be derived from Pan-American solidarity, he is only too prone to impute to us ignoble motives of self-interest.

The majority of Argentina's inhabitants have always been dead against any form of Pan-American union. They opposed it in the days of Bolívar, the great Venezuelan liberator, who dreamed that a sort of League of American Nations should meet every little while to discuss ways and means of furthering the welfare of all the States on the continent.

Argentine objections at that time were rather vague; since then, they have crystallized into a single, deep-seated conviction: *any form of Latin-American union with the United States, no matter how informal and non-binding it may seem to be, must necessarily mean, in the long run, our domination of Latin America.* That uneasy thought was in the minds of those who, when the Argentine delegation to Lima began its journey thither, reminded the world of traditional Argentinian policy. It was in the mind of Dr. Saavedra Lamas when he launched his recent book.

Long-dormant fear of American domination of Latin America woke up among the Argentines, as the date of the Lima conference drew near, until, on the eve of the conference, it had assumed an unfriendliness invisible only to the blindest of wishful thinkers. It was undoubtedly encouraged by German undercover work—also British.

Despite certain disquieting signs on their national horizon, the Argentines at that time were pretty cocky. Quite a number of them were making money, there was a growing feeling of national self-confidence; the I'm-as-good-as-anybody-and-better-than-most attitude that has characterized Argentines for years was becoming more self-assertive. It caused many of them to adopt a suspicious and carping tone toward Lima. During the conference there they believed, or acted as if they believed, that Secretary Hull, in league with President Roosevelt, would try to "put something over" on Latin America. Wherever I went in Buenos Aires I found evidence of that sort of point of view.

There was a tendency to sneer at American reminders of the German peril as transparent camouflaging of sinister designs in Washington to impose the hegemony of the United States on Latin America; and there was open assertion of the theory that danger of potential aggression against Latin America was to be looked for not in Europe but in North America.

There was resentment likewise at what were considered tactless and unintelligent endeavors on our part to turn Argentina, as well as the rest of the southern countries, against Europe before Europe had done anything specific against Latin America. This was clearly brought out in the Lima address of the Argentine Foreign Minister, José María Cantilo, when he called attention to the big cultural debt Argentines owed to Europeans, and pointedly mentioned, among the latter, Germans and Italians.

As a rule, people in Argentina absolutely refuse to consider the danger of aggression from non-American countries; and if they do, they like to insist that it would be well-nigh impossible for a hostile fleet to strike a blow at Buenos Aires, in view of its distance from the sea, the shallowness of the River Plate, which forms its harbor, and the ease with which that harbor could be sown with deadly mines. All of which feeds the self-starting cockiness of the average Argentine—and bolsters his anti-Americanism.

AT one of the most famous of the "parrilla" restaurants of Buenos Aires—grills, we would call them—a breathless waiter slapped a big steak in front of me, threw a knife and fork at me, and rushed away from me in a frenzy of bustle and perspiration—not that waiters in Buenos Aires are rude, but they have very little time indeed for their fellow-humans, especially customers.

I put a sliver of that steak in my mouth, and . . . the clouds rolled away from my private affairs, the sun shone upon me in golden radiance, pretty little birds, suddenly perching on my brain, burst into enthusiastic song.

I carved and chewed and swallowed, carved and chewed and swallowed, carved and chewed and . . . smiling beatifically . . . in Nirvana. . . .

The steaks of Argentina! They are the best in the universe. He who makes that statement will back it anywhere, anyhow, any time. There used to be steaks in the United States before cold storage put science into food and took flavor out of it. And there used to be a place in Paris which served steaks of the type that dreams are made of, but the last time he who is typewriting these lines was there he got a stringy slab of very dead ox meat.

The steaks of Argentina! They are firm. They are thick. They are tender. They are full of sap and kick and life. Succulence permeates them. Rich, delicious juice oozes down their sides.

And they are so big that a husky American, of impressive appetite, before whom a particularly extensive specimen of the breed had been placed, replied, after he had stowed away the first half pound or so of the elephantine delicacy, to the question "How's the steak?":

"Steak? That isn't a steak. It's a cow with the ears and tail cut off!"

Another visitor to Buenos Aires, just off the boat which had brought him from New York, was whisked without delay to another renowned "parrilla" establishment, and introduced forthwith to a most potent, grave and reverend Señor Steak. After a tremendous bout with it, the diner called the waiter and asked how much he owed.

"One peso and a half."

"Cheap enough. Only one dollar and a half, eh? If you had charged me three dollars and a half for Jumbo I wouldn't have objected."

"Wait a moment," interposed the friend who had brought him there. "A peso isn't a dollar."

"How much is it?"

"Less than a quarter."

"So that steak cost?"

"Thirty-five cents."

Once, twice, that American tried to speak. But the words wouldn't come. Finally, in an awed voice, he murmured:

"Good heavens! Think what I'd have got for three dollars and a half!"

* * *

President Roosevelt admires Argentine cows and bulls. As producers of steak he has the highest opinion of them—as he proved last Spring on the occasion of that lively controversy which arose in Washington as to whether it was patriotic for the United States Navy to eat canned corned beef from Argentina, the only kind of Argentine beef which, under existing regulations, can be imported into this country. Boldly departing from the points under actual discussion, he gave newspapermen, at one of the regular White House press conferences, the impression that he shared the sentiments of those American visitors to Buenos Aires whose emotions, on first looking into the subject of Argentine steaks, have just been recorded. The President's views, incidentally, were not based on hearsay. He was in the Argentine in person, it will be remembered, a few years back.

At the press conference the President told the reporters that he was unable to say just why South American beef was so much better than that produced on the prairies of the western United States, unless it was that some foreign cows were naturally better makers of beef than their American sisters. And he professed himself so sure of the superior quality of the South American article that he told his visitors to ask for it the next time they went on a camping trip.

His remarks raised an ungodly rumpus. Western cattle interests danced war dances and tore their hair out by the handful. They rose as a man to the defense of the virtue of the American cow and the valor of the American bull, on which, they felt, presidential aspersions had been rudely cast. At a subsequent press conference the President denied any intent to insult American live stock and placed himself on record as feeling enormous respect both for our cows and our bulls. The uproar subsided. Cattle interests calmed themselves. Peace returned to our prairies.

As for the Argentinos, they have no doubts whatsoever as to the merits of the meat of their native land. To them, it is a case of Argentine meat first and the rest nowhere. They get positively lyrical when they talk about the great cattle herds on their pampas, about the colossal weight of the cows and bulls stolidly grazing there, about the long list of fine points that make those cows and bulls the grandest repositories of potential rump and sirloin and tenderloin in the world.

Once I was partaking, in Buenos Aires, of a magnificent steak of superb flavor, which an expert Steakologist (my host) had commandeered to dispel any doubts that I might still harbor as to the unapproachable excellence of Argentine meat. I asked him for inside information as to the reasons for this excellence. Between two copious mouthfuls, he explained.

"You see, it's this way: Argentine cattle are fed right through their lives, on pampa grass, which is the best of all cattle foods, and the only time they ever take any exercise, from the moment they are born, is when they walk to the slaughter-house."

*　　*　　*

Most American business men in Buenos Aires favor one or the other of two local schools of thought, which, because of recent developments in American-Argentine relations, have been nicknamed the Wheats and the Meats.

The Wheats, who advocate more firmness and less politeness in our dealings with Latin America in general and Argentina in particular, were delighted at the recent attempt of an enterprising American trader to sell American wheat in Brazil, a country which, so far as sales of wheat are concerned, the Argentines consider their own private hunting-ground.

If Washington had allowed this trader's plan to succeed, growl the Wheats, it would have constituted a long-needed retaliatory measure on our part against Argentina, which persistently discriminates against imports from the United States in favor of other nations, especially Britain and Germany.

When the Wheats are told that such retaliatory measures might jeopardize the harmony of our relationship with Latin America, so auspiciously affirmed at Lima last Winter, they retort that they don't care a hang; that the sooner such retaliation comes, the better. And they often garnish their remarks with outbursts of peppery profanity concerning our Good Neighbor Policy which would profoundly shock President Roosevelt and Secretary Hull.

The Meats, on the other hand, recoil in horror when such rough tactics are advocated. Being all for conciliating our southern neighbors, particularly the Argentinos, they feel that things like that wheat business in Brazil, which loosed a tempest of indignation in Argentina, are extremely short-sighted and highly detrimental to Good Neighborism.

To insure the development of a more cordial attitude toward us in Argentina, they enthusiastically champion—and that is where they get their nickname—the ratification by our Senate of the so-called Sanitary Convention, between the United States and that republic, which would permit the importation into this country (along with canned products) of chilled meat from the Argentine.

Non-ratification of the Sanitary Convention is considered by the Argentines an insult to their national honor, since it places on the whole of their country the stigma of seeking to export meat from livestock suffering from hoof-and-mouth disease, whereas, in reality, that disease is unknown in certain zones.

Removal of the present stigma, it is argued, would not result in competition of any importance with Americans in the meat business, and would be such a satisfaction to the national pride of the Argentines that it would bring us valuable general trade with their country and increase our popularity with them. At least, that is what the Meats contend.

The discrimination against us in Argentina, which so angers the Wheats, has been worked this way: importers of merchandise from various countries, among them Britain and Germany, have been allowed to pay at the official rate of exchange, whereas those importing American goods have had to pay for them at the "free market" rate, and have had difficulty in obtaining import permits. After December, 1938, they found themselves able to obtain fewer import permits than ever before.

Endeavors to get treatment for our products in Argentina comparable with that accorded, under special agreements, to goods imported from Britain and Germany, had consistently failed—up to the time that these words were being written.

One of the main arguments of the Wheats is that pressure from the United States, similar to the recent contemplated sale of American wheat in Brazil, would make Argentina let down its barriers against imports from our country. But the Meats, in a panic, claim that the reverse would result, that the Argentines would raise those barriers still higher.

The now celebrated wheat deal with Brazil developed thus:

We had a huge surplus of wheat to dispose of abroad. An American trader wanted to unload part of it in Brazil. This so perturbed Argentine wheat interests that frantic long distance telephone calls from Buenos Aires to the Argentine Ambassadors at Washington and Rio de Janeiro abruptly stopped that trader's activities.

After this had been accomplished, the Argentines talked as if he would not be heard from again in the Brazilian wheat market. But some of the American "Wheats" in Buenos Aires, when I was there, were not so sure. They hoped that he (and others like him) by sailing in and getting a share of the wheat profits now being reaped by Argentina in Brazil, might bring an end to discrimination against us by the Argentinians.

But the Meats are horrified by all such talk. Would it be worth while, they ask, to risk losing Argentine good will merely for the sake of the few million dollars that would accrue to us from the sale to Brazil of surplus American wheat?

And that brings the Meats back to their favorite topic, the necessity for ratification by our Senate of the Sanitary Convention regarding Argentine meat. This would clear up a most unfortunate situation, as they see it, which stands as follows:

At present no meat, except canned products, may be imported into the United States from any part of Argentina because of hoof-and-mouth disease. The American-Argentine Sanitary Convention, which cannot go into effect without Senate ratification, would amend existing restrictions to allow meat imports into the United States from Patagonia, an Argentine zone where hoof-and-mouth disease has never appeared.

If, as a result of ratification, meat should come to us from Patagonia, American cattle interests need not worry, according to the Meats, since Patagonia raises sheep but virtually no cattle. Only chilled lamb would come into question in our market because Americans will not eat chilled mutton. Difficulties of transportation from remote Patagonia are such that, according to a recent investigation, it could not be laid down in New York under 20 cents a pound, against a prevailing price there, at the time of the investigation, of only 16 cents a pound for American and New Zealand lamb of superior quality.

Of course, the Argentine Government could and probably

would foot the deficit, or make the shippers do so, just to have the satisfaction of getting Argentine meat of some sort into the United States, where it has been so long under a stigma. But it is believed that governmental action of this kind, even if taken just after the ratification of the convention, could not last long, in view of the essentially uneconomic nature of the whole business.

What Argentina really desires is a new market for chilled mutton, not lamb, because the United Kingdom absorbs as much lamb as it can get, and Americans are adamant against consuming chilled mutton from Patagonia or anywhere else.

To sum up: ratification by the United States Senate of the American-Argentine Sanitary Convention, according to the Meats, would not thwart safeguards now existing for protecting livestock in the United States, since in Patagonia there never has been any hoof-and-mouth disease and all meat exported from there is carefully inspected.

Nor would ratification cause any except the most insignificant change in the status quo in the American meat market, because of the great difficulties in the way of meat exports from Argentine Patagonia. The only really important point involved, they say, is the fostering of good feeling between Argentines and Americans.

If we allowed Argentina to send Patagonia chilled lamb to New York—even so much as a single token shipment—our action would be looked upon there as a courteous gesture of good will, which might easily open up valuable Argentine outlets for American products.

"Our restrictions against Patagonian meat," declared an American in Buenos Aires, "seem as illogical as for an importing foreign country to bar Alaskan meat because hoof-and-mouth disease existed in Oregon, or as unreasonable as action by ourselves barring imports of meat from Denmark because there was hoof-and-mouth disease in France."

But the Wheats don't want our Senate to bother with ratification of the American-Argentine Sanitary Convention. What they want is rough stuff. If, for instance, we should pour American wheat into Brazil, they insist, it would do more good to us in Argentina in a business way—good will or no good will—than any number of polite gestures. That is where they differ radically from the Meats on how we should deal with the Argentines.

"Pat 'em on the back!" coo the Meats. "Soak 'em in the jaw!" snarl the Wheats.

*   *   *

It is a shock to an American who has just arrived in Buenos Aires from Brazil—where the United States and Germany are fighting tooth and nail for first place, commercially and otherwise, among foreign nations dealing with the Brazilians—to remember that, in Argentina, the principal rival of democratic America is not totalitarian Germany but democratic Great Britain.

In this most progressive and wealthiest of all the Latin American republics, we and the British may be classed as friendly enemies—but enemies we are just the same. It is certainly a strange paradox that Nazi Germany, the Old World's most formidable stronghold of totalitarianism, and the United States, the New World's most powerful citadel of democracy, are—so far as Argentina is concerned—in the same boat.

Both play second fiddle to Britain. Both welcome every setback to the British locally as a corresponding gain in their local importance. If it should ever come to a real showdown in Latin America between democratic and totalitarian ideals, the British would undoubtedly be found on the side of democracy. Nevertheless, they would undoubtedly continue, in Argentina, at least, to look upon American as well as German successes, whether economic, political or cultural, in the light of threats to a supremacy which they have been building up for a century and mean to maintain indefinitely—if they can.

For that reason they do not hesitate to try to influence Argentines against us. In this they are greatly helped by the latent feeling of anti-Americanism that exists among a large percentage of the people. Our friendly enemies, the British, know that we are not popular in Argentina; and they don't at all mind profiting from their knowledge.

This being so, it is most unfortunate that they are finding valuable aid just now in the fact that we happen to be in a particularly poor position for influencing the Argentines in our favor.

Trade talks more loudly than anything else; and in United States-Argentine trade a slump has come, especially in our purchases of Argentine products, which militates disastrously against arguments we use on the Argentines to enlist their cooperation in Latin America.

"But you don't buy enough from us," they retort—in suave, diplomatic Spanish, of course. And the British, "sitting pretty," smile. So do the Germans, for they also, compared with the United States, are "sitting pretty" in Argentina.

When one nation's balance of trade with another is favorable, the inhabitants of that first nation tend to forget the other's defects and go out of their way to find reasons for calling the latter a jolly good fellow. When, contrariwise, the second nation's books show a favorable balance, Nation Number One promptly gets out pencil and paper and starts trying to figure out whether Nation Number One is just bad or thoroughly lousy.

That's somewhat the way things are just now in business relations between Argentina and Uncle Sam. They have just turned from a status favorable to the former to one decidedly otherwise.

In the three-year period between 1935 and 1937 we bought from the Argentine merchandise to a total value of something like $225,000,000, whereas that country bought from us goods totaling in value only about $180,000,000, which meant a favorable balance for our southern neighbor, during those three years, of $45,000,000.

But—

In 1938, according to estimates of the U. S. Department of Commerce, our purchases from Argentina reached a total value of only $29,000,000 as against sales of American merchandise to Argentina worth considerably over $75,000,000. This signified a balance in our favor of $46,000,000, more than the total balance favorable to Argentina in her trade with us during the preceding three-year period.

In 1938, only 8 per cent of everything exported by the Argentine went to the United States. The British—as always in a class by themselves as buyers of Argentine goods—took nearly 32 per cent of all Argentina's exports, or nearly four times our total. Meanwhile, Germany, in 1938, absorbed 11½ per cent of Argentina's total exports—more than we took.

All of which accounts for a good part of the latest phase in Argentina's permanent grouch against Uncle Sam.

*   *   *

Argentina, like our West, is a land of vast plains, treeless and monotonous. It has the same mammoth wheat fields, the same huge herds of cattle. Cowboys like ours loaf around the shacks that serve as stations at the cow towns huddled around Argentine railroads. These railroads, built mainly by Englishmen, drive across the pampas in unrelieved stretches of straight track, with never a curve for dozens of miles. I was told in Argentina that the longest straightaway section of railway in the world is down there. I believe it.

Scattered over these plains are big *estancias*, on some of which enormously wealthy owners live in feudal magnificence. Here are bred the steers and cows from which come those best steaks in the universe. The biggest of these *estancias* are small countries in themselves, with a big managerial staff and a regular army of workers of different sorts. There, pedigreed bulls, fat as butter, roll an amiable eye on visitors. Sleek race horses stick their heads into the windows of visitors' motor cars, nuzzling newcomers in friendly welcome. At Chapadmalal, most luxurious of the lot, one is shown a horses' cemetery, with the grave of a renowned race horse which won races for its master in Europe and at home.

* * *

After the winning of independence in the days of San Martín, the national hero, the Argentine nation entered on a long period of civil strife and warfare with its neighbors. It also produced one of the most famous of South American dictators, Rosas. He reigned—*reigned* is the word—from 1829 to 1852. Like others of his stamp he eventually decamped to Europe and died in England, protected by free institutions such as he couldn't or wouldn't bestow upon his own country. After Rosas there was more turmoil, more fighting; nevertheless, Argentina fought her way steadily upward toward something like democracy. Immigration helped. Free-

dom took root. The idea of dictatorship waned. Yet, only a
few years ago, there was the dictator Irigoyen, who became
so convinced that he was the whole show that his fellow-
citizens finally pushed him out of the way.

In spite of the big power wielded by a small number of
families in Argentina, there is a lot of democracy. Indeed,
there has been such a trend away from Latin American traditions of violence that it is difficult to believe that this is the
land where Rosas ruled considerably less than a century ago.
One of the principal reasons for Argentina's progress is the
strong influence of the immigrants who began pouring into
the country in numbers such as had no counterpart on the
American Continent except in its northern half.

Most numerous of all were the Italians. The Italian strain
in the Argentine has tended to dilute the essentially Spanish
character of the population without basically altering it,
since both Italians and Spaniards are Latins. It is more noticeable among present-day Argentines than the strains of English, Irish and Scotch blood which have been also an important factor. As for the original Indians, the "gauchos" of the
pampas, they were never numerous and have left little mark
on the present-day population, except in rural regions far
from Buenos Aires. Argentina is emphatically a "white man's
country"—there is practically no trace whatever of African
blood.

American travelers who prefer, in their wanderings, to find
not differences but similarities, will be more at home in the
Argentine than anywhere else in South America. Despite
their strong affinity with Europe, especially France, and their
considerable tinge of anti-Americanism, the Argentinos are
much like ourselves.

They are business men to the marrow. They like short cuts.

During business hours they never suggest a desire for a siesta. Unlike Brazilians and natives of other Latin American countries, they don't let their attention stray, until after business deals have been definitely consummated, to little cups of coffee.

From the Argentine plains, men of daring, wielders of a power like that of our indomitable pioneers of big business, have wrested fortunes of a size rarely found anywhere except in the United States. Their descendants of today smash through the same obstacles, reach the same heights of success and affluence. They think themselves the Parisians of the New World. In reality, they are the North Americans of South America.

IN Argentina, at the southern end of South America, one's attention is constantly turned to the wars of independence waged there, at the turn of the eighteenth and nineteenth centuries, against European domination. So it also is, in Venezuela, at South America's northern end. That is because the two greatest heroes of those wars were a Venezuelan and an Argentine.

They—the wars and the heroes—had an epic quality.

Though the armies engaged were small, judged by our standards, they accomplished extraordinary things. Their leaders at times rose above themselves in the quality of their leadership, bringing off military coups of melodramatic sensationalism.

In those wars, the sinister mountain barrier of the Andes, rock-ribbed, snow-capped and precipitous, was crossed twice by little armies of South American patriots, pitted against the soldiers of the King of Spain, in marches that stand forth to this day as military classics of their kind. Once, in Venezuela, a reckless commander of cowboy horsemen, achieved the feat—probably unique in all history—of capturing gunboats with cavalry.

There were battles on plains broiling in tropical heat, on icy plateaus, on the rim of a volcano. Into these, unkempt and footsore regiments were urged by daredevil leaders with words of command now enshrined as integral parts of Latin America's language of patriotism. When a citizen of one of the more turbulent republics there becomes discouraged at its record of governmental chaos and militaristic dictatorship and chronic rebellion, just remind him of his country's War of Independence. That will strike sparks from his eyes, as he exclaims: "Yes, some of us may have done little with the independence that we won, but the winning of it—ah, *that* was our Heroic Age!"

In the brave company of men who led those wars against European royal masters, two names shine in unapproached splendor—Simon Bolívar of Venezuela and José de San Martín of the Argentine.

The careers of both show striking similarities. Both, destined to tear down the stately edifice of Spanish rule on the South American Continent, were born, not in the great colonies where that rule was proudly centered, but in obscure outlying portions of the huge colonial realm of Spain, remote from Lima, haughty "City of the Kings," and Mexico, bright with vice-regal pomp. Both, belonging to the ruling colonial class, might easily have won prominence in the Spanish service; instead, both staked everything to bring freedom to their fellow-South Americans.

In civil matters, both had vision; as generals, both combined the audacity to plan moves involving awful risks with the ability to crown their plans with brilliant success. Both climbed to the pinnacle of achievement. Both met—once—to part in mutual distrust. And both, having listened to frenzied popular acclamation, to the thundering cheers of soldiers whom they had led to victory, ended their lives in exile, their health shattered, their money gone, their dreams dead.

Venezuelans and others have leveled against San Martín the charge that, at the height of his career, he proved himself a quitter; Argentines and others have impugned the motives behind some of Bolívar's actions. But neither of these accusations, in the dozen decades that have elapsed since the two were laying the foundations of their renown, has sufficed to tarnish their achievements. Both emerge—from the mists and contradictions of history—fully worthy of the reverent admiration in which their fellow-countrymen, together with millions of other people all over Latin America, have enshrined their memories.

In their lifetime, the world heard much about them; since their death their story has been largely forgotten beyond the borders of the lands which they freed. It is a story that richly deserves re-telling. For it is heaped to the brim with thrill and drama; indeed, in the case of Bolívar, it is so romantic, so glamorous and so spectacular, as to be almost unbelievable.

Both grew into manhood when Spain and Portugal, lords of the southern part of the American hemisphere, were rounding out the third century of their rule. For a full three hundred years and more Spanish and Portuguese monarchs had governed there, in jealous exclusiveness, yet within the short space of the ensuing quarter of a century, that whole vast appanage of their royal crowns slipped from their grasp, with the lone exception of Cuba and Puerto Rico, where Spain maintained her sway to the end of the nineteenth century.

Some of the Latin American colonies were lucky enough to achieve independence peacefully: Brazil, without firing a shot, exchanged a Portuguese king for a Brazilian emperor; Paraguay left to Argentine armies the winning of her independence from the Spaniards; and the five republics of Central America passed without bloodshed from the tranquillity of Spanish despotism to a freedom stained (except in Costa Rica) with almost uninterrupted civil war.

Other lands had to fight hard before they saw the last of
their European overlords: in Mexico, the patriots Hidalgo
and Morelos, after leading Mexicans to victory in battle, died
before firing squads; in Haiti, swarthy Toussaint l'Ouverture,
also victorious in the field, eventually paid with his life for
his temerity in defying Napoleon Bonaparte; around Montevideo, stubborn Artigas held high, in savage strife, the banner
of Uruguayan patriotism; and in Cuba patriots struggled
dauntlessly until American soldiers and sailors helped them
to end the control of Spain.

But nowhere was the tie with Europe broken in warfare so
ruthless and devastating as in the regions which are now the
republics of Venezuela, Colombia, Ecuador, Peru, Bolivia,
Chile and Argentina, freed by armies in which numerous
brave officers—among them, to name only a few, the Venezuelans Sucre and Páez; the Colombians Santander and Córdova; Flores of Ecuador; Santa Cruz of Peru; O'Higgins of
Chile; Belgrano of Argentina—served under the supreme command of Simon Bolívar or José de San Martín. In these two
heroes the tenacious bravery of every fighter for independence in Latin America's Heroic Age, from the northernmost
point of Mexico to the southernmost tip of Cape Horn, rises
to martial climax.

Simon Bolívar was born July 24, 1783, at Carácas, the
capital of the Spanish province of Venezuela. He was a scion
of patrician stock. Also, he was rich—enormously so, by the
standards of his day—the heir to great coffee plantations and
troops of slaves. Instead of casting in his lot with Spain, however, he early decided to devote his life to freeing his native
land, and as many other Spanish provinces as possible.

This resolve he backed with gifts extremely well suited to
its realization. The most striking of these was perseverance;

nothing in the way of misfortune sufficed to deflect him from his goal.

Three times he was driven from the South American mainland by Spanish victories only to return from exile more determined and formidable than ever. He was a little man, scarcely five feet, six inches in height—but a giant in valor and endurance.

He despised money. When the Spaniards confiscated his rich estates, he remained indifferent; and when a twist of fortune put him at the head of South American republican governments, with the power to dip into the treasury almost at will, he remained poor. On the other hand, he was a lavish spender of public funds on public works.

Bolívar always admired the United States, but he believed that our American form of government was not the right kind for South America. Anglo-Saxons, he reasoned, could make a success of a federation of sovereign states, loosely bound together under a central authority. For South America, however, he felt that this would never do. Central government there, he thought, must necessarily be strengthened at the expense of state sovereignty.

* * *

In 1806, on his return from a trip to Europe, Bolívar visited the United States. What he saw there made him more discontented than ever with the state of affairs in his native land and he sailed from Charleston for Venezuela, determined to bring about a change. Once at home again, he threw himself heart and soul into rebellion.

Sent to England to enlist aid there, Bolívar, though he failed in the principal object of his mission, brought back with him Francisco de Miranda, a Venezuelan, who had already been working for the freedom of his country and had captained an expedition (fitted out, by the way, with American money in New York) to wrest Venezuela from Spain. Shortly after his arrival in Carácas, the veteran plotter lined up all the anti-Spanish elements and persuaded them to launch Venezuela's Declaration of Independence. This document was signed July 5, 1811.

One after another Spain's other colonies in the New World followed Venezuela's lead. Fires of revolt blazed up. Now came years of desperate fighting, wholesale destitution and hideous cruelty, with the South Americans battling obstinately for freedom, with Spain striving to the utmost to crush their resistance and punish their commanders.

Soon Bolívar pushed his way to the very forefront of leadership. Miranda, though he had held high command in the army of the French Revolution, proved unsatisfactory as a general. The Spaniards in Venezuela forced him to surrender. Bolívar and others, furious at what they considered perfidy, arrested him immediately after the surrender, intending to have him shot. But they were forced to flee the country, leaving Miranda in Spanish hands. Violating the terms of the capitulation, Monteverde, the Spanish commander, had Miranda shipped in irons to Spain, where he died a few years later, chained to the walls of a dungeon.

Bolívar escaped to Curaçao, in the Dutch West Indies. Thence, he got himself to Cartagena in New Granada (now Colombia), which was in rebellion against Spain. Placing himself at the head of a small army, he had the temerity to cross the mountains into Venezuela. There, after hard fighting, he routed the Spaniards in his path and made his triumphal entry into his native city of Carácas.

Triumph, though, was short-lived. The Spaniards reacted

savagely. Boves, a leader of extraordinary ability and cruelty, led a big force of wild horsemen from the "llanos," Venezuela's great plains, to the coast lands. After desperate resistance, they completely defeated Bolívar and the rest of the Venezuelan generals. Boves became master of nearly the whole of the country.

Bolívar was again forced to save his life by flight to foreign parts. He took refuge in the British island of Jamaica. He was nearly destitute. The Spaniards, long before, had seized his estates and cut off his revenues. He was forced to borrow money, a dollar at a time. He was half-starved, ragged, haggard. His piercing black eyes burning above sunken cheeks caused the English Governor of Jamaica to say of him: "The flame has consumed the oil."

Yet he never gave up. When everything seemed at its darkest, he penned, in the miserable Jamaican lodging-house to which fate had sent him, an epistle, a sort of open letter to the world, an amazing combination of splendid dreaming and prophecies uncanny in their accuracy.

"Though I aspire to see a perfect government in my native land," he wrote, "I cannot bring myself to the belief that, under present conditions, the New World can be governed as a great republic. Since this is impossible, I dare not desire it. Even less do I wish to see a monarchy in America, because such a thing, besides being useless, is also impossible. Abuses now existing would not be reformed, and our regeneration would be fruitless. . . .

"The American provinces are fighting to free themselves: they will eventually win freedom; some of them will make themselves into federal or centralized republics; in certain large sections of the continent it is well-nigh inevitable that monarchies will be established. . . . It will not be easy to consolidate a great monarchy; as for consolidating a great republic, it will be impossible. . . .

"Would it not be splendid if the Isthmus of Panama could be to us what the Isthmus of Corinth was to the Greeks? May we some day be fortunate enough to install there an august Congress . . . to deal with and discuss the high interests of peace and war with the nations of the other three parts of the world!"

Thus, Bolívar, exiled and apparently beaten beyond hope, not only never despaired of bringing freedom to South America but actually dreamed of creating something like an American League of Nations.

From Jamaica, he managed to reach Haiti, which had shortly before won freedom from France. From there he effected a landing on Venezuelan soil, set up a capital at Angostura (now Ciudad Bolívar) on the great Orinoco river, and again defied the Spaniards. They accepted the challenge.

Captained by Morillo, a veteran of Spain's wars against Napoleon, who had brought to Venezuela an army schooled in European fighting, they confronted Bolívar on the Venezuelan Plains. Battle after battle was fought, with Bolívar himself, Páez, the "Centaur," and British and other soldiers of fortune especially distinguishing themselves.

It was Páez who accomplished the extraordinary feat of taking a flotilla of Spanish gunboats with a squad of his "llaneros," Venezuela's cowboy riders.

The gunboats, anchored in the middle of the broad Apure river, barred Bolívar's army from crossing. "If only we could get them out of the way," groaned the leader of the patriots, who had no war vessels to engage them nor artillery to bombard them.

"That's easy," said Páez. He waved his sabre over his head, shouted, "Follow me, my children!" and spurred his horse into the river. The cowboys obeyed.

In a few minutes, the whole squadron, Páez at its head, horses shaking water from their manes, men brandishing lances and howling in maniacal elation, were alongside the gunboats. The Spanish crews, bewildered and terrified by this sudden attack, unprecedented in war, leaped over the sides of the vessels and struck out for shore, while Páez and his cavalrymen climbed over the rails.

A few minutes later the "Centaur" was back on the riverbank, saluting Bolívar.

"General," he said, "you wanted those gunboats. They are yours."

But rough-and-tumble fighting did not keep Bolívar's thoughts from high governmental problems; at his ramshackle capital of Angostura he convened a congress and drafted a constitution, which—had Venezuelans been capable of applying it to their country—would have made Venezuela a model among republics.

Hard-pressed by Morillo, Bolívar now conceived the most daring plan of his daring career—inspired by a similar idea which had occurred two years before to San Martín.

Keeping his adversary completely hoodwinked as to his ultimate object, he vanished from Venezuela, and at the head of a small army, crossed the formidable chain of the Andes in freezing Winter weather. Though they suffered terribly, the forces of the audacious Venezuelan surmounted the Andean heights, toiled down the Eastern slopes, and deployed on the plains of New Granada, to the amazement of the Spaniards there.

Though he was over the Andes, Bolívar still had a task before him almost as difficult as his crossing of the mountains. He must fight and beat trained Spanish soldiers before he could add New Granada to the territory under the control of the patriots. This he proceeded to do with his usual dash and brilliancy. In two furious battles—Pantano de Vargas and Boyacá—in which the fighting often became a savage hand-to-hand mêlée, with victory inclining first one way and then the other, he completely defeated Barreiro, the Spanish commander, and pushed forward to the gates of Bogotá.

Bewildered by his whirlwind advance, the Spanish Viceroy ran away. Bolívar, at the head of dirt-caked, ragged and exultant battalions, marched proudly into the New Granadan capital.

Thence he returned to Venezuela, and in 1821, on the plain of Carabobo, in one of the most spectacular and celebrated battles ever fought in South America, he routed the Spaniards and gave the death-blow to Spanish rule in his native land.

Reforming his little army, he marched through virgin jungle and over steep mountains, into the Spanish province of Quito (now Ecuador). Principally through the successful feats of his ablest Venezuelan lieutenant, Sucre—who won a battle close to the crater of the Pichincha volcano—he was enabled to make another triumphal entry, this time into the city of Quito.

Soon after, he met the man who now shares with him the loftiest rank in South America's roster of heroes. Journeying northward, as Bolívar marched southward, José de San Martín, liberator of the southern part of South America, was now to grasp for the first time the hand of him whom destiny had chosen as the liberator of the northern part.

Before reaching Guayaquil, seaport of Quito, and setting eyes for the first time on his fellow-liberator, San Martín had to plan campaigns as daring as those of the Venezuelan—the most famous of which is rated by some military experts superior in boldness of conception and precision of execution to anything emanating from the brain of Bolívar—to fight battles as fateful in their outcome as any fought in the North, to solve problems fully as baffling as any that arose there. All these tests he had passed with conspicuous success; on the day of the historic meeting of the two, San Martín stood as high in the south of South America as Bolívar stood in the north.

Born in 1778, five years before Bolívar, at Yapeyú, in the Spanish Provinces of the River Plate, now known as the Argentine Republic, he inherited from his father, a Spanish army officer, a taste for military life. He went to Spain, and began, at the age of eleven, to study military science at Madrid. After seeing active service in Africa, he took part in Spain's courageous struggle against the armies of Napoleon, including the Spanish victory at Bailén. There and elsewhere he gave evidence of such soldierly capacity that he was promoted steadily until he became lieutenant-colonel. But when the fight for independence in his native land assumed definite shape in 1812, he resigned from the Spanish service, returned home, and was promptly commissioned colonel in the forces embattled against the country which he had served so long and so honorably.

After some hard fighting on the Argentine side of the Andes, San Martín conceived the plan on which his military fame mainly rests—the passage of that lofty snow-covered mountain range to Chile—the march which inspired that of Bolívar (already described) two years later, over the northern wall of the same mountains, and which has been deeply studied and enthusiastically praised, like the Venezuelan's, by military experts in many countries.

Realizing that the power of Spain could not be definitely broken in the southern part of the continent unless the Spanish forces in Chile and Peru were crushed, San Martín proceeded to form and equip a small army in secret for the consummation of his daring project. He assembled them on the Argentine side of the Andes; and in order to deceive the Spaniards on the Chilean side, he caused himself to be appointed to a post in an entirely different part of Argentina and pretended that he had left to take up his new duties there.

All the qualities which went to make up the genius in San Martín did their bit in his preparations for his dangerous march over the mountains. Patience, which he had in good measure, helped him in the long weeks of waiting before he could start and in the disciplining of his followers and the assembling of munitions and provisions. His military skill—afterward to be tried in pitched battles with the Spaniards—was tested in the choice of a road for the invasion of Chile (he eventually selected the trail over the Uspallata Pass). His habitual caution made him see to the smallest detail of training and equipment; and his poise (some called it coldness) enabled him to keep order among unruly subordinates and compose the differences which regularly arose among them. This calm in San Martín stands out in vivid contrast to the fire in Bolívar's temperament—but both led their possessors to a like fullness of success.

San Martín was particularly clever in finding the right man for each job to be done. Somebody, for instance, told him that a certain monk, who had joined the army, knew how to make cannon. Immediately, the Argentine general put that monk in charge of a small and primitive foundry, from which strange warlike products soon issued, with little resemblance to normal artillery—but cannon they were, just the same. And having discovered an officer with a bent for chemistry, the general relieved him of his regular duties and set him, without further ado, to concocting gunpowder and other warlike necessities, of which there was urgent need if Chile was to be invaded and the Spaniards there, hidden behind the Andes, driven from their positions.

But where San Martín showed the keenest insight was in picking his main coadjutor. That distinction fell to Bernardo O'Higgins, son of a former governor of Chile and Viceroy of Peru, who now shares with his Argentine chief first place among the national heroes of the Chilean republic.

After resorting to a series of clever ruses, among them the misleading of some Indian tribesmen (who promptly told the Spaniards a false report as to San Martín's coming movements which the crafty Argentine had purposely given them) he took his little army of about 5,000 men through steep defiles, across dangerous gorges, over a pass 13,000 feet high. They braved the terrible "soroche," the dreaded sickness of the Andean heights, and were exposed constantly to attack from the trained Spanish regiments strung out along the mountainous Argentine-Chilean frontier.

Accomplishing his tremendous military feat in five weeks (airplanes, on regular schedule, now do it in a couple of hours) the Argentine general astounded the Spaniards by deploying his army against them on Chilean soil, only a few miles from the capital city of Santiago.

At Chacabuco the two armies met. There, on February 12, 1817, San Martín, after hours of bloody struggle, won a famous victory. It opened to him the gates of Santiago; and, seemingly, it added Chile to the list of the world's free nations.

But the Spaniards were tough. Rallying again to the defense of their king's Chilean domain, they inflicted a severe defeat on San Martín and O'Higgins at Cancha Rayada and threatened to hurl the Argentine leader back over the terrible mountains which he had so daringly scaled. But tough though the Spaniards were, San Martín was tougher. Again handling his forces with remarkable skill, ably seconded once more by the doughty O'Higgins, he crushed the Spanish army of Chile once and for all at the celebrated battle of Maipú. Never after that was the independence of Chile again menaced by the monarchy which had so long ruled it from across the Atlantic.

Next, enlisting the aid of Lord Cochrane, a recklessly brave Englishman who had distinguished himself in the Napoleonic Wars, San Martín, with his army of Argentines and Chileans, now swelled (like Bolívar's forces in the north) with volunteers from several European countries, proceeded by sea to Peru. There he maneuvered so skilfully that the Spanish Viceroy resigned, allowing his antagonist from the south to enter Lima, the Peruvian capital. The date of that entry was July 12, 1820. San Martín, within the space of less than two years and a half, had won freedom for Argentine and Chile and seemed on the point of assuring it to Peru. But he acted with his customary patience and diplomacy. He did not wish to stampede the Peruvians into joining him. They must do so of their own free will, he insisted, in their own good time.

Meanwhile, down from the north, the fiery Simon Bolívar was marching toward Lima. San Martín resolved to meet him.

At Guayaquil they saw each other for the first time, and at once went into conference. To this day nobody knows exactly what happened at their meeting. In any event, they did not hit it off with each other. San Martín, issuing from the conference with a glum countenance, returned immediately to shipboard.

The noble leader from the south found Bolívar disappointing as an individual; and the hard-boiled Venezuelan, jealous of his fellow-hero, audaciously resolved to continue his fight against Spain without help from the other.

San Martín sailed away to Peru. "The Liberator," he said, "is not the man we thought him."

Five months later, exasperated by the ingratitude of those around him and their cruel accusations against him, he resigned his post as "Protector of Peru" conferred upon him after his triumphal entry into Lima, and headed homeward. "Peru is not big enough for Bolívar and myself," he is said to have remarked—also: "I am tired of hearing people charge me with trying to make myself king."

After staying a few months in Chile and a couple of years in Argentina, he turned his back on the two lands which he had freed and repaired to Europe. There he traveled until, in 1829, weary and homesick, he took ship for Buenos Aires. His fellow-countrymen received him with insulting contempt. Impoverished, utterly disillusioned, he again crossed the ocean. Living from hand to mouth (his old comrade O'Higgins, on one occasion, generously sent him 3,000 Chilean pesos), assured of a roof over his head only by the kindness of a Spanish banker whom he had known in Spain, and who gave him a house in Paris, he passed melancholy years there, lovingly tended by his only daughter. At last, more than twenty years since he had seen his ungrateful native country, he dragged himself to Boulogne-sur-Mer, hoping that the sea air might check the fatal illness which he felt creeping over him. In August, 1850, he died in his daughter's arms.

No sooner was he dead and beyond consolation than the Argentinos woke up to the immensity of their debt to him;

and ever since they have vied with those honoring Bolívar in heaping tokens of affection and reverence on the memory of their national hero, the noblest and most upright of all the paladins of Latin America's epic wars of independence.

*   *   *

After his meeting with San Martín, Bolívar resolved to bring to fruition his daring plans for continent-wide independence.

Despite the hard knocks administered to her forces on Peruvian territory by San Martín, Spain was still far from beaten. An enterprising Spaniard, La Serna, proclaimed himself Viceroy (a piece of impudence later meekly confirmed by the Spanish King) and aided by a French adventurer, Canterac, assembled a formidable army.

Bolívar, still ably backed by Sucre, scotched La Serna and Canterac in a brilliant cavalry battle on the plain of Junín, where only sabres were used and not a shot was heard.

But just as the Liberator was preparing to force a decision, the Congress of Venezuela, his creation, jealous of his growing power, demanded that he leave the army and attend to civil affairs. He obeyed. Caught in the trammels of his own lessons to South Americans on the advisability of being law-abiding, he felt that he must practise what he had preached. So back to Lima he went.

It was his Venezuelan lieutenant, Sucre, who, on the wind-swept plateau of Ayacucho, thousands of feet above sea level, encircled by Andean peaks buried under a canopy of gleaming snow, fought and won the most renowned battle in all the annals of South America.

It was fought by his men and their foes in a sort of martial intoxication—by cavalrymen charging in a sort of madness,

[151]

by infantry regiments rocking with excitement, hurling themselves against equally fight-inspired Spaniards in a delirium of courage. All this was epitomized in the order shouted by Córdova, brave leader of New Granadan troops, when told to sweep his battalions into the crucial charge of the day. Ignoring the military etiquette requiring that a commander, in starting an attack, tell his men just how they are to hold their weapons and at what speed they must advance, Córdova electrified his men with the words:

"Arms as you please and step of conquerors!"

Thousands of schoolboys in Latin America recite those words to this day. And there are few grown-ups there, who, if challenged to repeat what young Córdova shouted on the field of Ayacucho, cannot come right back with:

"Armas a discreción y paso de vencedores!"

The victor of Ayacucho, chivalrous Sucre—ever a veritable Bayard—lowered the point of his victorious sword in homage to his absent chief. "The glory is yours," said he to Bolívar.

*　　*　　*

Ayacucho was the climax of Bolívar's dazzling career.

After the winning of the great battle there, in 1824, he started on the downward slope. But, though weakened by illness and meeting opposition on every hand from those whom he had thought friends, he never lost sight of his splendid dreams. He actually brought together a Pan-American Congress, which, had one of those dreams come true, would have been convened regularly, to discuss affairs of mutual interest to all the nations on the American Hemisphere.

It met in Panama. The United States sent delegates (they did not arrive, however); and England, scenting in Bolívar's scheme a plot against monarchy, turned watchful eyes on him and it. But her worry was wasted. Having met, the Congress did nothing in particular, adjourned, and promptly died of inanition. Bolívar was deeply disappointed. From now on, disillusionment clutched him ever more firmly.

On all sides friends abandoned him, revolts broke out. It seemed almost as if he had driven away the Spaniards only to loose worse evils in South America than any inherent in their domination.

Finally, in utter despair, he left his native land—never to return, except in his coffin. His health gone, penniless once more—he had spent the remnants of his private fortune and all that had accrued to him from high office—he dragged himself wearily to Santa Marta, on the coast of New Granada, intending to embark there for the United States or Europe.

But he never went further. Finding shelter in the home of a generous admirer, surrounded by only a few friends who remained faithful to the end, clad in a borrowed night-shirt, with bitterness eating into his heart and poisoning his last words, Simon Bolívar died on the 17th of December, 1830.

He had brought independence to his native Venezuela, freed three other South American countries besides—Colombia, Ecuador, Peru (the latter with the help of San Martín)—and had founded and given his name to a fifth, Bolivia. He had won acclaim far beyond the regions where he had fought and battled and governed for twenty years; he counted great men of his time among those paying him homage. He exchanged letters with Lafayette; received from George Washington's kin mementos of the North American Liberator in token of their admiration; tasted flattery at its most fulsome and glory at its sweetest.

Yet he died bitter in spirit and broken in body. Thanks to

his prowess, the red-and-yellow banner of Spain waved no more over the lands to which he had devoted life and fortune. But he had dreamed of giving them much more than bare freedom; he had dreamed of welding them, and the rest of South America, into a great union, composed of nations at peace, ably governed, united for mutual welfare by bonds of unselfish respect and amity. Instead, his dying gaze fell on a continent rent by dissension, plunging into political chaos, with freedom prostituted to base ends and the common good sacrificed to sinister personal ambitions.

"All we have gained is independence and we have gained it at the cost of everything else!" he cried, as the shadows of death fell darkly about him. And in an earlier bitter outburst of disillusionment: "I have plowed in the sea!"

Now, a century and more later, his memory is revered all over South America, his name honored all over the world. It has been given to streets and squares, regiments and ships, cities and provinces.

Bolívar's statues—there are scores of them—and the marble monument over his tomb in his native city of Carácas, Venezuela, are heaped on his birthday with magnificent wreaths, while the space around them rings to the sound of oratory, the cheers of crowds and the roar of cannon.

Yet, after his death, the nations of South America have not brought to Simon Bolívar the offering which he vainly dreamed of receiving from them in life. Today, as in 1830, when he died, there is no united South America; now, as then, in the lands which he freed, revolution still raises its head.

Other lands which he dreamed of seeing at peace and welded in amicable union, have also witnessed discord—including Argentina, the native country of his noble contemporary and fellow-hero, San Martín, and Chile, to which San

Martín also brought independence.

The latter shared Bolívar's disillusionment. His last years, like those of his great contemporary, were poisoned by the pettiness, selfishness and ingratitude of those around him. Writing to a Chilean friend from France, a few years before his death, the liberator of Argentina and Chile bitterly declared:

"The labor and the blood given for the independence of America have been, if not wasted, at any rate unfortunately spent, in most of the new States."

In summing up the two supreme champions of Latin American liberty, the famous Argentine statesman-historian, Bartolomé Mitre, wrote:

"In San Martín and Bolívar are combined, in unequal proportions, the two elements that make history: the active element, which produces immediate effects in deeds, and the passive element, from which springs the future."

AMONG my friends is a little man who weighs 120 pounds (when fit) and stands five feet four inches (when on tiptoe), with a mild eye, a drooping mustache, a feeble frame, and two hobbies. One is to push aside six-foot giants who get in his way; the other is to tell giant six-footers who happen to annoy him exactly what he thinks of them.

"Billy," I said to him once, "I have never seen anyone as puny, and at the same time as pugnacious, as you are. How come?"

He explained:

"When I was holding down my first job as an office boy the whole gang in the office bullied me. They made my life miserable. Finally, when I was just about ready to go out and hang myself, I overheard two of my office mates talking.

" 'It sure is terrible the way we treat that new boy,' said one.

" 'It sure is,' agreed the other, 'but—if anybody in this world lets himself get kicked around, he darned well *will* get kicked around!'

"Those words made me see a great light. The very next time one of the bunch started to bully me I walked right up to him and—well, the bullying stopped. It has been that way ever since with me."

And off he strutted about his affairs; years passed, and I scarcely gave a thought to that experience of his until I arrived in Uruguay.

LITTLE BUT LUSTY

Uruguay is the second smallest of all the Latin American republics. (Only El Salvador is smaller.) It is also the cockiest. You see, away back in their history the Uruguayans decided not to let themselves get kicked around. The decision was doubtless arrived at in a huddle pulled off by the seven families who founded Montevideo, Uruguay's capital, early in the eighteenth century. A century or so later that decision had already become a cornerstone in their attitude toward the rest of the human race.

So much so that, getting tired of Spanish domination, they told powerful Spain to quit kicking them around, and—Spain quit.

Then they told England (who had come snooping down to South America looking for likely new colonies) the same thing, and—England quit.

Then they turned to big Argentina and bigger Brazil, both of whom had designs on little Uruguay, and—both of them quit, nursing barked shins and rubbing bleeding noses with swollen fingers. And little Uruguay went strutting on her way.

She has been strutting ever since. If a Uruguayan walked in his sleep, he would strut—not offensively, for, like all Latin Americans, he is a pleasant and polite chap—but strut he would, nevertheless.

I had entered Uruguay from Brazil, where, when you meet somebody on the street, he says: "Good morning; Brazil is bigger than the United States," and if you ask a cop the way to your hotel, he answers: "First turning to the right, then second to the left; Brazil is bigger than the United States." So, knowing that the size of Uruguay was not far from infinitesimal, compared with Brazil and others, I rather expected to find the Uruguayans humble-minded—reasonably patriotic, if you will, and proud of this or that episode in their history or in their economic and social progress, but distinctly humble-minded.

My wife and I walked into a well-known shop on one of Montevideo's principal business streets. It is situated in cosmopolitan surroundings quite pleasing to the bewildered foreigner, alone in a faraway South American city—with an American bank opposite, and close at hand an Italian steamship agency and a big French concern. Moreover, it is owned by a man with a name which is both good English and good German. When we got inside we were attended by a youth, who, it turned out, was the son of the proprietor. I asked him:

"Are you English? Or German?"

He looked at me.

"My father is German," he replied, "but I'm Uruguayan—thank God!"

Perfectly polite, mind you—perfectly calm—yet he gave me the feeling that I had been planning to kick him around. Before I had been twenty-four hours more in Montevideo, I realized that his remark summed up the general attitude of Uruguayans.

There are only 2,000,000 of them, against 13,000,000 Argentines, on their southern and western borders, and 45,000,-000 Brazilians to the northward. Argentina is one of the most pushing and successful nations in the world, and Brazil one of the biggest and richest, and beyond them lies the world which includes the United States and Great Britain, France and Germany, Italy and Russia. But the Uruguayan, from his pretty capital city or from the rolling purple plains which girdle it, looks upon all these nations with a cold eye. "I'm Uruguayan, thank God!"

What is there about his native land to make the Uruguayan so cocky? A lot—make no mistake about that—a lot.

Until some forty years ago Uruguay was torn every few months by revolution; its record was such that even natives of other parts of Latin America, to whom revolutions were the most ordinary events imaginable, were shocked. Yet now, Uruguayans proudly tell you, their country is one where "votes have taken the place of knives."

Yesterday Uruguay was filled with bloody, cruel and meaningless fighting, which emptied the national treasury and paralyzed business; today she boasts that serious civil warfare has become a memory of far away and long ago; that she has paid her debts and (until the depression caught her) prospered at a rate that would have made the eyes of the original settlers pop out of their sockets in amazement.

After Artigas and other leaders had freed Uruguay from Spain, back in 1828, she had a total of only sixty thousand inhabitants, who without delay, leaped at each other's throats. "Blancos" and "Colorados," two political parties which detested each other, kept the country in a state of strife for eighty years. It is difficult for even the most careful student to make head or tail of their quarrels which were conducted with terrible cruelty.

Here is a story which gives a clear idea of what the Blanco-Colorado epoch was like. After a skirmish on the Uruguayan plains, a young Colorado was captured by the Blancos. He was treated with elaborate courtesy. At a dinner in his honor, his hosts pressed the best food on him and repeatedly drank his health. Then one of them turned to the guest, bowing politely.

"Of course, you know we are going to shoot you?"

"Of course, I do," said the youth, with an equally polite

bow.

He tossed off another glass of wine, again toasting his captors. He walked out into the open. A firing squad was waiting. In a few minutes he was dead.

But there is no such Uruguay any more.

She has done wonders of late years in bettering herself. Her people have made daring experiments in advanced social legislation. Her schools are good. Like Argentina, she has profited from immigration. In her capital, attractive windswept Montevideo, one breathes the air of enlightenment. It is too bad that her leading man of letters, the late Señor Rodó, didn't like the United States.

He was passionately attached, however, to Ancient Greece, and always tried to imbue his students—he was a professor—with an appreciation of Greek beauty. His pupils adored him, made their adoration into a cult. One of his most famous lines is: *La antigua Grecia fué una sonrisa de la historia*—Ancient Greece was a smile of history.

Uruguay had a taste of dictatorship a few years ago when President Terra got rough with the local parliament. But it was only a little taste. Incidentally, Señor Terra was president when Secretary Hull headed the American delegation to the seventh Pan-American Conference at Montevideo, in 1933. I saw Mr. Hull escort him down the front steps of the Parque Hotel, where the Uruguayan executive had paid our head delegate a visit. It was a toss-up which was more courtly—the Latin or the Tennesseean.

Little Uruguay has been lucky enough to produce a big man. His name was José Batlle—pronounced, in accordance with the peculiar Uruguayan treatment of Spanish, pretty much as we would pronounce "Barjy."

When he died a few years ago, he was acclaimed by enthusiastic admirers as the most remarkable statesman of the whole American continent. In the domain of social reform he initiated legislation which would be considered audacious anywhere, but which, in a South American republic, was positively sensational.

He was instrumental in abolishing capital punishment. He introduced the eight-hour day for workers. ("Nine-hour and ten-hour days," he used to say, "are equivalent to suicide for the employed and to murder for the employer.") To him is largely due the suppression in Uruguay of bullfighting, cock-fighting and other diversions involving cruelty to animals.

He fought hard (this time, though, without success) for the granting of equal rights to Uruguayan women. He did more than any other Uruguayan to promote clean elections and get the workers their rights. "Workers will find the vote more efficacious than firing shots or throwing stones," he declared.

All this, one would think, he would have considered achievement enough. But he did not. He also put through political reforms which, for anyone who knows South America and the deep-seated forces against which he struggled, seem positively miraculous.

Batlle became convinced that the main reason for the constant revolutions in Uruguay, as in other Latin American countries, was the enormous power wielded by the President, which tempted those reaching the presidency to stay there as long as they possibly could, in defiance of constitution, Congress and public opinion.

So he drafted a new constitution, *abolishing the job of President!* That was too much even for his most ardent adherents; they prevailed upon him to modify it, leaving the presidency in existence, but vesting most of the powers formerly exercised by the President in an executive council.

In this form the new constitution was adopted. One of its most important clauses provided that no President, after serving one four-year term, could serve another until eight years had elapsed from the date of his quitting office. It also expressly forbade running for a third term.

Marvelous to relate, the new constitution worked! Election after election was held without serious disorders. One President after another stepped down, after his allotted four years, and relapsed peacefully into private life, instead of sticking to the presidential chair, or laying dark plans for climbing into it again as soon as possible.

But a few years ago a President of Uruguay, Señor Terra, (he who did that Alphonse-and-Gaston act on the hotel steps with Cordell Hull) returned to something like the dictatorial authority yielded by his predecessors in the old days before Batlle got busy clipping presidential wings and trimming presidential claws. Following a rumor of impending revolution he suppressed the council in whose hands had been placed most of the executive power.

Meanwhile, irrespective of what set of ideas triumphs ultimately in his native land, the Uruguayan goes on being inordinately proud of it. He goes on holding up his head in sturdy independence. At times, his cockiness brings amusing consequences.

For instance, I was told about a little Uruguayan girl, Carmencita by name, who having absorbed much concerning the glories of Uruguay from her parents and other adults, got into a discussion with a little girl from the United States as to the relative importance of their countries. It was finally decided that the little American should go to her mother, obtain the latter's verdict in the matter, and impart it to Carmencita.

In diplomatic but firm language the American mother declared that the United States was more important than Uruguay. Off trotted her little daughter to her Uruguayan playmate. Shortly afterward the American mother asked what had happened.

"Mother," answered the little American girl, with the shadow of a great and disturbing doubt on her countenance, "Carmencita says you are quite wrong!"

* * *

Though, as I remarked, there are only 2,000,000 human beings in Uruguay, I found myself, on the occasion of a recent visit, in the midst of some 9,000,000 head of cattle and 20,000,000 sheep. At least I was told that I was so situated— a sobering thought. The country's frozen meat industry is one of the most important anywhere. Out at Fray Bentos, in the midst of prairies rolling away in all directions, there is a gigantic plant for preparing meat extract which has earned the nickname of "the biggest kitchen in the world."

The Uruguayans are practically all of pure European stock. Most of them are descended directly from the original Spanish settlers; and since the days of Spanish rule, thousands of immigrants—Italians, Spaniards, Germans, and others—have settled in the country. Of Indian and Negro blood there is scarcely a trace.

Much of Montevideo's downtown section has grown up out of the original Spanish settlement. It is a place of narrow streets crossing at right angles; of pleasant plazas, flanked by old churches and public buildings, built when the King of Spain was overlord; of sudden vistas of ships, loading and unloading at docks only a stone's throw from the banks and shops where the foreign visitor transacts his business.

Once you are out of the old town, you get into a region of fine avenues and brand new buildings, so cosmopolitan in character that, were it not for the shop signs in Spanish, it might just as well be part of a modern French or American city.

In the midst of all this cosmopolitanism, one thing essentially Spanish has survived—the patio. Practically every house is built around a patio. A dash in a mad Montevideo taxi is enlivened constantly by glimpses of pretty interior court-yards, tucked away behind half-closed front doorways, where fountains play and birds sing and flowers riot.

Montevideo's beaches—gay Pocitos, rocky Malvín, fashionable Carrasco—are linked by a magnificent driveway, stretching from the city proper more than ten miles along the shore of the bay, affording beautiful views of distant lighthouses, ships big and little, and the sparkling, white-flecked sea.

At short intervals brightly painted kiosks shelter vigilant policemen, part of whose job is to see that the precepts of Mrs. Grundy are observed by visitors to the various bathing establishments—for there is, in the Uruguayan, for all his Latin blood, a touch of the Puritan. Once a young American girl of my acquaintance was severely reproved by a beach constable for wearing a bathing suit which—though hardly of a sort to cause a false impression as to how she was built—would have passed muster on any North American or European beach. And an American youth who appeared at Carrasco, most exclusive of the beaches, in nothing but swimming trunks, so shocked a Uruguayan policeman that he chased that brazen northern nudist back into his bathhouse and wouldn't let him come out until he promised to put on something more.

The natives of Montevideo are proud of their late dinner hours. Each evening, seven, eight, nine o'clock strikes—and still they sip coffee or beer at a café, blissfully unconscious of any necessity for dining. When the 1933 Pan-American Conference was in session the members of the American delegation were driven almost crazy by the lateness of the local dinner hour. Sometimes, when they finally sniffed soup approaching, they were in a condition of near-starvation.

*   *   *

Montevideo is the only big city in Uruguay. All the rest of its more important towns come nowhere near the capital in size; they are merely country centers, scattered about amid the vast plains of which the republic is almost entirely composed.

On the Uruguayan plains, the millions of cattle and sheep, which constitute the principal wealth of the land, are now kept behind wire, instead of being allowed to roam at will as they did during the first period of Uruguayan history. In those days the great herds of wild cattle were killed merely for their hides and tallow; the Uruguayan landscape was dotted with the skulls and carcasses of slaughtered animals.

Scattered over the great plains of Uruguay are *estancias*, or country houses, usually low-roofed structures, often standing with no other building within miles. Around these, and clustered about the crossroads stores, typical of rural Uruguay, may still be seen the *gauchos*, descendants of the original settlers—sturdy, tough, sun-tanned individuals who have much in common with our cowboys but who, like the latter, are not as picturesque in costume or habits as they used to be. However, one may still see Uruguayan *gauchos* wearing bright-colored shirts and gay scarfs wrapped around their necks—and still, of an evening, they congregate in towns, or outside the general stores, and dance, to native tunes, the *gaucho* dances that go back to the days when these plains, like those of our West, were without railways or roads, infested with bandits, and acknowledging no law but that of gun and knife.

* * *

When I returned to Montevideo last Winter, I found that it was no place for Cordell Hull. That arch-foe of bilateralism in trade between nations was much better off at Washington, with the length of a whole continent between him and Uruguay.

For that up-and-coming republic had turned itself into a regular little citadel of bilateralism. It had applied (and is still applying) in its international business relations that famous saying of Artemus Ward: "You scratch my back and I'll scratch yours."

Under the guidance of Señor César Charlone, Finance Minister and Vice-President, Uruguay is stubbornly buying almost entirely from those countries that buy from her. And as the United States has been buying very little of late from Uruguay, the latter is buying practically nothing from the United States.

A few years ago the total annual value of American-Uruguayan trade ran to almost $40,000,000; in two successive recent years we sold to the Uruguayans merchandise to a total annual value of $28,000,000. Now that trade is in a state of paralysis. Quite recently 95 per cent of the automobiles imported into Uruguay were American; later in 1938 less than 40 per cent of them were. German cars had largely taken their place, also cars of English makes virtually unknown to Uruguayans in the heyday of our trade with them.

Great Britain, Germany, Italy and other European nations had gobbled up the bulk of the business that was ours before bilateralism à la Dr. Schacht raised its head in Uruguay.

Britain buys heavily from Uruguay, whose principal articles of export are chilled fresh meat—which we cannot take at all under present regulations, since hoof-and-mouth disease exists among Uruguayan live-stock—canned corned beef, wool, hides, packing plant by-products, and linseed.

Germany also is a heavy buyer. So is Italy. Therefore, Uruguay, true to the basic tenet of bilateralism, buys big quantities of goods from those European competitors of ours.

When I was last in Montevideo (1938) high government officials suggested that we remedy the sad mess into which our trade had fallen by stabilizing our purchases from Uruguay, so as to give exporters there a firm basis on which to make their calculations. Before stagnation of United States-Uruguay trade set in, they complained, we would buy a large amount of some Uruguayan product—wool, say—thereby encouraging local exporters to base their plans for the future on a similar annual demand from us. But—the very next year perhaps—our purchases would drop sharply, without warning, to the dismay of exporters, who often suffered severe losses.

European nations, on the other hand, were acting quite differently. The totalitarians, Germany and Italy, were guaranteeing to Uruguay a certain fixed yearly total of purchases of her products. And Britain, though unable, like European States run dictatorially, to provide a similar guarantee by the simple expedient of ordering British importers to import this or that quota from Uruguay, was easily absorbing, year in year out, all the Uruguayan meat allowable under the Ottawa agreements.

"Why do you not follow European examples?" Americans in Montevideo were being asked. "Why do you not scrap your theories and get back your business here?"

Uruguayans insist that, in their country, there is no hostility toward us, commercial or of any other sort—our democratic ideals appeal to them, and our great men command their enthusiastic admiration. Uruguay makes bilateral agreements with Europe, they explain, solely because she is obliged to do so.

Europe calls the tune to which Uruguay must dance. How can that little republic be expected to antagonize European nations, which are the heaviest buyers of the products that it must sell in order to live?—nations, which, if antagonized, would promptly buy elsewhere what they now get in Uruguay, thus bringing ruin to the Uruguayans.

"Buy more from us," Americans in Montevideo are told, "and watch the situation change."

Increased purchases by the United States, they point out, would greatly benefit our local sales of goods formerly disposed of in large quantities by American exporters—manufactured and semi-manufactured articles, machinery, lumber, petroleum products, sugar, structural steel, automobiles, etc.

I was informed by one of the most prominent government officials in Montevideo that investigation had proved that the total of all the meat products imported into the United States from all the foreign countries exporting such articles to us— even including hams from Poland—would suffice to feed our population for only three days in each year. He added:

"Make your imports of these products, from Uruguay and our neighbor, the Argentine, big enough to feed all Americans *one week each year* and there will be a very different story to tell in our trade relations."

Meanwhile, every three months, the Bank of the Republic of Uruguay makes a careful compilation, and then—strictly in accordance with this compilation—the bank calculates what Uruguay shall buy from each foreign nation. Which means that we, rigidly consistent in our adherence to anti-bilateralism, are almost entirely out of the running when Uruguay apportions her commercial favors.

Not long before I was in Montevideo, American goods were piled high on the docks of that seaport, because those who had ordered them simply could not get permits for introducing them into the country. Subsequently, the Uruguayan Government allowed these goods to be cleared in driblets, and for sometime these driblets constituted all there was of United States exportation to Uruguay. Later, when even those dried up, American-Uruguayan trade fell into a state of coma.

American-Uruguayan trade relations strongly resemble the corresponding picture of relations between the United States and Argentina. Uruguay, like Argentina, has been tumbled from an advantageous position in her trade with us into one that she finds distinctly disadvantageous. This is convincingly shown by the following figures, from official Washington sources, covering the situation during the last few years:

From the beginning of 1935 to the end of 1937 we sold to Uruguay merchandise worth some $15,000,000 and bought from her goods worth over $20,000,000. That meant a favorable balance for the Uruguayans of about $5,000,000.

In 1938, on the other hand, we sold to Uruguay merchandise aggregating in value more than $5,000,000 and bought from her products worth only about $2,000,000, the equivalent of only 40 per cent of our sales.

Germany, during 1938, bought from Uruguay merchandise worth nearly $13,000,000 and shipped to that country German goods totaling in value $7,000,000, which meant a highly favorable balance for the Uruguayans. Great Britain also got into their good graces by taking imports from Uruguay worth $14,000,000 and exporting to her British products worth $8,000,000, thus allowing the Uruguayans to book a favorable balance of $6,000,000, as big as the one in German-Uruguayan trade for 1938 and contrasting strongly with the big deficit for Uruguay in her transactions with us for the same year.

Italy, too, bought more from Uruguay during 1938 than she sold. But the Japanese got into our class as a pain in the neck to Uruguay by selling to that republic in 1938 merchandise worth over twice as much as the total of their purchases of Uruguayan products.

An interesting point about the situation in Uruguay is that quite a number of American residents there feel no resentment at the Uruguayan attitude. Indeed, they consider it largely justified. Among them, there is little or none of the clamor, typical among Americans in Argentina, that we should crack down hard on recalcitrant Latin American republics that balk at playing the international trade game according to Washington's desires.

Various ways out of the present mess were suggested by members of Montevideo's business colony when I was there. Some advocated reduction of our tariff barriers against certain Uruguayan products; others advanced pet theories that seemed to them the only solution; still others came out flatly in favor of bilateralism, or something like it. They even used, in their arguments, that word so out of favor in Washington nowadays—barter.

But they usually admitted that, after all, little Uruguay

was far from important enough to justify any drastic change in our theories of international trading. Therefore, as a rule, they were resigned—merely waiting for something or other to turn up that might make prospects more promising.

The existing state of affairs, they feared, could not last much longer without serious consequences. I attended a luncheon at Montevideo at which several leading American business men were present—men of varied experience, broad outlook, keen intelligence.

"Either Uruguay gets out of the present situation," said one, "or we get out of Uruguay."

Another, a philosopher endowed with a sense of humor that all the business discouragements of recent years had not sufficed to shake, chuckled grimly:

"If I saw any figures nowadays which did not show that my business was in the red, I wouldn't know how to read them! My only hope is that I continue to get together enough money to buy red ink for making entries in my books!"

No, Uruguay, in its present bilateral phase, is not for Secretary Hull. He would not enjoy hearing leading Uruguayans now in the saddle expound—and extol—the Charlone you-scratch-my-back-and-I'll-scratch-yours system of international trade. But Dr. Hjalmar Schacht would.

* * *

In the heart of South America, west of Uruguay, is one of the most primitive, interesting and mysterious countries on the American Continent—Paraguay. Tucked away hundreds of miles up the great Paraná and Paraguay rivers, she has let the rest of the world make little impression on her.

When Buenos Aires freed itself from Spain, Paraguay slipped into freedom under the Argentine wing, without having to do much of anything about it herself. Buenos Aires had to fight in kicking the Spaniards out; but up along the wild reaches of the Paraguay river, they just picked up their hats and went away, without any fuss at all.

In 1813, Francia, *El Supremo*, started on a long career of dictatorial despotism. He had his good points. So did his successor, López the First. But whatever good they did to Paraguay was largely trampled under foot by López the Second, who set a record for dictatorial ruthlessness seldom equaled in Latin America.

Around the grim figure of this fantastic tyrant centers an extraordinary chapter in Latin American history: the war waged, single-handed, by little Paraguay through five terrible years (1864-69), against Brazil, Argentina and Uruguay.

López provoked that war. Justice was not on his side. He treated his soldiers, of the sturdy Guaraní tribes, with shocking cruelty. Once a Paraguayan officer reported to López his valiant defense of a position against overwhelming enemy strength, but instead of praising him the tyrant thundered: "Why weren't you killed?" and immediately had him shot.

Yet the Paraguayans fought superbly. Emaciated, bandaged, hungry, they stopped their foes in their tracks; and when beaten, they lay on the battlefield, dead, in such heaps that a Brazilian general declared: "When you say you have defeated a Paraguayan army, you mean you have exterminated it." Women, taking rifles from their dying men, died in their turn.

Eventually, López, hunted down like a wild beast, perished with his Parisian mistress, Madame Lynch, in a burning hut. There were scarcely any men left in Paraguay. For years the little country lay crushed under the weight of that awful war. Why did her Indians fight as they did? Nobody knows.

Long years afterward, Brazil, Argentina and Uruguay, in a spontaneous gesture of admiration, sent back to Asunción, Paraguay's capital, the torn flags captured from the indomitable regiments of López. And all South America applauded.

A little over thirty years later poor Paraguay was up to her neck in another conflict, the bloody and ruinous Chaco war against Bolivia. This time she came out the winner—if there was a winner in that futile struggle. It was horrible beyond belief; one picture sure to haunt all who ever read of it, was that of a whole Bolivian army, several thousand strong, lying on a parched desert, dead of thirst. The war finally terminated in 1935, after efforts at mediation by several countries, including the United States.

Things have been better of late in Paraguay. And her future seems to bear promise. Some months ago, her President, General Estigarribia, hero of the Chaco war, received a substantial loan of United States dollars for the economic development of his country in pursuance of the Roosevelt-Hull Good Neighbor Policy.

AMERICAN interests in Chile, with an investment of something like three-quarters of a billion dollars—second only in Latin America to our stake in Cuba—face the possibility of serious trouble if the ambitious plans for social reform of the present Popular Front government, headed by President Aguirre Cerda, are eventually put into effect.

Señor Aguirre Cerda came to power through that rare thing in Latin America, a bona fide election. He really seems to have got to the presidency (believe it or not) because the majority of Chilean voters wanted him there and were able to make good their wish at the polls. That alone makes him interesting—presidents so elected are still almost as rare in South American republics as a panda or an okapi in a North American zoo. But equally interesting, at least to people in the United States, is the ultimate effect of his election on our Chilean investments.

Most of those with whom I talked, both Chileans and Americans, when I was in Chile early this year, considered drastic steps improbable. On the other hand, they could not help asking themselves where the money was to come from for the financing of the Popular Front program for the better- ment of the lot of Chile's workers unless from the pockets of foreign investors. Either one or the other—the program or the foreigners—seemed sure to suffer.

The new President is backed by a hodgepodge of political elements with conflicting ideals. According to which way they make him turn, his course is sure to have an effect on our huge Chilean investments.

If he goes far to the Left, as extremists of the Popular Front want him to do, it may presage both Rightist exasperation and governmental action aimed against the big and powerful American copper and nitrate companies in Chile, along lines similar to those followed by President Lázaro Cárdenas of Mexico toward American oil interests in that country.

If he sticks to the middle of the road, shunning both Left and Right turns, those big American business concerns there will probably continue to fight successfully against the dire consequences of Chile's 1932 collapse.

If he veers to the Right, joining up with reactionary and other anti-Leftist elements, he may so infuriate Leftist extremists that they may stage a revolt and involve everybody and everything in Chile, including hundreds of millions of American dollars, in one grand, unsettling, profit-devouring, free-for-all fight.

Our stake in Chile consists of close to $500,000,000 in direct investment, and at the highest estimate, about $300,000,000 more, representing indirect investments. Most of this enormous amount is invested in the copper mines of northern Chile, which are among the richest in the world, and in the nitrate fields of the same region.

Should the Chilean government elect to follow the course strongly hinted at recently by her neighbor, Bolivia, big American business interests in Chile are certainly heading into rough weather.

Bolivia, it will be remembered, in so far as the national attitude toward Americans is concerned, has shown signs of wanting to be, in the southern part of Latin America, what

Mexico is in the northern part. Having already expropriated holdings on Bolivian territory of the Standard Oil Company, the government of Bolivia, it was announced early in 1939, had made a deal for turning over Bolivian oil in large quantities to Germany. Germans, it was announced at the same time, had agreed to build a pipe line from Bolivia's oil fields to a point in the Chaco (scene of the recent Bolivia-Paraguayan war) on the Paraguay river. Should the plan be carried out, Bolivian oil could easily be supplied to Argentina and other republics east of Bolivia, thus competing with American interests there. There was also talk of a big air base, to be built by Germans (with the express sanction of Dictator-Colonel Busch of Bolivia) on Bolivian soil, providing easy access for planes to neighboring South American countries. The Bolivian government promptly denied having ties with Nazi Germany—a denial to which different values are attached by different people.

Already the Aguirre Cerda régime in Chile has taken over the distributing in that country of American oil—a course which possibly may be a forerunner of similar action (or, at least, of action not quite so sweeping, but drastic nevertheless) toward American copper and nitrate concerns. These are far more important than our Chilean oil stake and represent a much heavier investment of American dollars. The average run of American investors in Chile would get a bad jolt if the Chilean President started earmarking ex-American oil, or copper, or nitrate, for Nazi Germany.

When I was in Chile he was anything but pro-Nazi. Indeed, he had come to power as a pretty-far-to-the-Left Leftist, backed by some elements avowedly hostile to everything savoring of Nazism. Eloquent evidence of how the new government felt about that sort of thing was given by the enthusiastic reception (I saw it) accorded to Indalecio Prieto, one of the principal leaders of the Spanish Loyalists, on his visit to Santiago. That left little room for doubt as to where Aguirre Cerda's régime (and, presumably, that gentleman himself) stood on the issue of Nazi-Fascism.

Yet hostility to American big business interests, in Latin America, is no mere matter of "ideology." That Bolivia should expropriate Americans, and then turn, with an ingratiating smile, to Adolf Hitler, was no cause for surprise, for the late Colonel Germán Busch, Bolivia's dictator, was the son of a German and made no secret of his pro-German leanings.

But how about President Cárdenas of Mexico? If he is not Leftist, who is? So one must not let the "ideological" set-up in Chile unduly influence guesses as to what the Chilean President—who certainly was elected on a Leftist platform—will do toward American business in his country. If he proves himself indeed a Leftist, he will be against the "exploitation" of Chile by foreigners; but he will also oppose letting Germany benefit from anti-American actions on his part. If he goes Rightist, he may not only wallop Americans but also play (à la Busch of Bolivia) into Hitler's hands.

Prophecy, nowadays, is at a discount. Nevertheless, for what it is worth—basing myself on the views of competent analysts of the situation in Chile—I venture the guess that, in the long run, nothing really drastic will be done there. And I guess that some way out will be found in the long run, to satisfy those decrying "exploitation" of the country by Americans, which, at the same time, will permit American interests to continue doing business in Chile at a reasonable profit.

By the time this is published the answer may have been given. And events may have knocked what is said here into a cocked hat. That would be just like events nowadays! The best that a writer can do in a fluid world—and Latin America is as fluid as the rest—is to take note of fundamental tendencies. That I have tried to do—and may the gods be with me!

There are points about President Aguirre Cerda's record, moderate though it has been in the main, that cause doubts in many minds. Some of his pre-election statements seemed to presage trouble for foreign investors in Chile—as, for instance, the following, published in *El Mercurio*, the leading Santiago newspaper:

> "Times have been changing and there is need for carefully revising the privileges obtained by foreign capital in other days. . . . If it threatens to leave the country, let it! . . . and the sooner the better! But I do not think that foreign capital, invested in concerns extracting products from our soil, especially North American capital, will prove to be stupid, and fail to understand the times in which we live.
>
> "If it wishes to continue doing business, it must yield wherever yielding is just. No more privileges! Or, if there are to be any, they must be for Chileans. Foreigners engaged in the above-mentioned lines must realize clearly that it is no longer sufficient that they pay us salaries and a certain degree of tribute.
>
> "No! We wish to share the wealth, which, up to now, they have taken away. Moreover, did not President Roosevelt say, a short time ago, that North American capital had not behaved well in these countries of ours, and that the time had passed forever when, behind each dollar, well or badly acquired, there were warships and cannon?"

In dealing with contemplated Popular Front educational reforms, Señor Aguirre Cerda also alluded to what he called "stupid commercial schools which manufacture office workers by the gross for foreign merchants."

Another source of worry for American interests in Chile, when I was in that country, was the assiduity shown by the Chilean delegation to the Eighth Pan-American Conference at Lima in working for the adoption, as an accepted principle of international law on the American Continent, of the thesis that, in case of confiscation or expropriation of property owned by foreign companies or individuals in any country on that continent, those companies or individuals should have no legal recourse not also available to nationals of the country decreeing such expropriation or confiscation.

In other words, the Chileans at Lima fought against the old idea that foreign investors had special rights—against the theory that intervention of the country of which they happened to be citizens was permissible in case they got into a dispute with the country in which they had investments. Our Good Neighbor Policy expressly disavows all intention, on the part of the United States, to stage any such intervention; but there are those in Latin America who still lack confidence in that policy.

Chilean activity at Lima afforded striking additional proof of the close attention being paid throughout Latin America nowadays to the recent expropriation of American oil interests in Mexico and to the arguments of the Mexican government in defending its course. It also clearly expressed the increased antagonism among Latin Americans to foreign capital invested in their native countries, and the strong feeling among them that foreign investment tends to exploitation of national resources primarily for the benefit of foreigners, and that, therefore, it should, if permitted at all, be hedged about in future with regulations precluding the possibility of such exploitation.

The above considerations, coupled with the fact that the present Chilean Government came into power on the heels of a short but bloody revolt, tends to make Americans in Chile apprehensive as to just what lies around the corner for them.

President Aguirre Cerda's anti-capitalistic remarks may be construed either as hostility to foreign interests in his native country or as mere pre-election vote-getting violence of language—according to taste. Taken all in all, his utterances, coupled with the activities of the Chilean delegation to the Lima Conference, aroused a slight feeling of uneasiness in the American community of Santiago, the Chilean capital. Most of its members were in favor of those sections of the Popular Front program calling for improvement of the miserable condition of the Chilean masses, the poverty-stricken "rotos." But they hoped that this improvement might be effected without serious dislocation of business.

After the election of Señor Aguirre Cerda, hero of the Popular Front in Chile, he was inaugurated last Winter with much pomp. Crowds of his holiday making fellow-citizens lined the streets of attractive Santiago to cheer the winner of the close and hard-fought contest of the preceding Autumn and boo the outgoing executive, Arturo Alessandri. They also booed the German and Italian Ambassadors, whose countries did not exactly stand high just then in Popular Front favor.

Thousands of the soldiers of the Chilean army paraded before the Congress building, in which the inauguration ceremony was enacted—also the cadets of the Military Academy. in spiked helmets, light blue tunics and white trousers, looking as if they had just stepped across twenty-five years of time out of the Kaiser's martial pre-war Germany.

But what impressed me most, as I stood on the side-lines,

was an unofficial parade of elated young Chileans, who marched around Santiago's main plaza singing socialistic songs, yelling socialistic battle-cries, and shouting, at the top of their lungs: "*Viva el nuevo Chile!*" (Hurrah for the new Chile!)

Their elation served as a reminder that the new President had been put into office partly by elements determined to effect revolutionary changes such as will (if introduced) shake to its foundations the old social structure of Chile.

Two Chileans were standing close to me watching the inauguration festivities. As they heard those exultant yells of "Hurrah for the new Chile!" one exclaimed impatiently:

"Pooh! I've heard that before. Never comes to anything."

But the other shook his head.

"This time," he muttered, "they mean it. Trouble ahead for the old system."

Whatever may be the fate of vested American interests in Chilean copper and nitrate, as a result of the advent to power of the Popular Front, one thing seems certain: it will doubtless continue to foster the country's attempts to industrialize itself, to manufacture more and more of the articles formerly imported from other parts of the world.

Even the most sanguine advocates of this course have grave misgivings as to its ultimate possibilities; even they can hardly envisage a new Chile with a purchasing power, among its masses of "rotos," high enough to justify confidence, among local manufacturers, in eventual big profits. However, Chile, the third most important South American republic south of the Panama Canal—where she is outranked only by Brazil and Argentina—is just now going through an acute attack of incipient autarchy.

In this she resembles some other South American lands, especially Brazil. But nowhere in South America is the movement toward economic self-sufficiency more intense than among the Chileans.

The foreign visitor is made aware of it instantly. When I arrived in Santiago I found that I had run out of shaving cream, so I dispatched a boy to get some.

"Mind you, it must be American," I warned him.

He returned in an hour with a tube of American shaving cream in his hand and a look of dark mystery on his face.

"Smuggled!" he hissed. "Domestic products only for sale. Chile now makes shaving cream. Price of the national product, eight pesos. This cost four times as much. Smuggled!"

Pocketing the Chilean equivalent of one dollar he sneaked away with the air of an international conspirator.

When shaved, I sallied forth and was almost run down by a street car bearing on its side in big letters the proclamation "Made in Chile." Judging from the clanking and wheezing and grinding with which it progressed it was about to be unmade there, too.

I read so frequently on shop windows "Buy only Chilean wares" that I began to be afraid that some patriot would demand where I had bought my shirt and rip it off my body if I answered "New York."

A Chilean to whom I sang the praises of the waterfalls I had seen in the Andes on my way into his country agreed absently, "Yes, beautiful," and then added, with sudden animation:

"Think of the power in them! Think of the number of factories that might be operated if all those waterfalls were harnessed!" And he fell into a deep dream of autarchy.

Despite the apparently slim prospects of genuine success in her campaign for industrialization, Chile has undoubtedly made considerable strides in that direction. The total number of Chileans engaged in manufacturing (according to recent statistics) ranks second to those in agriculture: 38 per cent of the working population are in the latter and 22 per cent in the former.

Most of the country's manufacturing is concentrated in three regions: around Santiago, the capital; near Valparaiso, the principal seaport; and in and about Concepción, one of the principal cities of south central Chile. This last named region was seriously damaged by the terrible earthquake which devastated the south central district early in 1939.

Santiago, with its adjacent territory, does more than nine-tenths of all the republic's manufacturing. It has brought local industrialization to such a degree of development that imports from abroad of the following articles have been nearly eliminated: shoes and leather goods, textiles, clothing, candy, biscuits, flour, soaps and perfumes, matches, enamel and glass-ware, cigarettes, beer and sugar.

The Valparaiso district, in addition to some of the above, manufactures cement, tobacco, canned milk and refined sugar. The country's largest sugar refinery is at Viña del Mar, the famous fashionable resort just outside Valparaiso.

The Concepción area produces chiefly textiles, glass and chinaware.

Neither in volume nor in value of output is Chilean manufacturing at all impressive as yet. As a sign, however, of which way the country may be headed, the record thus far achieved is certainly worth careful attention—especially from Americans. If it becomes apparent that Chile's attempts at autarchy are futile, that they must be shattered eventually against the rock of low purchasing power among the Chilean masses, what then?

Whence is the money coming for the Popular Front program of social reform which helped sweep Señor Aguirre Cerda into office?

Whence, if not from foreign interests, among them the American copper and nitrate concerns which have invested those hundreds of millions of American dollars in Chile's copper mines—or in her nitrate fields, whose wealth was once the meal ticket of the whole country?

Thoughts like these were in the heads of the elated youths who sang their socialistic songs and shouted "Hurrah for the new Chile!" on the day of the new President's inauguration.

"Pooh! Heard it before! Never comes to anything!"

"This time it *does* mean something. Trouble ahead for the old system."

*　　*　　*

It is not only in trade that one runs up against Germany in Chile: the hand of the Teuton is also seen in the shaping and disciplining of the Chilean army.

Chile (likewise Argentina) has had her army trained by German officers in the German tradition. Bolivia also entrusted the training of her soldiers some years ago to German experts. But in all three, the Germans show signs of being on the way out.

In Argentina, German instructors of the Argentine army are meeting competition from the members of the American military aviation mission. The work of the latter has been so successful that the Argentine Government wants us to send more of our officers to instruct Argentina's military fliers.

In Chile, where successive German military missions have been employed to train officers and soldiers for more than half a century, the last remaining instructor from Germany recently left for home and has not returned; nor had he been replaced, up to a short time ago, by another German.

As for Bolivia, whose army is the only one of the three that has seen actual fighting, German military influence is under a cloud because, in the recent war in the Chaco between Bolivia and Paraguay, the German-trained Bolivians got much the worst of it at the hands of the French-trained Paraguayans.

Chile's German-trained regular army totals about 18,000. The principal units in the navy are two battleships, three cruisers, eleven destroyers and nine submarines. Her air force as about 200 planes.

Chilean interest in German military methods goes back to the victorious war against Peru in 1879-83. As a result of German success against France in the Franco-Prussian War of 1870-71, Germany had acquired, before the Chilean-Peruvian conflict, considerable prestige among South American military leaders, so much so that German officers straying to South America in search of more fighting found ready employment.

One of these, named von Moltke (said to have been a cousin of the famous German Commander-in-Chief against the French) who had joined the Chilean army in the 70's of last century, so distinguished himself fighting the Peruvians, that he attracted the attention of General Sotomayor, one of the Chilean commanders. Von Moltke was killed in the fighting outside Lima, Peru's capital, but the impression he had made on General Sotomayor was so great that, after the war was over, the general was instrumental in having the Chilean government invite a German officer to serve as military instructor to Chile's army.

This officer, Captain Koerner, of the regular Prussian army, reached Chile in 1885. He was the first of many, who, arriving singly or in groups, soon gave the Chilean army the Germanic imprint which it shows to this day. Captain Koerner did not content himself with instructing Chileans in the military art. He also mixed in Chilean politics and was one of the principal leaders of the rebels who, in 1891, overthrew the government headed by President Balmaceda.

Among the officers who, at one time or another, helped give the Chilean army its Germanic stamp, were a number belonging to famous German military families, some of whom afterward achieved prominence in the World War. One was von Lettow-Vorbeck, who led the German African campaign until he was finally defeated by the South African contingent of the Allies under Generals Botha and Smuts.

Others, whose names will be immediately familiar to all who have followed German military history, were von Alvensleben, von Buelow, Bronsart von Schellendorf, Count von Koenigsmarck and Count von der Schulenburg.

Six German officers who were in Chile as instructors in 1914, returned to their country when the World War started and were killed at the front.

The number of these instructors gradually dwindled after the World War. Finally, only one, General von Kiesling, remained. He also returned to Germany a short time ago. So now, for the first time in many years, there is no one to carry on the Prussian tradition among Chilean soldiers—a favorable opportunity, it would seem, for instructors from other nations to step in.

Argentina has employed German military instructors for many years. How highly Argentines think of them is shown eloquently by the fact that, at present, there are eighteen Argentine officers studying in Germany and only five in France. Recently, Italy has tried to work her way into Argentine military circles, especially in aviation, but her efforts to have Italian aviators appointed as instructors to Argentina's military fliers have failed.

Nevertheless, there is a considerable tinge of pro-Fascism among the officers of the Argentine army, one of whom was recently disciplined for ostentatiously giving the Fascist salute in public. Among the younger officers there is a tendency to sing the Italian Fascist hymn, and otherwise show pro-Fascist leaning. This sort of thing, however, need not be taken too seriously in a country like Argentina, where there are hundreds of thousands of citizens who have Italian blood.

Italian elements there have sought to counteract the influence of the United States Military Aviation and Naval Missions now instructing army officers in the Argentine Republic, but they have made little headway.

Our Aviation Mission, when I last visited Buenos Aires, consisted of eight officers, detached from their regular duties for this special assignment. Two more, it was expected, would soon be added. Our Naval Mission had three members at that time (the Winter of 1938-39).

Germany's military mission in the Argentine Republic was officially composed then of one general, two colonels, one lieutenant-colonel, one major and one captain. Of the eighteen Argentine officers studying military methods in Germany, one was a general, four were majors, eight captains and four lieutenants. Only one colonel, one lieutenant-colonel and three majors were studying in France.

The Argentine regular army, to which these various foreign officers were devoting their expert attention, consists of about 3,000 officers and 50,000 rank and file. In the reserve are 5,000 officers and 200,000 men. About 30,000 conscripts join the colors yearly.

Argentina's military aviation corps is a separate unit, consisting of some 1,500 officers and 2,000 enlisted men. It has about 150 planes. The navy possesses two battleships, three cruisers, sixteen destroyers, four submarines and a considerable number of smaller auxiliary vessels. It has a separate aviation force, with about 750 officers and men, and 100 planes.

The rough handling received by Bolivia's German-trained troops from the French-trained Paraguayans in the recent Chaco war has caused many a chuckle among anti-German South Americans. One of the main reasons, according to some observers, for Bolivian defeats, was the over-confidence of many of the Bolivian officers, who felt that their men, trained by Germans in the methods that had brought Germany's army such marked military efficiency in the past, must necessarily triumph over their foes, who knew nothing of such methods. But they were mistaken.

There were also other causes for Bolivian reverses. Two of these were particularly detrimental to the forces of Bolivia: the fact that her soldiers, accustomed to high mountainous regions, were compelled to fight in the low, swampy, pestilential Chaco, and the extraordinary military prowess of the Paraguayans, who are born fighters, as they proved in the famous war waged by them against the combined forces of Brazil, Argentina and Uruguay.

One of the German military experts who helped train the Bolivian army, by the way, was Captain Ernst Roehm, who, after he returned to his native Germany, became one of the leading aides of Adolf Hitler, and, later, the principal victim of Hitler's ruthless "purge" in June, 1934.

In her Golden Nitrate Age, Chile was in complete control
of the world's markets for pure nitrogen, indispensable in the
manufacture of fertilizer and explosives. The reason for her
monopoly was that the prime source of nitrogen—nitrate—
was to be found only in her northern deserts, wrested by the
Chilean armies from Bolivia and Peru in the "War of the
Pacific," which ended in 1883. The export tax levied on
nitrate by the Chilean Government brought in an average of
$25,000,000 yearly—"easy money" if ever there was any!
Over a period of nearly half a century nitrate paid about half
the total of Chile's official expenditures. The country was
indulging in a wild nitrate jag, it was living on nitrate, making whoopee on nitrate.

But clouds were gathering.

Manufacturers of synthetic nitrogen were getting to be
more and more of a threat to the Chilean monopolists. Even
as far back as 1912, Chile, which had been supplying a full
100 per cent of the world's pure nitrogen, saw that figure cut
to a mere 57 per cent. But just as her nitrate magnates were
beginning to get really alarmed, the World War came along,
the demand for nitrate, as a base for deadly explosives, became
frantic, and the reign of easy money in Chile took on new
vigor.

Production of Chilean nitrate rose steadily. Just before the
World War it had reached in one year almost 3,000,000 tons,
which yielded some 450,000 tons of pure nitrogen. This fig-

ure was surpassed during the war, in 1917, when an all-time high of 486,000 tons was made from the nitrate sent from Chile that year to the Allied belligerents. For several years after the return of peace, nitrogen was sought with similar eagerness, as a fertilizer for the fields which had been neglected while millions of tillers of the soil were busy killing each other.

But in 1926 the situation changed with tragic suddenness.

Germany, having been cut off by the Allied blockade from her Chilean source of pure nitrogen, had turned to synthetic nitrogen as the only hope of salvation from surrender. In 1915, her chemists had succeeded in producing 200,000 tons of the synthetic substitute; by 1918 they had raised the output to 400,000 tons. Other nations, deeply impressed, had begun to imitate the Germans. Within a few years, the principal consumers of nitrogen, foremost among them the United States, Britain, France, Italy, Japan and Russia, were well on the road to self-sufficiency in the manufacture of synthetic nitrogen.

Chile woke up to find herself on the brink of ruin.

In 1929, the former monopolist was caring for only about 20 per cent of the world's needs in nitrogen! Later she tobogganed still further down hill, reaching, at one point, such dismal depths that her nitrate beds—which used to produce 100 per cent of the world's needs—supplied a puny 8 per cent! No wonder revolutionary disturbances followed each other in quick succession on her soil!

The good old days of the Chilean nitrate bonanza are doubtless gone forever. But there is a strong probability that pure Chilean nitrate will always be in demand as a basis for certain kinds of fertilizer; that no matter how great may be the improvement in the manufacture of synthetic forms of nitrogen, the product derived from Chilean nitrate will, to some extent, maintain its superiority.

Of late the situation has improved somewhat, largely owing to the successful working of Chile's nitrate deposits, and profitable marketing of their yield, by Americans. But it is realized on all sides that the country can never again depend on nitrate as the main source of its revenue.

As for copper, the situation has oscillated between conditions bringing enormous profits to copper mining interests, notably those financed by American capital, and cataclysmal slumps, which have swept away millions of dollars of American investments. At present both the nitrate and copper interests in Chile are progressing satisfactorily, though uncertainty as to how the Chilean Government is going to act toward foreign investors is clouding the outlook for the latter.

They are wondering whether Chile is destined to move along new roads to new economic, social and political objectives, or continue to exist under conditions she has known for decades.

Along those new roads lie social regeneration for the country's working class, and a process of industrialization which, if thoroughly developed, may greatly decrease Chile's volume of imports. But if those new roads turn out to be blocked by insuperable obstacles, Chile will remain, though probably not quite to the extent of earlier years, a nation in which a rich and powerful landowning aristocracy of a few families, allied with a strong agglomeration of capital from abroad, dominates several millions of working people, unable to rise above the abject poverty and backwardness in which their forebears lived, toiled and died.

The plight of the Chilean "rotos" today is much what it was when the land was a Spanish colony, administered by

Spain primarily for whatever profit was to be made out of it.

They are unschooled, unwashed and almost unclothed. A good look at the garments of a "roto" makes you realize that the art of patching in other countries is in its infancy. Many of the lowest class, especially street urchins in the towns and the ragamuffins who abound along the roads, wear clothes which are so tattered that it seems impossible for them to hang together another hour, and so alive with vermin that it seems out of the question that their wearers can endure them another minute. Stitches, itches, patches, scratches—that sums up much of the life of the "rotos" of Chile.

Yet most of them are cheerful enough. They have a rough and ready wit of their own, are not particularly enthusiastic about work when they find it, prefer drinking deeply of the potent native "chicha" and wines to scheming for advancement and better pay. And there is one really bright spot in their lives: food in Chile is plentiful and cheap. Many "rotos" raise their own food. Along the roads you constantly see their little shacks, set in the midst of diminutive truck gardens, whence ragged but apparently contented children survey you amicably as you pass.

"Nobody need go hungry here," a "roto" informed me, smiling as if his existence was all beer and skittles. He told me further that a few centavos would buy meat or fish enough for a good meal; and, as for vegetables—"why, señor, at any market you can get onions and carrots and tomatoes and potatoes at prices which almost everybody can afford. As for fruit"—he smacked his lips—"have you tasted our Chilean peaches, señor? Well, there are good peaches in any market at a few centavos a dozen and at fewer centavos still for those not so good. And plums—has the señor tried the Chilean plum? Why, a few pesos will buy as many as you can carry away with you!

"And don't you know our shell-fish, señor? Ah, try some, be sure to try some!" Again he smacked his lips and rolled his eyes and kissed his finger tips to invisible mollusks, while he rattled off a whole list of locally celebrated marine specimens—*locos, erizos, camarones, langostinos*. All of them, he vowed, were fit for a king yet within reach of a "roto."

"Nobody need go hungry in Chile," he repeated. And I can well believe him.

Chileans have the reputation of being cooler than other South Americans. Some say this is due to the strain of English blood in their make-up. "They drink tea," one is told. Owing partly to the national coolness of temper, a few aristocratic families have managed to keep Chile in their pockets most of the time since San Martín and O'Higgins won independence for the country more than a century ago, without arousing the hot resentment which might have boiled up in more effervescent Latin communities.

O'Higgins staged a nice little dictatorship for himself after the Spaniards had been driven out, but other Chileans threw him out in his turn. After he had gone, Chile saw lively days, politically, though revolts there were not as frequent as in the republics roundabout.

But when Chile had wars she had good ones—tea or no tea. In the thirties of last century she took on Peru and Bolivia, to the great detriment of both. In 1879, she again tackled them, and after a war replete with astounding feats of bravery on both sides, utterly defeated them, took away big slices of Peruvian and Bolivian territory, and left a rankling dislike for herself in Peruvian and Bolivian bosoms which bodes ill for future peaceful relations. In 1891, Chile was torn asunder by one of the bloodiest of South American civil wars, between

President Balmaceda and the Chilean Congress. Balmaceda, after getting decisively beaten, killed himself.

Since then there has been considerable trouble in Chile, but again not as much as elsewhere in her neighborhood.

* * *

Germany is doggedly pushing ahead in her campaign to get the lion's share of Chilean trade. Though the United States occupies first place, both as an exporter to Chile and an importer of Chilean products, whatever gains there have been recently in foreign business with Chile have been registered largely by our German competitors.

But there is one point about the situation from which Americans can draw consolation—Germany's advance has been not so much at the expense of the United States as at that of Great Britain.

In Chile, as in other Latin American lands, the German drive for trade is based largely on bilateral agreements and on the employment of "Aski" marks.

Chileans, like other Latin-American exporters, are forced to take German merchandise in lieu of money when they ship their products to Germany. To make such dealing attractive the Germans sell "Aski" marks at temptingly low rates.

But that is not the only reason for their success. In Chile, as in other parts of Latin America, they get the business away from Americans and Britons—especially from the latter—by the method eloquently illustrated in the following anecdote, told me by the head of a mining concern in Santiago, the Chilean capital:

His firm wanted to import a big lot of machinery. They first approached a British machinery company. The Britons quoted a satisfactory price.

"What terms will you grant us?" asked the Chileans.

"Forty-five days."

"Couldn't you give a little more time?"

"Not one day. Sorry."

So the Chileans went to an American concern. There, too, the machinery and price were to their liking.

"What terms?" asked the Chileans.

"Three months."

"Couldn't you make it four?"

"Impossible."

So the Chileans went to a firm of German machinery manufacturers. They quoted most attractive figures. Then came the crucial question:

"What terms?"

"How long do you want?" asked the Germans.

"Well—how about six months?" said the Chileans.

"Pooh! That's not long. Let's make it one year."

The Germans got the order.

That story is typical of what is going on all the time nowadays in Latin American countries.

There is hardly anything that the Germans will not do to book orders. They are utterly unable to understand the rigid conservatism of the British or the casualness of the Americans.

Their methods have been winning success, temporarily anyhow. Despite this success, it must not be forgotten that German exports to Chile fell off in January-February, 1939, as compared with those for the corresponding months of the previous year.

Turning to imports from Chile, for 1938 there was a sharp drop in purchases of Chilean products—copper, nitrate, wool, hides, etc.—by all three of Chile's principal foreign customers compared with the corresponding period of 1937. But the

Germans succeeded in holding their own better than we did.

In 1938 we bought only 60 per cent as much from Chile as in 1937. In that year British imports from Chile totaled 80 per cent of what they had been for 1937, a much better showing than ours.

The Germans managed to take from Chile, in 1938, merchandise aggregating in value nearly 76 per cent of the total taken by them in 1937, thus maintaining themselves almost as well as the British and with far greater success than their American rivals. Expressed the other way around, American purchases of Chilean products for 1938, compared with the corresponding period in 1937, dropped 40 per cent, those of Britain 20 per cent, those of Germany 24 per cent.

The Germans did even better than these figures show because nitrate exports from Chile are kept secret and it is well known that, in 1938, Germany took a large part of the Chilean nitrate production.

These large German importations of Chilean nitrates may surprise those who remember that it was Germany who, before and during the World War, nearly ruined Chile's nitrate industry—which had previously been a world monopoly—by inventing and developing the process of making synthetic nitrate. But despite this invention and its subsequent intensive development by the Germans, synthetic nitrate remains inferior to the Chilean product as a fertilizer for potato crops, and since potatoes are among the principal food staples of Germany, she continues to import Chile's nitrate in large quantities.

Here are some statistics showing the record made in Chilean trade by the United States, in 1938 and 1937, compared with that of her principal rivals. The figures used have been compiled by the United States Department of Commerce at

Washington, and are the latest complete statistics available covering this section of our foreign business transactions.

TOTAL VALUE OF MERCHANDISE IMPORTED INTO CHILE

	1938	1937
From the United States	$28,634,000	$25,711,000
From Germany	26,666,000	23,014,000
From Great Britain	10,911,000	9,633,000
From Italy	2,754,000	1,688,000
From Japan	2,581,000	2,287,000

TOTAL VALUE OF MERCHANDISE EXPORTED FROM CHILE

	1938	1937
To the United States	$22,143,000	$43,918,000
To Germany	14,097,000	18,575,000
To Great Britain	30,655,000	38,177,000
To Italy	5,680,000	8,912,000
To Japan	2,183,000	3,081,000

Germans have been doing particularly well as suppliers of machinery and synthetic organic chemicals to Chile. In the field of machinery exports to Chile, according to recent statistics, the United States retains an impressive lead, but the Germans are pushing forward with great energy. As for the British, they are slipping badly.

In 1934, we exported machinery to Chile to a value of 16,000,000 Chilean pesos (a peso is worth between 3 and 4 cents). In 1936, the value of our exports in this line was nearly 38,000,000 pesos, a gain of 137 per cent. In 1937, we dropped back somewhat from this high mark, but our machinery exports, nevertheless, were still 135 per cent of the 1934 figures.

German exports to Chile of machinery, meanwhile, leaped from a total value of a little under 6,000,000 pesos in 1934 to nearly 17,000,000 pesos in 1936—a gain of 185 per cent as against ours of 137 per cent over the same period. In 1937, Germany, like the United States, dropped back a bit, but her exports in this line still totaled in value nearly 16,300,000 pesos, or 176 per cent more than in 1934, as against our gain for the same period of 135 per cent.

During those years Great Britain lagged far behind. In 1934 the total value of the machinery she exported to Chile was worth a little over one-half the value of Germany's exports and only about one-fifth of ours. For 1937, exports of British machinery to Chile slumped still further, representing in value considerably less than one-fifth of those from Germany and less than one-tenth those from the United States.

For the whole year 1938 the percentages of the total imports and exports of Chile, which fell to the three principal competitors in the Chilean market, stood thus:

	Imports	*Exports*
United States	27.8	23.2
Germany	25.9	9.2
Great Britain	10.3	20.5

One reason for the slump in Chile's purchases of British goods is illustrated by the following story, told with relish by Chileans:

A South American firm placed a large order for machinery with a highly conservative British concern manufacturing machinery, one of those that had been in existence a century. All was moving smoothly until the South Americans asked the Britons to paint the machinery red instead of green. The Britons gasped with horror.

They said frigidly, "Our machines have always been painted green."

"But can't you, for the sake of this big order, paint them red just once?"

"Impossible; our machines have always been painted green."

So the South Americans cancelled their order and transferred it to a German firm, which, in its correspondence with those South Americans, clearly implied that if necessary it would paint the stuff in alternate streaks of purple, blue and yellow.

As for Chilean imports of synthetic organic chemicals, Germany has elbowed herself into the lead, though in a few lines, notably mining chemicals, we are keeping her down in second place. According to the 1937 figures—the latest obtainable—Germany sold Chile synthetic chemicals worth $761,000; our sales totaled $193,000 and Great Britain's $185,000, which means that the Germans sold nearly four times as much as the United States and more than four times as much as the British.

In the sales of some of these chemicals Germany's lead was overwhelming, as, for instance, in dyes and colors, Chile having bought from Germany, in 1937, nearly nine-tenths of her total consumption of these products.

In short, Germany's fight for Chilean trade is just as bitter and as ruthlessly conducted as her fight in Brazil and Argentina and all over the rest of Latin America. This was proved vividly by the experience of an energetic American who, having just arrived in Santiago, sallied forth from his hotel, full of determination, to book orders for his firm. He returned at lunch time in a state of deep dejection.

"Many Germans around?" I inquired.

"Many?" he snorted. "Why, man, they're as thick as flies!"

When you start from the Alameda station in Santiago on the southbound night express, you know perfectly well that you are in Chile. But when you look around you next day, you think for one bewildered moment that you are in Germany.

Instead of churches built in Spanish colonial style, mixed up with modern office buildings, you see trim villas with freshly painted walls and window-boxes filled with flowers—like enlargements of those toy houses that German toymakers fashion for children all over the world.

Instead of liquid Spanish greetings, from Chilean swains to Chilean señoritas and vice versa, you hear a fat individual grunt *"Wie geht's, Herr Schultz?"* and another mutter, *"Ach, Herr Schwartz—guten Morgen!"*

Out of the train steps a bunchy woman, in a squarely cut dress and squat hat, wearing a big brooch fastened to an antediluvian bodice. She falls into the arms of another, similarly attired.

"Ist es warm in Santiago, Gretchen?"

"Ja, es ist sehr warm, Trudchen."

Together they advance, in mass formation, on the exit. A little tow-headed girl, with most Teutonic blue eyes, a most Teutonic pinafore, and hair braided into two most Teutonic pigtails, watches them solemnly.

It is just like that at station after station served by the southbound express—at Valdivia and Osorno, at Frutillar and Llanquíhue and Puerto Varas. Germany wafted 10,000 miles across the ocean! Of course, you also see Chilean "rotos" in their rags, and hear Chilean station masters bawling out orders in Chilean Spanish. But they cannot drown the German note.

What tempting material for Hitler, if and when he should decide to follow up Nazi economic penetration of Chile with an intensive drive for Nazi political penetration! As a matter of fact, he has already made some preliminary passes. But he has encountered—and undoubtedly will continue to encounter —obstacles that may easily wreck all his plans.

The temptation to Hitler in south central Chile is obvious. To his impulsive, go-getting nature, it must seem like fruit ripe to pluck for Nazidom.

Here, eighty or ninety years ago, a few hundreds of Germans who had decided to leave home for various reasons (some because, as republicans, they had become mixed up in the events of 1848 and were marked men to the police of the monarchical Fatherland), settled, with their families, in almost untouched, uninhabited solitudes. They built neat towns, turned virgin forest and untilled hill slope into smiling farmland, prospered through industry and thrift, became the most substantial element in the whole region, and tucked away money in the bank.

As most of the native Chileans in the vicinity were poor and illiterate laborers, some of them Indians, there was little intermarriage. The German nucleus, its numbers increased hardly at all by subsequent reinforcements from Germany, developed, through succeeding generations, into a compact, isolated Teutonic community.

On the roads around Osorno, a district that is primarily agricultural, and in the villages fringing southern Chile's enchanting, beautiful lakes, well-to-do Chilean-German farmers —Francisco Wiedenhold, Antonio Rudloff, José Adel—may be met riding to town, wearing broad-brimmed hats and bright ponchos and high knee boots—cowboys made in Germany! They bestride wiry little nags, with saddles like those of our West—but never do they lose their essential, unalterable, thick-necked, bristly-haired, grandpa-came-from-Wuerttemberg look.

In Valdivia, the biggest town of Chile's Little Germany, in a group of notices inserted in the local newspaper by eleven physicians, I counted one English, one Italian, two Spanish and seven German names. A stroll around Valdivia's pretty main plaza revealed the following: Lebermann's shoe store; the office of Erwin Kleinknecht; Mueller, the tailor; Schuetz's department store; Carlos and Max Noelke, druggists; the Deutscher Verein; the Hotel Schild; Adolfo Schwarzenberg's dry-goods emporium; the Bischoff arcade; and the German Transatlantic Bank. A stone's throw away were the Hotel Schuster, the Hotel Haussmann and the Hotel Pelz.

On the waterfront, two blocks distant—Valdivia is attractively situated on a big river a few miles from the Pacific—a diminutive tugboat puffed importantly, trying to live up to its name, *Bremen*. On the opposite shore rose Anwandtner's brewery, behind a big sign proclaiming the presence of Pilsner. And the Chilean military band, huddled together in the kiosk in the middle of the plaza, played a German song that was immensely popular in Berlin a few years ago:

> "Das ist die Dolly Wood,
> Sie sitzt in Hollywood,
> An einem Tisch,
> Mit Lillian Gish,"

and followed it up with a German overture called *Soldatenleben*.

Local Chileans, immersed in this sea of Teutonism, seemed, as a rule, to be taking it calmly. After all, Germans have always been part of their lives and of the lives of their fathers. But now and then one of them gets fed up with it all; as, for instance, the barber working at a place closer to the Valdivia plaza, who growled into my lather-swabbed ear:

"The Chilean Government ought to issue a decree absolutely forbidding everybody in this whole region to speak German! Oh, how sick I am of the German language! I wish I might never have to hear another word of it as long as I live!"

The ground looks so promising to Berlin for Nazification that Nazi agents are already at work in Valdivia and Osorno and points south. Some of the younger element of the population, especially among the few who emigrated from Germany after the war, are keen for Hitler. There is also a certain degree of ferment among older people, caught by the breathless tempo of the Fuehrer's spectacular doings.

There is even grumbling talk of Chile's "German minority" and its rights; and one may hear about the great destiny supposedly in store for Nazi doctrines. But this sort of thing is neither widespread nor deep as yet. And it is seldom correlated with local political issues. If Hitler and Goebbels count on such sporadic manifestations as a basis for the Nazification of Germanic Chile, they certainly seem to be in for bitter disappointment.

Movements like Hitlerism are built up on defeat and discontent and despair of which the Germans of Chile know practically nothing. For several generations they have bothered very little with politics, especially foreign politics. They have concentrated on their daily toil, on narrow local interests, on the necessity for wringing from the soil enough for food and clothing and shelter, on the urgency of providing for tomorrow.

"If my grandfather earned thirty cents a day," a German-Chilean of Valdivia told me—we were drinking Chilean Pilsner on Valdivia's river shore—"the daily expenses of the whole family amounted to thirty cents—or, no, that's wrong, I take it back—he spent twenty-five cents on himself and his family, and put aside five cents."

Such thrifty methods soon gave the newcomers from Germany a pride in their new home. They felt they had a stake there, that they must do nothing rash to jeopardize the hard-earned fruits of their labor. And though their essential Germanism persisted—and was handed on to their descendants—they developed a robust belief that they were Chileans. They began more and more to sense a solidarity between themselves and the republic for which they had abandoned the monarchical land of their ancestors. Little by little, the tie that bound them and theirs to the old country became a mere sentimental memory of a Germany that was dead, a Germany that had nothing to do with the World War, the early post-war era, or the era of Hitlerism.

A steady stream of new immigrants from the Reich, bringing new ideas and new theories, might have altered the situation. It might conceivably have injected the virus of changing Europe into the sons and grandsons of Chile's transplanted Teutons, who were still reciting the poems of Goethe learned from their grandmothers and still dimly recalling stories told them by their grandfathers of marching with Carl Schurz, back in '48, to bring democracy to Bavaria and Prussia and Saxony. It might, finally, have made the new generation around Valdivia and Osorno forsake the prudent ways of their forebears and plunge into headlong pursuit of the will-o'-the-wisp of Nazi ideology.

But no such stream of immigration came. In all the length and breadth of Germanic Chile those of the inhabitants who were born in Germany are remarkably few; and by no means all of these are militant Nazis.

Recently, when Hitler held one of his plebiscites, all Germans living in Chile were commanded to vote. The polling-place was a ship moored off Corral, the port of Valdivia, just outside Chilean territorial waters. The total number of sons of the Fatherland—from all over those districts of Chile where people of Germanic blood predominated—who went out to that ship to cast their ballots was barely 350.

And here is a detail which I observed when I was wandering about in those districts a short time ago, that is more significant than any amount of voluminous reports and solemn statistics: in the show-windows of bookshops on the main plazas of Osorno and Valdivia, the proprietors of which, one may certainly assume, would not deliberately hurt trade by outraging local public opinion, there was a prominent display of books by Sigmund Freud, Emil Ludwig and—*Thomas Mann!*

A good guess, it would seem, is that a Nazi bid for political ascendancy in South America, if it comes, will be based not on southern Chile but on southern Brazil. In the latter, Germans and near-Germans are far more numerous. Moreover, Brazil is much nearer Europe than Chile is; and it is also the nearest land on the American Continent to the west coast of Africa, where, in their dreams, Nazi extremists see the German flag flying over a vast German colonial domain of the future, lavishly studded with naval bases and airdromes.

After all, Chile's Little Germany is 10,000 miles away from the Wilhelmstrasse. And in mental outlook most of its inhabitants are even farther away than that from the bluster and ballyhoo of the Third Reich. In Valdivia, the grandson of one of the Teutonic settlers of last century, mockingly raising his arm in the Nazi salute, said to me:

"We haven't time for that sort of thing around here!"

He spoke, I believe, for the majority of his Chilean-German brothers. Hitler has a lot of spade work ahead of him before he can make Nazis out of these people.

* * *

American globe trotters, who constantly rush off to far-away places of Europe, Asia, Africa and Australasia, in restless search for the thrills that come from the contemplation of beautiful scenery, fail to realize that right here on their own American Continent, in the southern part of the republic of Chile, there is a practically unknown region filled with scenic wonders of such superlative merit that it is sure to become celebrated before many more years go by, as a first-class, top-notch, Grade A tourists' Paradise—if there is justice on this earth.

It is a land of enchantment, where lakes as lovely as those of Switzerland or California lap the bases of snow-covered volcanoes, looking like Japanese prints come to life. These lakes are as blue as the sky, or as green as the emeralds in a monarch's crown; and the peaks above them are so neatly curved and smoothed and rounded off as to seem deliberate productions of an artist instead of haphazard works of nature.

On verdant shores, in the shadow of towering summits, little villages, trim and hospitable, offer simple food and shelter; and for those to whom travel is palatable only when hedged about with luxury there are palatial hotels, modernistic in architecture, air-conditioned, swarming with bell-boys studded with brass buttons—yet whose proprietors, despite all this gadgetry, have not been able to bring themselves as yet to charge beyond three or four dollars per person per day for room, bath—AND MEALS! As for those little lake-fringing, volcano-hugging villages, you can sleep the sleep of the just and eat yourself out of shape in any one of half a dozen of them for a dollar, or a dollar and a half, a day—word of honor! And all this is a mere week from New York, if you are in a hurry, or somewhat over a mere fortnight, if you are not.

More and more American tourists every year make the circuit of South America, especially now that Europe is behaving so badly. They either begin with the east coast—visiting Rio de Janeiro and Buenos Aires first, crossing the Andes to Santiago, the capital of Chile, and returning by way of Peru and Panama—or else they reverse this route, heading first for Chile, via the west coast of South America, going over the Andes from Santiago to the Argentine and Brazil, and thence northward and homeward.

In either case Santiago is their Farthest South.

They get back to the United States rich in unforgettable impressions of engineering marvels (provided by the Panama Canal); of massive Inca ruins and quaint relics of Spain's colonial empire of yesteryear (gathered in Peru); and of metropolitan rush and energy (Buenos Aires). But they reach home comparatively poor in memories of magnificent scenery, since, on the whole long trip, natural beauty, belonging to the A1 tourist classification, has met their eyes scarcely anywhere except during the short hours of the passage of the Andes and in matchless Rio de Janeiro.

Yet, a day's railroad ride south of Santiago, is the scenic wonderland of the Chilean lakes. Even a hurried globe trotter can get a superficial idea of it by adding a brief five or six days to his itinerary—though, he is hereby warned, two extra weeks would not exhaust its treasures.

A fine express train, with steel-built sleepers (equipped even with shower baths!) and dining cars in which copious meals—with good Chilean wines and including the waiter's tip—are served at the fantastically low cost of 50 cents, leaves Santiago early every evening for Chile's Switzerland-plus-Japan Southland. Next morning it reaches Loncoche, whence a branch runs to the lake of Villarica and the volcano-dominated resort of Pucón, which has a luxurious hotel and is the center of an almost untapped Utopia of river and lake fishing. But I am not concerned here with the joys of detours—this chapter is aimed at tourists who follow the main lines of travel. These, ignoring Villarica and Pucón, will push on to Puerto Varas, 650 miles from Santiago, which the southern express reaches the afternoon after leaving Chile's metropolis.

For several hours before reaching Puerto Varas the train traverses delightful landscape—rolling farm country, well-wooded and well-watered, sprinkled with clean little towns. Shortly after leaving Osorno, the first of the volcanoes, which are one of the most striking and most attractive features of the region, leaps into visibility on the far horizon, to the left of the railway. It is the Osorno volcano—its lower part all green vegetation, its tapering upper half encased in gleaming snow. As the train puffs southward, one gets glimpse after glimpse of this mountain, all different and beautiful. Finally, after the tourist has alighted at Puerto Varas and installed himself at the grandest hotel in Chile south of Santiago, it bursts upon him, as he steps out on his private balcony, in clean-cut symmetry, grandiose yet delicate, as if painted on the canvas of the evening sky by the light strokes of a subtle brush—Fujiyama playing truant!

Below it shine the waters of Lake Llanquíhue (pronounced Yan-keé-weh) deep blue, stretching away eastward to where other volcanoes majestically ring its shores—blunt three-pronged Calbuco; pointed Puntiagudo, stabbing the heavens like a pencil of sharpened rock, and far in the distance, massive Tronador, "the Thunderer." But the tourist who has just arrived by the Santiago express cannot stand drinking in these wonders for long. Soon darkness falls on waters and mountains. He bathes, changes, goes downstairs, to scan a dinner menu printed in French and listen to American dance tunes played by a swing orchestra.

With the big Puerto Varas hotel as headquarters, American visitors (unless they are in a dreadful hurry) can spend several days profitably on the shores of azure Llanquíhue. They can make the circuit of that lovely lake on a puffing little steamboat, explore pretty rivers which flow toward it through fields alive with bright flowers, get acquainted with the funny little Teutonic-Chilean settlements lining its shores, which rejoice in Spanish-German names like Puerto Fonck or Puerto Klocker. Moreover, they do not by any means have to stay at that swell, bell-boy ridden *caravanserai* at Puerto Varas. Down at the other end of the lake, at Ensenada, the semi-German proprietor of a charming little hotel is all ready to feed and house them for a ridiculously low sum—that is also true of the proprietors of other similarly modest and well-located little road-houses, all of them singularly unexacting in the matter of charges for room and board, though they have a beautiful lake just beyond their front yards and perfectly enchanting volcanoes sticking up out of their back yards!

When the visitor has had enough of navigating Lake Llanquíhue, after a few days at Puerto Varas, he can charter a motor car and proceed to Ensenada by road.

The road in Chile! Here's to it! Farm and river, village and lake, mountain and cascade and sparkling blue sky. Miles of jolting through deep silent forests, filled with magnificent trees and covered with flowers. No use to ask their names. The driver simply answers with an incomprehensible local word, which doesn't make sense in any language with which you are acquainted, and leaves you just where you were before. But what's the difference? Flowers and flowers and still more flowers. And right and left the sharp pinnacles of volcanoes, white with eternal snow.

"That one over there," volunteers the driver, "was in eruption a few years ago. And, a little later, it was making such dreadful noises inside itself that scientists came rushing down here to find out what ailed it and said it was soon going to erupt again."

You look at the volcano with respect.

"What is that grayish stuff all around it?"

"Lava—from the last eruption."

You look at the volcano with apprehension. But it remains fast asleep in the sunlight.

Wheat fields. Corn fields. Children waving cheery greeting. Lone riders, riders in twos and threes, each wearing a poncho, that compact mixture of cloak and coat, sometimes drab and old, sometimes new and bright. Brown ponchos. Yellow ponchos. Blue ponchos and red ponchos. Riders prodding unruly herds of cattle, or frightened droves of sheep. Riders, with little sons or daughters on the pommel of the saddle in front of them, half-hidden in dad's poncho. Riders trotting on their way, with wives perched uncomfortably behind them. Riders roping steers in impromptu rodeos.

Wooden shanties. Hovels with rough thatched roofs. Oxcarts creaking along at a mile an hour. Small automobiles, of incredible antiquity, rattling past them in lordly disdain.

And Germans. (Here they are again!—simply can't get away from them!) Though the riders one meets wear those Chilean ponchos, the like of which Germany never saw, and stick their toes into stirrups like wooden boxes, which would give a German horse fits, the Teutonic tinge over the region makes it almost seem like a bit of Bavaria, or the Black Forest, which has cut loose from the Fatherland and floated across the Atlantic.

At Ensenada one is whisked by car to Petrohué, on the shores of Lake Todos los Santos. That lake, I here and now declare, with the backing of practically everyone who has seen it, is one of the most enchanting sights in the whole world, capable of galvanizing the most jaded tourist into instant and voluble enthusiasm.

Now the volcanoes have narrowed their ring. They seem to be crowding to the very shore of the lake, right into the waters of emerald, their snowy pinnacles flashing in the sunlight.

"If only they don't erupt!" mutters an American lady nervously, as the diminutive steamboat chugs boldly in and out between them, valiantly ignoring their scowls.

"Well, if they do," I reassure her, "the lake will make a good fire department."

Peulla is the boat's destination. One lands there, amid meadows smothered in flowers, amid swarms of big, handsome red-and-brown gnats, in front of a nice little hotel (all there is to Peulla is that hotel, dozens of volcanoes, thousands of gnats, and millions of flowers). Most tourists are content to stop at Peulla only one night. But that same American lady of the boat, completely recovered from volcanophobia, had become so enthusiastically Peulla-conscious that she warbled ecstatically:

"Some day I'll come back here and stay the rest of my life!"

From Peulla the American tourist who is circling South America may either retrace his steps to Santiago and cross the Andes from there to Argentina, by plane or rail-and-motor, or he may continue eastward, over the Pérez Rosales Pass, which traverses a primeval forest absolutely carpeted with flowers, yet wrapped in deep silence, because there are no birds in it. This will bring him to the counterparts, in the Argentine, of the lakes of Chile.

These are Laguna Frias, nestling at the foot of enormous mountain walls, and Lake Nahuel Huapí, the biggest of all, which vies in glorious and variegated loveliness with Lake Todos los Santos. Close to its shores the Argentines have just put up a big modern hotel de luxe, in the same class with that grand *caravanserai* at Puerto Varas, on the Chilean side, which can serve as a starting point for half a dozen delightful excursions on Nahuel Huapí and in its neighborhood—unless cheaper quarters (also available) are preferred.

From Bariloche, on Lake Nahuel Huapí, an express train with sleeping car accommodation, runs several times weekly to Buenos Aires in about forty hours. Other trains take longer.

Honesty compels the admission that this part of the lakeland trip has nothing whatsoever to recommend it, since it consists almost entirely of dust, heat and horribly unattractive desert. But that is the only flaw in the entire journey—and, after all, the Chilean lakes, with their Argentine side-partners, are well worth even those hours of desolation.

NORTH AMERICANS are too hard on South Americans. They are good at spotting defects in the latter, bad at noting virtues. They are glib about the numerous revolutions which mar the South American record, indifferent to the early handicaps (without counterpart in the history of North America) which made those outbreaks of militaristic violence unavoidable. In strict justice, these northern critics of southern neighbors should have transferred, in the past, much of the blame heaped on nineteenth-century Mexico and Cuba, Central America and Venezuela and the rest, to the Spain of the sixteenth and seventeenth centuries—not forgetting a similar shifting of hard words and thoughts, leveled at the Brazil of recent times, to the Portugal which, over a period of some three hundred years, shaped Brazilian character.

Our ancestors of the thirteen original North American Colonies were luckier than the people of Latin America. They had political sense. They came from a land where resistance to governmental encroachment was second nature to millions, where opposition to autocratic rule—both royal and ecclesiastical—was in the very blood of the inhabitants. Thus, when they came to the New World, they were, to some extent, already qualified to hand down to their descendants the capacity to profit peaceably from independence, after it had been won on the battlefield.

That was not so in Latin America.

The great majority of Spaniards who ventured across the

ocean to the new dominions opened up to their kings by Columbus and those who followed him, felt no urge for freedom of any sort. Most of them wanted, above all things, gold —lust for wealth, in the form of precious metals and precious stones, filled their minds to the point of mania. It shaped their actions with such overwhelming power that one tribe of South American natives, according to legend, having captured a grasping and cruel Spanish conquistador, poured molten gold down his throat until he perished in agony, taunting him as they did so with these words: "So you want gold? Well, here's gold!"

Leaders of Spanish expeditions to the New World nurtured no dreams of future home rule, of even the most shadowy autonomy, for the lands which their swords were annexing to Spain. What they wanted was gold, more gold, always gold, gold in limitless quantity for themselves and their king waiting, greedily, in his great palace of the Escorial.

A state of mind, this, certainly not analogous to the feelings, which sent so many of the forebears of present-day North Americans to the "stern and rockbound coast" of New England, or to other parts of the northern region destined, in time, to become (like Latin America) a home of the brave, but also (unlike its neighbor to the southward) a land of the free.

Then, too, there was climate.

In the north, climatic conditions were, as a rule, rather a help than a handicap to early settlers. In the south, on the other hand, or in most of it, climate proved a thing of such detriment and insidiousness that it wore down even some of the steeliest of those men of steel, the conquistadores.

The seeds of Latin America's turbulent and backward nineteenth century were heedlessly sown not alone by despotic overseas kings and their rapacious henchmen, but by corrupt government officials and bigoted churchmen, to such an extent that the efforts of far-seeing and honorable civilians, soldiers and priests—of whom there were splendid examples throughout the days of the Conquest—were powerless to counteract them.

Many have paid attention in their reading to the great voyages undertaken by European navigators, which resulted in the discovery of the West Indies, and of Central and South America. In the minds of most of us something has lodged permanently that has to do with Columbus's first discovery of America; and with his three subsequent voyages; and with Balboa's first sighting of the Pacific; and Cabral's first glimpse of the Brazilian coast; and that renowned first circumnavigation of the world, which—begun by a Portuguese, Magellan, and ended by a Spaniard, Elcano—revealed a sea passage skirting southernmost South America and threw wide to conquest and commerce the vast regions fringing that ocean on whose tranquil waters Balboa, first among Europeans, had laid wondering eyes.

Similarly, we know how Cortez, with a puny force of resolute fellow-Spaniards, crushed the great Aztec Empire of Montezuma in Mexico; how Pizarro presented his king with the territory and treasury of the Inca Empire of Peru, wrested from the luckless Emperor Atahualpa, with the help of a little battalion of Spaniards as weak and as audacious as the men of Cortez; how Alvarado conquered Central America; how Valdivia overran Chile; how De Soto found the Mississippi; how Ponce de Leon sought youth in Florida; how reckless Portuguese adventurers took vast Brazil for their king; and how hardy Frenchmen added Haiti (and what is now the Dominican Republic) to the domain of the

French Crown.

But, in comparison, little attention has been paid by most of us to how European monarchs jealously followed up discovery and conquest, haughtily curbing the ambitions of navigators and conquistadores, restricting the privileges of those venturesome individuals, everywhere asserting the supremacy of the monarchy, everywhere setting forth in solemn documents, and implementing in ruthless action, the theory that the main reason for a colony's existence was to provide revenues for the royal treasury, at no matter what cost to local freedom and local prosperity.

On the eve of the voyage which resulted in the discovery of America, Christopher Columbus stood in high favor with royal Ferdinand and Isabella of Spain. They had dubbed him admiral, promised him one-half of whatever profits might accrue from his coming great venture—early testimony to the craving for New World gold which ever actuated both adventurous Spanish voyagers and stay-at-home Spanish monarchs.

But soon after Columbus had reported his discovery, the equally strong royal urge for undivided authority vigorously asserted itself. Those special privileges which had been dangled before Columbus before he set sail were taken back by the royal donors. And they lost no time in sending out, on the heels of the Genoese navigator, Spanish officials vested with powers to govern the new realm in the royal name. One of these, after a dispute with Columbus, sent him back to Europe in chains. The man who had been the first to sight the New World was also the first to feel the weight of royal displeasure at even the smallest encroachment on autocratic kingly privileges.

It was the same with conquistadores as with navigators.

Hernan Cortez, with his band of marauders, wrecked the Aztec Empire. But it was not he who ruled in place of luckless Montezuma. It was a viceroy, first of many, directly representing the faraway monarch, dispatched across the ocean just as soon as the news of Cortez' unbelievable exploit became known in Madrid.

Pizarro, too, felt the irresistible weight of Spain's royal authority. After he had conquered Inca Peru, after he had fallen out with his fellow-conquerors and been assassinated by them, no member of his family, nor any other among his comrades in conquest, governed the great territory which he and they had overrun. It was again a Viceroy sent from Spain. Direct representatives of the Spanish King also landed, armed with credentials admitting of no sharing of authority, in every other part of South America won by Spanish swords. And, meanwhile, in Brazil, every budding ambition of Portuguese conquistadores to keep for themselves what they had won, was nipped, with similar promptness, by the King in Portugal.

Nowhere did anybody carve out domains for individuals, islands of freedom—no matter how tenuous. Instead, royal masters in the Old World put on their territories in the New World the colonial stamp, sucked up all local life, made perfectly clear to all and sundry, in the harshest of language, that it was the duty of every colonial to obey without question.

By this insistence on royal prerogative the Spanish and Portuguese Crowns paved the way for the dictatorial régimes in many of the Latin American "republics," of our times. These, through decades of instability, found that they had exchanged European despotism for governments which, though administered by natives, were scarcely less autocratic. In ex-

alting the king above everything, in staking out for Spanish
aristocrats most of the highest and most lucrative posts in
their overseas dominions, in arrogantly excluding colonials,
even the most prominent and most pro-Spanish, from all but
inferior positions, the monarchs of that Spain which conquered and administered Spanish America in colonial centuries were largely responsible for some of the gravest blem-
ishes in the Spanish America that we know—where presidents
of independent nations sit in the seats of Spanish viceroys
and captains-general. What has happened there, to a considerable extent, is that the king's prerogatives have been merely
taken over by the descendants of those colonial upper classes,
which had been denied authority under Spanish rule. And
when a leader from the lower classes has fought his way to
power, he has seldom shown the slightest interest in bettering
the condition of his fellows, but instead, has proceeded to imitate his "white-collar" fellow-citizens of the upper class in
oppression and peculation—a direct heritage from Spanish
concentration on despotic rule for the profit of the king.

Spain, unflinchingly true to her determination not to foster
even the most elementary political sense among colonials,
early curbed the power of the "cabildos," or municipal coun-
cils, which, in the New World, had become the typical repositories of local administration. These bodies had, at times,
vested in themselves a semblance of home rule; had they
been left alone, or better still, encouraged from across the
ocean, they might have developed a kernel of democratic
autonomy which might later have blossomed into genuine
democracy. But the "cabildos," severely repressed by the
monarchs in Madrid whenever they showed signs of self-
assertion and local consciousness, soon lapsed into that in-
ertia, that spineless acquiescence, which lasted in Latin Amer-

ica, almost unbroken by attempts at change on the part of colonials, from the discovery by Columbus to the beginnings of the Spanish American wars of independence.

And that goes, *mutatis mutandis*, for Portuguese Brazil. Rio de Janeiro, of the 16th and 17th and 18th centuries, as well as Bahia and the rest of Portugal's coastal Brazilian settlements, were as much under the thumb of the king in Lisbon as were haughty Lima and opulent Mexico and battery-girt Havana under that of the despot of Madrid, ruling through his viceroys and his other obedient yes-men of the famed Council of the Indies.

Spanish America, under Spain, was long divided into two vice-royalties, New Spain (Mexico) and Peru. The viceroy of the former resided at Mexico City, built on the ruins of glittering Aztec Tenochtitlan; the viceroy of Peru held court at Lima—"City of the Kings"—founded by Pizarro after he had obliterated the Inca Empire from the map.

Both viceroys lived in pomp and splendor. And both were expected by their king to see to it, above all else, that the flow of revenue from the New World into the royal treasury remained copious and regular. The arbitrary freakishness of Spanish rule was illustrated in the vice-regal realm of New Spain by the fact that it comprised not only the Mexico and Central America of today but also the distant Spanish West Indies, and even settlements established by early Spanish explorers along the coasts of the Caribbean, in what we now know as Venezuela and Colombia.

The viceroy at Lima, thanks to a similarly arbitrary dispensation, exerted his king's authority not alone over Peru and the territory now comprised in Ecuador, Bolivia and Chile, but likewise over huge regions stretching eastward to Paraguay and to the River Plate—the latter on the shore of the Atlantic. This state of affairs made Venezuela (though remote alike from "New Spain" and the West Indies) dependent for financial and political administrative decisions on Mexico or Santo Domingo; and it brought about the even more bizarre subservience of Buenos Aires, on the Atlantic coast of South America, to Lima, on the Pacific side, though there were hundreds of miles of almost pathless mountainous tracts between the two. Merchants of Buenos Aires were for many years strictly forbidden to trade over the Atlantic with Spain, being confined instead to importing and exporting entirely by way of Peru. This, of course, besides entailing all sorts of dangers and inconveniences, raised the price of European goods in the River Plate region to fantastic figures. There are tales of cloaks and coats imported from Europe, which were looked upon by those who had ordered them from across the seas as something so precious that they were handed down to descendants through several generations, since none of the successive wearers of these prized garments could bear the thought of paying the price of new ones ordered (via Lima) from Spain.

But there was nothing to be done about it. It was the king's will!

Finally, Spanish rule in Latin America grew so unwieldy and caused (even among the generally docile colonials) such vehement protests, that two new vice-royalties were created, one on the River Plate, the other in New Granada (now Colombia). New captains-general, with new local powers, were also installed at several of the more important colonial centers, and permission to trade directly across the Atlantic was grudgingly given, under severe restrictions, to merchants of Buenos Aires.

Thanks to the highly efficient follow-up methods of the

Spanish monarchy, it had staked out for itself, even before all those who had sailed with Columbus were dead, a vast American Empire. And it gradually achieved exclusive domination over that immense area, making possible the survival of autocratic Spanish authority, with scarcely a single concession to liberalism, until the late eighteenth century. Then the effects of the French Revolution made even obdurate Spain realize that something had to be done in the way of reforms. But by that time it was too late. Centuries of uncompromising despotism had done their work. Independence was at hand.

During those centuries of despotism Spain met an astonishingly small degree of local self-assertion in Spanish America. Whatever revolts happened—and there were quite a number, notably the uprising of Tupac Amaru, descendant of the Incas, in Peru—were soon crushed.

Corruption among colonial officials soon grew to alarming proportions. Many of these retired, after their tenure of office, with fortunes in their pockets. It must be remarked, in justice to Spanish monarchs, that at intervals they tried hard to correct abuses. For example, they demanded (in recurring eras of reform) a strict accounting from retiring colonial officials. But these measures had little lasting effect. The king was too far away. There were too many ways for corrupt officials to make gold stick to their fingers, without arousing too much embarrassing royal attention. And clever servants of the Crown, from whom accounting was demanded, found means of wriggling out of serious personal consequences. Moreover, the tremendous royal thirst for revenue only too often nullified royal corrective measures.

In Spain's New World the official Spanish-born class was cock-of-the-walk. Its members strutted proudly through the streets of Lima and Mexico, Carácas and Quito, Santiago in

Chile and Santiago in Cuba. They looked down on every other class in the local population—on the wealthy proprietors of landed estates and on the operators of mines, the next highest category, who bitterly resented the airs of these Spaniards and their monopoly of the best official jobs; on the free people of the lower strata—artisans, shopkeepers, farmers, laborers; and on the lowest of all, the thousands of Negro and Indian slaves. And in the classes despised by the Spaniards, each sought to look down on the next lower, thus engendering a state of affairs by no means unpleasing to Spanish masters, who felt that royal authority could be imposed more easily on a community divided against itself.

The Inquisition, introduced into Peru and Mexico in the sixteenth century, proved a valuable aid to autocratic Spanish control. Just as settlement in the New World was restricted to Spaniards, so also was no religion tolerated there except the Catholic—a restriction vigorously maintained by New World inquisitors.

Priests, following the conquerors, everywhere baptized the natives in the Catholic faith. Like their civilian and military colleagues, some of these ecclesiastics were corrupt and cruel. But their delinquencies fade before the shining achievements of the good men among them. Beginning with the renowned Bartolomé de las Casas, "Apostle of the Indies," a long line of saintly priests labored, with no thought of earthly reward, for the spiritual and bodily welfare of the natives.

Their deeds were not confined to the Spanish dominions. They were accomplished, with equally conspicuous success, in Portuguese Brazil. In the jungle lands of that colony, Jesuits and others established settlements where, with unflinching devotion, they assembled and taught the Indians. In so doing they braved not only hostility and climate, but also the enmity of the hideously cruel "bandeirantes," the slave traders of Brazil, who looked upon Brazilian Indians as articles of commerce especially created for their profit and detested the missionaries because of their disinterested efforts to save these unfortunates from slavery.

In much of the Latin America of today there is a shocking cleavage of class. The upper classes have everything, the lower nothing. The former are socially elect, educated or enabled to become so, rich or in a position to get rich—or, at least, to live in comfort. They are tended in illness by competent doctors, guarded through infancy, supervised in childhood, protected in adolescence and maturity and old age, and decently buried in death.

But the lower classes, to this day, in many parts of the Latin American lands, are still, in the grim words of the "Internationale," *forçats de la fortune*—convicts of destiny. They are despised by their "betters"; they are mostly entirely illiterate and bereft of means of achieving literacy; they are lucky to earn enough to keep from starving; they cannot pay for medicines when ailing; they "jest grow" out of childhood; they work without happiness or solace or hope, through life almost to senility; and after the last breath has left their weary and dirty bodies, they are carted to paupers' graves.

Thus—not always, of course, but far too often—lives and dies the "roto" of Chile, the "peón" of Mexico, the "gaucho pobre" and "hombre del pueblo" of other parts of Latin America. For these miserable conditions, and for the altogether too strongly contrasting good fortune of those living on the other shore of the Gulf of Class, the Spanish and (in Brazil) the Portuguese forerunners of Latin American "republican" governments of our day, are largely to blame.

From the earliest days of European rule in Latin America

the natives were looked upon as things to exploit, without human attributes or rights. Cruelty to the Indians stains the entire Spanish record in the New World. The massacre of Columbus's followers, left behind by him on the Island of La Española (Hispaniola), after his first voyage, was largely due to outrageous conduct toward the Indians inhabiting the region around the first Spanish settlement.

The system of "encomiendas," through which exploitation of the natives reached its most revolting heights, was introduced by Spain soon after the discovery of America. By this system, the conquistadores and other Spaniards, who had achieved prominence in the New World, received, as their personal property, entire tribes or groups of Indians. These, doomed thenceforth to hard labor for their European masters, were denied the most elementary individual privileges. Women of enslaved Indian tribes were often turned over to the conquerors, the number of these concubines being proportioned to the importance of each Spaniard and to his supposed deserts.

The "encomienda" system soon became general. Abuse eventually became so atrocious that the faraway Spanish monarch was forced to attempt reforms. One of the main instigators of these was the "Apostle of the Indies," Las Casas, who, himself, in his early life, had been granted a lot of Indians.

The Spanish king's reforms did not get very far. At first, "encomenderos" found their cruel activities in exploiting Indian serfs considerably limited; and under the watchful eyes of Spanish officials, especially appointed to carry through the reforms, they had to mitigate their cruelties. But soon the old abuses returned. Under the best of conditions, it was hard for Madrid to exact one hundred per cent observance of its

decrees in remote and semi-savage Spanish America. Now—
with the incentive of profit ever before them—"encomenderos" became adept at evading royal curtailment of their authority. And the officials set to watch them soon nodded—
perhaps, in some cases, with well-filled pockets as a reward for
laxness.

Especially in the mines of the New World forced labor
continued, under various modifications of the original system.
It was employed in some places so mercilessly that tribes of
Indians upon whom it was imposed were almost wiped out,
or, at least, woefully reduced in numbers. Instances of this
occurred in the famous silver mines of Potosí, in what is now
Bolivia, also in present-day Venezuela, where greedy Spaniards exploited the pearl fisheries of the island of Margarita.

All this brought cynical disregard of human rights. Even
the most cursory survey of the Latin America of the present
shows the unhallowed trail of these inhuman methods. Right
through the nineteenth century, dictators in some of the
southern republics have oppressed their soldiers; rich employers have used employees as chattels; influential planters, feeling immune from interference by governments as conscience-
less as themselves, have kept their hundreds of miserable
laborers, their pickers of coffee, cutters of sugar, and tenders
of cattle, in a state differing practically not at all from
actual slavery.

Spanish and Portuguese kings lost no time in imposing the
most rigid trade restrictions on their American dominions,
as a most efficacious means of running these as private royal
estates.

During most of the period of Spanish domination all li-
censes to import goods into the colonies, or to export them
from Spain's American Empire, were given exclusively to

Spaniards. Moreover, all goods sent to the colonies over a long period, had to be shipped from Seville and from nowhere else. Later, Cádiz took over this special privilege; and toward the end of Spanish rule, certain other Spanish ports were granted restricted rights to trade with the Indies.

In addition, merchandise could be sent from Spain across the ocean only in the vessels of two merchant fleets, which sailed each year—one to Vera Cruz, in Mexico, the other to Porto Bello, on the Isthmus of Panama. Everything thus transported was marketed at two big fairs, one at Jalapa, Mexico, the other at Porto Bello itself. Profits sometimes ran as high as five hundred per cent.

For the return voyage, the ships of the two fleets took on great quantities of colonial products, which had been assembled at Vera Cruz and Porto Bello, the only ports in Spanish America allowed to trade with the mother-country, and through her, with the rest of the world. These shipments included even those products from the remote River Plate region which might perfectly well have gone directly over the Atlantic.

Shipments from the New World by the two great merchant fleets comprised—in addition to the gold, silver and precious stones so keenly coveted by the king in Madrid—cocoa, tobacco, hides, indigo, and other (at that time) outlandish wares. The king, of course, was especially interested in precious metals and precious stones, as well as in the product of the pearl fisheries of the New World.

At first, the "cut" of the Spanish Crown on such shipments reached even to two-thirds of the yield. But there was such a roar of protest at this, from the usually long-suffering merchants, that the Spanish monarch, afraid to kill the goose that was laying such valuable golden eggs, scaled down his share gradually until it was only one-fifth of the output—from which comes the Spanish term "quinto," applied to the royal percentage. Toward the end of Spanish rule in Latin America, there were times when the king took even less—as little, in fact, as a meager ten per cent. In periods when trade was going strong, and the "quinto" was flourishing, the royal overlord of the Americas probably raked something like $2,500,000 yearly into his coffers.

Throughout the Spanish era in Spanish America there were serious commercial frauds and an enormous amount of smuggling. In fact, even early in that era it is said that the proceeds of smuggling were higher than the total proceeds of legitimate trade.

It took Spain a long time to let any other nation in on her New World graft. Finally, after smuggling had become rampant, she began cautiously to extend trading privileges to non-Spaniards.

The English, especially, were the beneficiaries of this change in policy. Early in the eighteenth century they were granted a monopoly in introducing African Negro slaves into Spanish America. Later, they got other business concessions, including the right to send one trading ship yearly into Spanish American waters.

These privileges, instead of curtailing smuggling, gave it a great impetus. The Britishers showed themselves most skilful at sneaking goods past Spanish customs guards, and at swelling, by all sorts of tricks, the tide of contraband trade between the Spanish colonies and Europe.

In addition to such depredations on his revenues, the king of Spain had to contend against a regular epidemic of piracy. This eventually became so serious that Drake, on one occasion, intercepted and plundered a homeward-bound Spanish

treasure fleet. And Sir Henry Morgan capped all earlier pirati-
cal feats by conquering and savagely looting the rich city of
Panama, where the Spaniards had assembled, for shipment
across the Isthmus of Porto Bello and thence to Spain, a vast
quantity of treasure destined for his sovereign master by the
viceroy of Peru.

The Spanish Crown also loosened up occasionally to the extent of giving monopolies of trade to certain privileged colonials, which also brought flagrant abuses.

All this sort of thing played an important and fateful part
in placing the imprint of centralized control and of governmental corruption on the heirs of Spain, the Latin American
republics. In these, Spanish monopoly of trade found its
counterpart in the monopolizing, by dictators and their
satellites, of varied lines of commerce for their own benefit. I
remember, in my childhood days in Venezuela, how neatly
the dictator of the moment had turned the trick of enriching
one of his favorites. First, the dictator decreed that all house-
holders in the better parts of Carácas, the Venezuelan capital,
must put down cement pavements on the streets fronting their
houses. Then he decreed that nobody but the favorite could
sell cement.

Further analogy between the corrupt days of Spanish rule
and the equally corrupt régimes of independent Latin America—when it was at its low water mark of maladministration
—may be found if one compares the smugglers of Spanish
days to revolutionists of our own era. The smugglers were
the *outs* of the past, just as the revolution plotters are the
outs of the present. The *ins* of Spanish days were, most emphatically, the king of Spain and his greedy entourage—just
as the *ins*, as we know them, are the dictatorial, monopoly-
hunting, money-crazed governments, which so often have

made a farce out of Latin American "democracy."

In Brazil, the Portuguese king acted much as did his confrère in Madrid. Most rigid control was imposed on Brazilian trade with Europe, all of which had to go through Lisbon. None but Portuguese could trade with the rich Brazilian colony. Most onerous regulations were loaded upon every trader. Not until after Napoleon Bonaparte had driven King John VI from Portugal to Brazil did the Portuguese monarchy, in a sudden rush of belated liberalism, open up Brazilian ports to a less restricted form of overseas trade.

Social conditions in Spanish and Portuguese America were bad—worthy counterparts, in fact, of the backward political and economic situation. The masses were cynically left in almost complete ignorance; the percentage of illiteracy, high enough now, was, in colonial times, appalling.

In the course of the three centuries and more of Spanish rule in the Spanish Indies a number of universities were established there. The first of these, that of San Marcos at Lima, founded in the early part of the sixteenth century, is still in existence, and lays claim to the proud title of oldest university on the American Continent. The University of Mexico, founded in 1551, antedates by many years both Harvard and Yale.

These universities catered practically entirely to sons of the upper class. For lower class colonials to get into any one of them was almost a miracle.

Like their successors in the Latin American republics, the inhabitants of Spanish America (and of Portuguese Brazil) were an emotional lot, giving little scope to reason in the determination of their actions. Men in all classes were sexually lax—a trait in which Spanish Americans of the era of independence have, if anything, gone them one better.

Women were emphatically classed as in an inferior category to men—a conception of the relation of the sexes, which, even in the most progressive parts of Spanish America, persists to this day. Among the lower classes, under Spanish rule, there was more freedom for women than among those of the upper class; indeed, the happy-go-lucky state of affairs among the "criollos" of inferior social status made it possible for them to dispense, to a considerable extent, with the formality of marriage.

Nor has political independence brought change in this. Marriage remains, in some parts of Latin America, largely a luxury for the upper class.

My mother, a New Englander from Boston, who often made long visits to cocoa plantations along the Venezuelan coast, owned by relatives of my Venezuelan father, on which patriarchal (and shocking) social conditions prevailed, used to tell with great glee the following story about one of these plantations:

The cook there had for something like a quarter of a century lived with the majordomo in what was, to all intents and purposes, a happy and permanent union. They had ten children, or thereabouts.

"Why don't you marry him?" my mother used to inquire.

"That's what he keeps asking me," the cook would invariably answer, "but I always say to him: 'No, Ramón, I won't. It's no use proposing to me. I can't see anything in marriage. I was born to be single.'"

And my young brother, while staying on another big plantation, attended a festival of the laborers at a nearby village, and was visited by a deputation of workers, who asked him to make a speech in honor of the occasion. Standing on the steps of the village church, he gave the crowd a terrific scolding because, for years, there had been very few marriages in the village.

"The priest feels very badly about it," he wound up. A number of men in the crowd nodded approvingly. Several women muttered: "Young Mr. Ybarra is right." And that week, and the next, and the next, a serious epidemic of marriage broke out in the vicinity.

In Spain's dominions women of the upper class lived and died according to the most rigid code of etiquette and morals. The education they received was, as a rule, of the sketchiest; and the way their men sought to isolate them from real life would have won enthusiastic approval from a Turkish pasha. Under the Spaniards in Peru, a young girl was denied absolution by a priest because of outrageous conduct unbecoming a Spanish lady: *she had learned French!*

Even stiff-necked Spaniards had to make exceptions now and then. Sister Juana Inés de la Cruz, that Mexican nun of the seventeenth century whose fame stands high as a poet in Spanish literature, was graciously allowed by the authorities in her native city of Mexico to study subjects usually beyond the reach of her sex—including that terribly dangerous thing, the Latin language!

Even now, similar conditions may be found here and there in parts of South America, though it is many years since the last Spanish viceroy and last Spanish prelate packed up and sailed home.

Divorce, for instance, absolutely uncountenanced in Spain's America, is, to this day, a disgrace even among some Latin Americans who are in constant touch with North America and Europe, and, hence, well aware of the crumbling of old traditions in those countries. I remember well one happening in a Spanish American republic which portrays admirably the never-say-die Spanish attitude toward divorce still existing there. A beautiful young girl of the local aristocracy, having become divorced from her husband in Europe, returned to live in semi-disgraced seclusion in her mother's house. She gave up all social life—scarcely left home, in fact. Yet this self-imposed punishment did not seem a sufficient penance to "right-thinking" members of the community. Her every move was criticized.

"But what would you have her do?" asked a foreigner, of one of her critics.

"Shoot herself," he replied.

It is wrong, of course, to blame the Spain and Portugal of the colonial period for all the shortcomings of the heirs to their overseas empires. The latter, despite the bad record of their European ancestors, ought certainly to have made, for their countries, a better nineteenth century than they did. It is unpardonable that they should have reared such mountain-ous obstacles in the paths of those fellow-countrymen of theirs, ever more numerous, who today are setting themselves the task of building a better Latin America.

Nevertheless, Spaniards and Portuguese cannot, in justice, be entirely exonerated. The seeds sown by them have brought crops of bad government, bad morals, bad business methods, bad social conditions. It must be admitted that they had an appalling task before them—but they made an awful botch of it.

AMERICANS are sitting pretty in Peru. In business they are doing well. They are getting along famously with the Peruvians. They sell them a lot of goods and buy a lot of goods from them. In the battle with competitors in the Peruvian market—Germans, British, Japanese—they are more than holding their own.

And in semi-hostile, semi-amiable, non-commercial sparring with resident Fascist Italians the Americans seem to be winning on points.

When I went through Lima early this year, the bouts in this running sparring contest were largely being staged, on the one side, by Italy's Aviation Mission, and by the Italian officers training the Lima police force; and, on the other, by the American Naval Mission to Peru. In their endeavors to keep Fascist stock high, Italian officers on duty there were inclined to act like little Mussolinis—there was much striking of martial attitudes among them, much squaring of shoulders, flashing of eyes and protruding of chins, many gruff statements of opinion on European current events.

As for the Italians teaching Lima's police how to be honest-to-goodness cops, there was a growing feeling among Peruvians that the efforts of these individuals savored at times too strongly of out-and-out Fascist propaganda. And the Italian habit of pinning medals on Peruvians at the slightest pretext, in the hope that these decorations would make the recipients good little pro-Mussolinians, aroused considerable sly snickering—"penetration by decoration" one irreverent individual called it.

Meanwhile, the members of the American Naval Mission did no strutting, acted like good fellows at social functions (while the Italians were giving an imitation of the March on Rome), didn't spring anything startling, like the Fascist salute, on an unsuspecting public; stuck closely to their work; and kept their powder (and sense of humor) dry.

All of which was helping Uncle Sam's progress in the thing which, in Peru as everywhere else in Latin America, beats all other things in importance. That's trade.

As an exporter of merchandise to the Peruvian market, the United States has a commanding lead over all competitors. In fact, when it comes to exports of automobiles, radios, electric refrigerators, certain types of machinery, motion pictures and motion picture equipment, we have practically a monopoly.

Some idea of our steady progress in the Peruvian market may be gained from the following facts:

In 1920, American exports to Peru were worth, roughly, 79,000,000 soles (one sol is equivalent to about 20 American cents). In 1932, at the worst of the depression, they dropped to about 22,000,000 soles. Then they shot upward—to 46,000,-000 in 1934, 59,000,000 in 1935, 64,000,000 in 1936, 83,000-000 in 1937. In 1938, they dropped back again, but remained, notwithstanding, well above those of any year between pre-depression days and 1937.

The Germans have also been doing well in Peru. They remain far behind us there in total value of exports, but in percentage of gain in exports, they have been running ahead of the United States.

From our depression low, in 1932, the climb to our 1937 export total represented a nearly fourfold increase. But the

Germans, over that same period, fought their way upward from a depression low (1932) of 8,000,000 soles to over 46,-000,000 soles, more than five and one-half times the value of their 1932 exports to Peru.

The British, before the depression and for a while after it, yielded only to the United States in sales to Peru (chiefly of textiles, machinery, tools, metals, inks, colors, dyes and other chemical products). The Germans lagged far behind. But from 1934 onward, Germany's gains in the Peruvian market at the expense of Britain have been sensational.

In that year, British exports to Peru were almost double those from Germany. The very next year, however, the position was dramatically reversed. Germany forged ahead of the British and has not only held the lead ever since but has materially increased it. In 1937, she sent to Peru goods worth $11,800,000, whereas British exports totaled in value only $6,000,000—about one-half the German figures.

In percentage of total imports into Peru from all foreign countries the United States has been gaining year by year. It went from 26.9 per cent in 1934 to 35.3 per cent in 1937. Our percentage of total Peruvian imports for 1938 was 34.3 per cent, a slight drop from the preceding year.

The Germans also have been climbing. In 1934, their share of Peru's total imports from abroad represented in value only 9 per cent. In 1937 it had jumped to nearly 20 per cent, and for 1938, to slightly over 20 per cent. But Britain's slice of the Peruvian import melon dropped from 17.4 per cent, in 1933, to 10.2 per cent, in 1937, and still further, to 10.1 per cent, in 1938.

Next to the United States, Germany and Great Britain, as an exporter to Peru, comes Argentina, followed by Japan and Italy. In 1938, Peru's purchases of Japanese products represented only 3.3 per cent of her total imports, and those of Italian products only 2.1 per cent.

In purchases from Peru, Britain was long the leader. A few years ago (1928-31) the United States was ahead—and in 1935, we nearly passed our British competitors. In 1936 and 1937, however, the United States could not equal British absorption of Peruvian products—principally cotton, wool, petroleum and sugar.

In 1937, the British bought from Peru to an aggregate value of $20,965,000, while our purchases aggregated $20,422,000, chiefly for copper bars, lead, silver ores, vanadium and zinc.

But in 1938, we bought Peruvian goods to a total value of $20,560,000, representing 26.8 per cent of Peru's total exports, whereas Britain bought to an aggregate of only $15,335,000, or 20 per cent of the total value of all Peruvian exports.

Germany, meanwhile, who had been climbing steadily for several years, showed signs of a recession in her purchases of Peruvian merchandise (cotton, hides, sheep and alpaca wool, lead bars, gasoline, etc.). They fell off in value from $12,850,-000 in 1937 to $8,091,000 in 1938. The percentage of total Peruvian exports which went to Germany in 1938 was 10.6.

Japan's purchases from Peru, by the way, had slumped so sharply, when I was in Lima some months ago, that they totaled only 0.6 per cent of all Peruvian exports, whereas, Japanese sales to Peru represented 3.3 per cent of all that country's imports. This situation was causing much resentment among Peruvians, who failed to see advantage to their country in such one-way trade.

As for Italy, she was about in Japan's class as a buyer of Peruvian wares; but on the other hand, she had not been dumping her products on the Peruvian market as the Japanese were accused of doing.

To sum up: Americans are doing nicely in their trade with Peru. So are the Germans—at a considerable distance in our wake. The British, far behind us for years in sales to the Peruvians, are falling back still farther, and are also losing ground to the Germans. Japan, after throwing a scare into all competitors in 1934 and 1935, has failed to reach her records for those years as a seller of goods to Peru, yet she still sells so much more than she buys there that the Peruvians are getting sore.

The Italians, outranked in Peru's foreign trade by many nations, seek to offset this by activity in other directions.

Furthermore, it may be stated that the Peruvians feel no special hostility toward the Germans, considerable toward the Japanese, a little toward the Italians, practically none toward us; that shop signs in our language, worded in a way to lure American visitors, are multiplying in Lima; that one can find more American magazines on sale there than almost anywhere in South America; and that Donald Duck is being run by one of the local newspapers—only he is called "el pato Pascual!"

* * *

After the two non-Peruvians principally responsible for Peru's independence—San Martín, of Argentina, and Bolívar, of Venezuela—had returned home, the Peruvian republic had to wait a full fifty years before it got a civilian president. Every occupant of the presidential chair was a military man—and he usually needed every bit of his military knowledge to keep his seat. During that half century, Peru's history was six of autocracy to half a dozen of anarchy. Dictators, good and bad, mostly bad, in a long procession strutted and fretted their little hour upon the stage, while the poor country pathetically tried to get along.

[237]

In this tempestuous era, the principal figure was Dictator Santa Cruz. Not content with civil warfare, he mixed into international strife as well, against Bolivia and Chile, which did him no good.

Better days came in 1845 under General Ramón Castilla. This general was a good dictator. Every foreign visitor to Lima knows the bronze statue to him—very small, as if in homage to his diminutive stature—which adorns one of the central squares of that city. Castilla's main job was financial regeneration of the republic. This he brought about largely by finding international markets for the huge deposits of guano—bird manure—which millions of sea birds had been piling up for many years on the islands off the Peruvian coast, and on that coast itself, without the slightest idea of what they were doing for their country. Around this same time the nitrate fields of southern Peru, destined to become one of the greatest South American headaches, began to be intensively exploited.

After a slight unpleasantness with Spain, which included a snappy bombardment of Callao, Peru's main seaport, by a Spanish admiral, Peru, after more financial disorder, got her first non-military president, Pardo. But all the good he did was spoiled by the worst chapter in Peru's history, her disastrous war against Chile. It culminated, after four years of desperate fighting, in the victorious entry of the Chileans into Lima and the loss to the victors of the Peruvian nitrate fields. To this day, Peruvians are sore about that war. "Those Chileans stole even the benches from our parks in Lima," a Peruvian once growled to me. And they love to tell foreigners that Chile is a land where wickedness grows luxuriantly because the Spaniards had a penal colony there.

Political and financial disorder continued. In 1919, Colonel

Oscar Benavides—now Peruvian dictator—headed a revolt against the dictator of the moment, an individual with the very un-Spanish name of Billinghurst. Billinghurst's abrupt exit brought in Leguía, who ruled for eleven years. He was friendly to the United States, but large bodies of his fellow-countrymen were anything but friendly to him. So much so, that the dictator, after a dash to escape them, was captured and jailed. Suit was then brought against him and his sons to recover enormous sums which they were said to have appropriated. While the case was on, Leguía, who had become seriously ill in his cell, was transferred to a hospital, where he died in 1932. His successor, Colonel Sánchez Cerro, was murdered the next year, on the Lima race track.

That brings us down to Oscar Benavides (already mentioned as the colonel who chased away Billinghurst) who became the next president. He is now a general and very much boss of Peru—at least he was when I started writing this.

During his régime, his opponents, especially the Apristas, Peru's Labor Party, have had a tough time. Many of them have been jailed and others forced to decamp.

The principal event in the reign of Oscar the First of Peru was the Eighth Pan-American Conference, held at Lima, his capital, in the Winter of 1938-39. Exactly what this conference meant to our relations with Latin America is still a matter of feverish dispute. But there can be no doubt about one thing: it brought a round of social festivities, conducted with genuine Latin enthusiasm by the Peruvians, which almost paralyzed some of the visiting delegates.

"Once we sat down to dinner at one o'clock in the morning!" the pale and weary United States Ambassador to Peru told me.

* * *

Under the Spaniards, two big slices of South American territory now forming independent republics—Bolivia and Ecuador—were long included in the viceroyalty of Peru. Therefore, this seems an appropriate place for appending short sketches of their history and development.

Having, under the orders of his fellow-Venezuelan Bolívar, set off Bolivia from Peru, as an independent state, Antonio José Sucre, victor of Ayacucho, became its first president much against his will—he was more soldier than statesman. He left Bolivia in 1828, after narrowly escaping assassination. Shocking anarchy and bloodshed then swept over Bolivia. She had sixty-odd rebellions, nearly a dozen constitutions—and half a dozen of her presidents were murdered. One of the toughest of Bolivian dictators, Melgarejo, actually killed one of his foes with his own hands.

In 1883 Bolivia, having sided with the loser, Peru, in the Chilean-Peruvian war, lost her only seaports to victorious Chile. And, in 1933, her unsuccessful Chaco war against Paraguay was disastrous in its consequences. But between the two wars, the Bolivians did not do as badly as in the first part of their history. In fact, as a British historian admiringly remarks of those years, "most of the presidents completed their terms."

As for the old Spanish province of Quito, now the republic of Ecuador, it followed the course of New Granada (Colombia today) by severing connection, in 1830, with the confederation which had formed Bolívar's "Gran Colombia" (Venezuela, New Granada, Quito). Dictatorship at once reared its head under General Flores, comrade of Bolívar. One of Ecuador's dictators, Garcia Moreno, took the curse off autocratic methods by really remarkable political enlightenment, for which his final reward, in 1875, was assassination.

The darkest spot in the recent history of Ecuador was the awful episode known as "los arrastres"—the draggings. General Eloy Alfaro, long prominent in the republic's chaotic politics, was taken from a Quito prison, in 1911, by a mob, which, having murdered him, together with several of his adherents, dragged their bodies through the streets.

To offset this and other disgraces, Ecuadoreans point to a number of creditable achievements, among which the almost complete suppression of yellow fever at Guayaquil, the country's principal seaport, is the most meritorious example. At one time that deadly tropical ailment was so prevalent there that Americans, appointed to the Guayaquil Consulate, used to show their appointments to friends with the remark: "My death warrant." Now year after year passes with scarcely a case of the disease in the whole Guayaquil district. Credit for this is largely due to the Rockefeller Foundation.

HE was one of those traveling Americans who simply won't take anything on hearsay.

"About this Peruvian harbor that's supposed to be a German submarine base," he remarked one afternoon, when we were both killing time in the lobby of a Lima hotel. "Before I left the United States, I heard right and left that it was no better than a South American branch of Hitler's navy—that it was being used also by Japanese submarines as a regular port of call for discharging cargoes of spies and taking on cargoes of information about the Panama Canal. Now there's only one thing to do, as I see it; I'm going to find out for myself."

He disappeared, leaving no trace. For several days I neither saw him nor had news of him. At last he turned up again. He looked tired. But on his face a look of quiet satisfaction, as of one who has, in spite of formidable obstacles, done his duty.

"Well?" I queried.

That look on his face slowly transformed itself into a contented smile.

"Say, listen," he said. "If that place we were talking about is a German—or Japanese—submarine base, *so is Jones's Beach.*"

Later I met another American, a well-known traveler-explorer, and asked him where he had been keeping himself.

"On the west coast of South America," he replied. "I got

myself a sailboat, and poked her nose into one little inlet after another, and landed on the shores of every one of them, and explored the whole region roundabout."

"Didn't you have to push aside Japanese army corps before you could take a step?"

He gave me a look—a long, searching look. I returned it. I grinned. He grinned. Complete mutual understanding suffused our minds.

"How is it possible," he remarked, after an eloquent pause, "that a nation like ours, which claims to possess a sense of humor, can believe some of the things that it does?"

And that was that.

Germans may be based, in menacing numbers, on the coast of Peru. German submarines may be sneaking in and out of Peruvian inlets and harbors. Their officers may be planning to wrest sovereignty from South American republics and transfer it to Fuehrer Adolf Hitler, for the greater glory of Nazidom and the eventual annihilation of the Panama Canal. Emissaries of Japan, teeming with sinister thoughts, may be encamped all along the west coast of South America. At a clarion call from their Mikado, they may be ready to embark on a shocking series of reprehensible deeds.

But if so, these Germans and Japanese are the most marvelous camouflagists in all history. They are not content with the ordinary classic line of disguises. Not for them to snoop around garbed as fishermen or peasants, waiters or barbers or shopkeepers. They must be impersonating trees or rocks or Peruvian guano birds. Some day, when I have time, I mean to sneak up on suspicious-looking trees in Peru and suddenly yell "Heil Hitler!" If they convulsively stretch out a branch in the Nazi salute, I shall then chop them down with an axe (brought along by me for that express purpose) disguised as a fountain pen. And I mean to approach guano birds, silently at work in the Peruvian gloaming, shout "Banzai!" and—if they show all their teeth and draw in their breath with an Oriental hissing sound—I mean to whip from my pocket a machine gun (disguised, until that moment, as a handker-chief) and end their commercial usefulness forever.

But not this evening. I'm too busy.

For the present I must limit myself to stating that, if the Germans or the Japanese are really preparing large-scale naval, military and air operations on the west coast of South America, I'll eat my hat.

Having got that off my chest I must add that there *are* Japanese (and Germans) in Peru, and that their activities there deserve a considerable amount of attention from Uncle Sam.

In fact, Peru is about as good a place as there is in all South America for studying what there is of Japanese penetration of our continent. With the exception of São Paulo, in south-ern Brazil, the little men from Nippon are nowhere no notice-able, or present in such compact lots, as on Peruvian soil.

In Lima, some of the principal shops are owned and oper-ated by Japanese; they have Japanese clerks and specialize largely in goods from Japan. The position of the Japanese, to be sure, in Peru's trade, is not what it was. There, as else-where in South America, they are in retreat. "Recession" is a mild word for describing what has happened to them in the Peruvian market during the past few years.

They remain, nevertheless, an element to be reckoned with in Peru. Years ago they drove away the Chinese, formerly strong there, and seemed to be on the road to playing a lead-ing rôle in local commerce. But after their brightest years—1932-34—they have lost ground badly. Of course, they may stage a comeback. But up to early this year, they were showing no signs of it.

To make matters worse for them, the Peruvian Government recently threw a couple of monkey wrenches into the machinery of Japanese penetration of Peru. The first jarred the commercial part of that machinery. The second put a crimp into another section of it, designed to further Japan's noncommercial activities.

Of course, the astute Japanese will try to repair the damage. But there are those in Peru who, with sly winks, assert that efforts in that direction will be futile.

"You see," they explain, "the Peruvian Government has not run out of monkey wrenches."

Monkey Wrench Number One was the quota restriction recently imposed by the Peruvian Government on Japanese textiles, the chief article of export from Japan to Peru. Monkey Wrench Number Two was the persistent refusal of that government to grant Peruvian citizenship to some born in Peru of Japanese parents, although the law of the country expressly states that children born there of foreign parentage are to be regarded, when they come of age, as Peruvian citizens.

Two reasons lay behind the imposition of a restrictive quota on the importation of textiles from Japan. The first was the fact that they were flooding the Peruvian market and threatening to put Peru's budding national industry entirely out of business. The second was the rising resentment among Peruvians at the one-way nature of Japanese-Peruvian trade.

For several years it had shown a big balance in favor of Japan. In other words, the Japanese were selling far more to Peru than they were buying from her. And the Peruvians were getting very sore about it.

A few years ago, Japanese-Peruvian trade leaped to unprecedented heights. A flood of cheap Japanese goods burst over the country, so cheap that they not only menaced home manufactures but endangered the position, in the Peruvian market, of some of Japan's foreign competitors.

Incipient Peruvian misgivings due to this new state of affairs were allayed when Japan bought unprecedented quantities of the products of Peru. In fact, during one year, the total value of the latter imported into Japan actually exceeded that of Japanese goods introduced into Peru.

This, however, according to disgruntled Peruvians, was just a "come-on" game; the canny Asiatics, they warned, would soon prove that they were out to line their own pockets exclusively. Sure enough, Japanese purchases of Peruvian products suddenly took an abrupt tumble. Alarmed at last, the government of Peru clamped down its quota restrictions, limiting importation of Japanese textiles.

This elicited from Japan promises of increased Japanese purchases of Peruvian wares, notably wool and cotton. But they were not made good. And, meanwhile, Japanese exporters continued to pour merchandise into Peru and stuff profits into their pockets, blandly disregarding the fact that Japan was buying virtually nothing in exchange.

To Peruvian expostulations, Japan hinted unofficially: "Remove restrictions against Japanese textiles and we will buy your goods." Such hints merely angered the average Peruvian. He recalled, only too well, earlier Japanese promises—still unfulfilled. So instead of yielding to pressure from across the Pacific, the Peruvian Government, at the time I was about to leave Lima last Winter, seemed to be reaching for another anti-Japanese monkey wrench.

As for Monkey Wrench Number Two, already thrown

by the Peruvians, it affords proof of the realization, in Peru, that commercial curbs alone are not enough to prevent the spread of Japanese influence.

The total number of residents of Peru born in Japan is not much more than 11,000. But the total of persons of Japanese parentage living in the republic is at least twice as large. The clannishness of these two elements and their tendency to form a separate unit, alien to the rest of the population, have not been lost on the Peruvian authorities. And the advantages, to residents in Peru partly Japanese in race, of Peruvian citizenship, are only too apparent.

Therefore, though such persons are indeed citizens, according to Peruvian law, we have the strange paradox of Peruvian Government officials defying their country's laws in the belief that, by so doing, they are acting for the good of Peru.

In vain the Japanese point out the illegality of such procedure. In vain they indignantly demand that the legal rights of persons of partly Japanese blood be no longer denied by Peru. The Peruvians turn a deaf ear to their clamor. Once Japanese, always Japanese, they insist—even though the laws of Peru seem to run dead against that theory.

But the Japanese do not despair. They work resolutely toward the achievement of their purposes, commercial and noncommercial. They ask prominent Peruvians to visit Japan, at no cost whatsoever to said Peruvians. They stage diplomatic receptions and dinners on a lavish scale in Lima, to which scores of important local personages get bids.

Meanwhile, the Peruvian Government recently summed up its position in the current Peru-Japan controversy as follows:

"Japanese exporters are presenting themselves once more in the markets of Peru, sending heavy lots of textiles and cotton garments, cement, foodstuffs and miscellaneous goods, proving that they are still carrying on the commercial game of former years.

"We believe in close commercial relations between Peru and the Japanese Empire, but we desire also that such relations develop within the limits of fair and reasonable interchange. It is right, we think, that Peruvian consumers should accept Japanese merchandise; but, reciprocally, Japanese manufacturers, who already know Peruvian products, must not forget that the future of their trade with us depends upon the timely and well-considered purchase of Peruvian export commodities."

A strong hint, that, to Japan. It certainly seems to mean that unless she changes her tactics, Peruvian monkey wrenches may soon fly again.

As a colony of permanent residents in Peru, the Japanese have some importance. By hard work, extending back over many years, many of them, originally poor immigrants, have bettered themselves so amazingly that, in some parts of the country, they have become the richest element in the community. This is particularly true of certain districts along the Peruvian coast.

I can think of no better way of giving a clear idea of the position which the Japanese have achieved for themselves in such districts than to quote from a remarkable document shown to me recently in Lima.

It is a letter, written by a humble Peruvian worker to a prominent American in the Peruvian capital, describing Japanese infiltration in the provincial town where he lives and in the rich agricultural region surrounding it.

The writer of this letter naively hoped that it would be brought to the attention of the American delegation to the

Pan-American Conference, then in session at Lima. The United States, he felt, ought to protect its interests by taking some sort of action against the rising tide of Japanese penetration of Peru.

From his letter two things emerge with distinctness: the astounding capacity of the Japanese to get ahead in a foreign land, and the helplessness and defeatism, in the face of Japanese competition, of Peruvians of the working class, descended from those subjects of the Incas, who, four centuries ago, allowed their native land to be conquered by Spaniards as alien to them as are the Japanese to their descendants of today.

Before quoting from this letter one thing must again be repeated: *there is no Japanese peril in Peru.* The total number of residents there who are wholly or partly of Japanese blood, is probably below 35,000. The great majority are humble folk—shopkeepers, barbers, small farmers, plumbers, gardeners, etc. Only a few have risen to affluence. Practically none mix in politics. They are just frugal, thrifty, hard-working people.

Nevertheless, they have prospered, multiplied and asserted themselves to such an extent in certain regions that some Peruvians think them a menace. One of these, most emphatically, is the man who wrote the above-mentioned letter.

In closely-scribbled pages, in Spanish often misspelled and ungrammatical, he tried to express the animosity and foreboding aroused in him by the settlers from the faraway Orient, who were besetting him and the rest of the Peruvians of his district, on all sides.

Here is a translation, somewhat condensed, of that Peruvian workingman's letter:

"With all due respect, I am taking the liberty of telling you, from a workingman's standpoint, how Japanese activities are developing along the Peruvian coast. There is a saying that nobody feels anything as much as one who suffers; and in this case it is we, the workers of Peru, who suffer most from the misery and unemployment forced upon us by the Japanese monster, the wild beast who most seriously menaces South America.

"The Japanese are multiplying here in the most astonishing way. Every one of them came first to this country as a youth, alone, having studied at least eight years in school, already qualified for some calling or profession. After a while, each brought out a wife from Japan, and at the end of ten years, each had at least six children.

"Peruvian politicians do not realize that the Japanese employ tactics different from those of Fascists or Nazis. They keep perfectly silent, pretend to be stupid, yet they are the cleverest of all. They don't mix in politics before they have thoroughly overrun commerce and agriculture. After that, they assert themselves politically, under some sort of pretext, as they did at Shanghai.

"When South Americans finally want to oppose them, it will be too late; they will find the Japanese well-based, fully militarized, served by numerous spies, in control of business and agriculture, in possession of the most valuable strategic points in the country.

"All the glory in this world, goes to those who have money, and become, thereby, fortunate in love, and prosperous. That same world is hellish for the poor, who cannot find happiness in love nor prosperity, the two most important things in life.

"Here the Japanese are living in glory and the Peruvians in hell. The former are gobbling up nearly all the plantations in this valley. They get hold of 'haciendas,' and chase out all the Peruvian workers by trickery or actual force, since the local authorities side with them.

"In the principal town of this valley nearly all the stores, restaurants, barber shops and such-like, are run by Japanese. Other Japanese raise vegetables, such as yucca and corn, also fruit; and all support wives and children and send the latter to school in automobiles.

"And whenever they deal with Peruvians, they close their mouths tight, show overweening pride and despotic manners, and when asked a question, they pretend to be deaf. If they finally answer, they tell a lie or say something malicious, and just as soon as they can, they get away from the Peruvian with whom they have been talking. Sometimes they insult us by saying, 'Peruvians are good-for-nothing; they're donkeys and dumb brutes.'

"All the Japanese around here are proprietors and capitalists, and they employ Peruvian girls as servants.

"Among all the foreigners who come to Peru only they come without capital, and take everything in sight, and instead of showing gratitude, they act outrageously, behaving well only toward the government, but showing brutality toward the Peruvian people. Only in a country like Peru, where most people cannot read or write, would such folk be tolerated.

"Some old Japanese here, who came as workers or servants, are today solid business men or planters. One of them owns six 'haciendas.' They live in the center of the town, in the best houses, which they own; they put in modern plumbing, and spend the Summers at the seashore.

"Meanwhile, the Peruvian is just a 'peón.' He earns barely enough to buy food. Economically, he is enslaved, badly fed, held in low esteem; and lastly, he is despised by women, because women heed only those who have money or a good job. If a Peruvian worker gets ill he has no money with which to stay abed, buy medicines, or summon a doctor. And all the while, the Japanese multiply, because not one of them is sunk in misery. Not one is a 'peón.' All are employers.

"And the Peruvians are humiliated and close their mouths because they are ignorant, and an ignoramus must keep silent, not because he agrees with others, but because he does not know how to express himself.

"The Japanese, though they earn lots of money here, boycott the country, keep away from moving picture houses and theatres, and buy only Japanese wares. The Peruvian must wander about like a gypsy, trying to find work.

"Peruvian owners of plantations are a lazy lot, who want nothing but life in the big city, where they just loaf and amuse themselves. They sell or lease their plantations to the Japanese.

"People in this neighborhood endure all this injustice in silence; there have never been strikes around here of any sort. There is one Japanese planter here who must earn about a million soles a year, from his six plantations alone, to say nothing of what he gets from his shops, etc. He lives in a little palace and does nothing but run around in a motor car overseeing his plantations. Yet if anybody asks for a raise of only a couple of cents, he is called an agitator, a Communist, and he is sent off to prison.

"I think that it behooves the United States, more than any other nation, to take action. It would not be to the advantage of the United States to have Peru invaded by some other power, or to have a puppet government here."

Few people in Peru are as jittery about the Japanese as the writer of that letter. Nevertheless, there is considerable anti-Japanese feeling there and a rising tendency to curb further "invasion" from across the Pacific.

HERE and now I proclaim myself among those who dislike the term "Latin America" as a name for the twenty republics to the south of us. But what can be used in its place to cover them all?

If you say "South America," ten of them are left out in the cold. If "South and Central America" is used, what about Mexico, which is in neither; and what about Cuba, Haiti and the Dominican Republic, which are in the West Indies?

"Spanish America" blandly ignores the fact that the biggest of the lot, Brazil, speaks Portuguese, and that Haitians speak French. And if "Iberian America" is substituted (Spain and Portugal are on the Iberian Peninsula) French Haiti still will trip you up.

So Latin America it must be.

On the mainland of the American Continent, seventeen of the twenty Latin American nations stretch, in unbroken sequence, from the Rio Grande, separating Texas from Mexico, to Cape Horn. The only mainland territories south of the Rio Grande not comprised in those republics are British Honduras, in Central America, and the three Guianas—British, French, Dutch—in South America. Off the eastern coast of the latter, the British own the Falkland Islands, long a matter of dispute between them and the Argentine Republic. The three West Indian nations of Latin America—Cuba, Haiti and the Dominican Republic—lie in the midst of numerous islands, big and little, owned by the United States, Britain, France, or

Holland.

By the end of the nineteenth century's first quarter, all Latin America, with the exception of Cuba and Puerto Rico, had been swept clear of European domination. But the independence won by the former colonials was not independence from their Latin heritage. That was woven intricately into the texture of their personal lives and the structure of their community development. Many a patriot of those new-born States, witnessing the departure of the last transport loaded with soldiers homeward bound to Europe, thought that the troubles of his native land, born of the past, were over. In reality, they had just begun.

Some of those troubles were with the United States.

At one time or another, our southern neighbors, especially the nearer among them, have been involved in serious arguments with us. Against one we waged actual war. On the soil of others we landed armed forces. These, in several instances, stayed years. When Latin Americans are feeling especially anti-Yankee, they like to remark: "You North Americans have been guilty of most of the aggression against us since we became independent republics."

Here are brief biographical sketches of each of our near neighbors in Latin America—with the exception of Cuba, who has a chapter to herself. They include the countries in whose affairs we have intervened most actively—Cuba, Mexico, Haiti, the Dominican Republic, Nicaragua. Also included are Nicaragua's Central American neighbors; also Colombia and Panama, much in the limelight when we were building the Panama Canal; and Venezuela, which, in 1895, inspired Presisent Grover Cleveland to the most forcible assertion on record of the Monroe Doctrine, which has governed our general relations with our southern neighbors for more than a century.

In each of these sketches there is a short mention of American intervention as applied to the country described.

Historical sketches of the rest of the Latin American nations are scattered through other parts of this book. All of them are presented, I am uncomfortably aware, with such outrageous paucity of general data, such ruthless condensation of historical facts, that some Latin American readers, in a ferocious fit of wounded patriotism, will probably want to skin me alive. But it can't be helped.

* * *

MEXICO, having achieved independence from Spain in 1821, after years of hard fighting, slid into an era of revolts of assorted sizes, with the usual dreary alternation of dictatorship and anarchy. Chaotic conditions led to the loss of Texas, and in 1846-48, to war with the United States.

Despite brave resistance to the invading Americans, Mexico's badly-trained soldiers were beaten. As a result of the treaty which ended the war, she found herself bereft of enormous territories inherited from Spain, including California.

Chaos continued. From it arose a commanding figure, the Indian, Benito Juarez (Italy's dictator, Mussolini, was named after him), who had to face not only the usual maddening complications of a Latin American statesman's life, but also serious foreign aggression. In 1861—while we were very busy with our Civil War—French, British and Spanish troops landed in Mexico. Spain and Britain, whatever they may have wanted to do at first, soon lost interest in this strange venture and got out of it.

But Napoleon III was in earnest. Spurred on by the uncomfortable feeling that a nephew of the great Napoleon must necessarily achieve big things, he took a leading part in persuading the Archduke Maximilian, the dashing and likable brother of Emperor Francis Joseph of Austria-Hungary, to become emperor of Mexico.

Maximilian, with his wife, Carlotta, went to Mexico and was crowned emperor. He never had a bit of luck. His position, false from the beginning, soon became impossible. Juarez met him with stern resistance. Another Mexican destined to resounding fame, Porfirio Díaz, once actually beat French troops, that were backing Maximilian, in a pitched battle.

In 1865, the American Civil War ended. Secretary of State Seward, voicing long pent-up American feelings, practically said to Napoleon III, "Get out!" The French emperor—Napoleon le Petit, as Victor Hugo had cruelly called him—after taking a good look at the million veteran Union soldiers, still under arms in the United States, decided not to defy Seward. He withdrew all French troops from Mexico, leaving poor Maximilian to his fate.

It was not long in overtaking him. He was captured by Juarez near Querétaro, where he had joined his Mexican supporters. Disregarding the frantic appeals of Carlotta—thinking himself not so much the judge of Maximilian as the avenger of European aggression against Mexico—Juarez refused to save the hapless Austrian. With two Mexican adherents, he was executed on a hill outside Querétaro. That ended one of the most romantic, ill-advised and pitiful episodes in the history of the Americas.

Juarez died in 1872. The supremacy which he had exerted in Mexico passed, in 1876, to Porfirio Díaz, one of the most extraordinary products of Latin America. In him were combined, to a remarkable degree, two clashing traits that go into the making of most dictators—the ability to exert iron rule and the inability to utilize it as a bridge to future democratic government. Díaz broke all Latin American records. He was supreme boss of Mexico for thirty-five years, from 1876 to 1911, with the exception of a short interlude between 1880-84, when, from behind the scenes, he pulled the strings that manipulated a marionette president.

Crystallization of anti-Díaz feeling, coming with astounding suddenness, swept the old despot in 1911 to exile and death in Europe, and placed in the presidency Francisco I. Madero, an idealist, the purity of whose ambitions was only exceeded by the tragedy which they brought to him. Pitchforked into the midst of discordant events which he could not control, outwitted by hard-boiled leaders of armies which were often no better than huge bands of brigands, Madero, after heroically endeavoring to bring better days to Mexico, was ousted and murdered by a revolt headed by men whose names were soon to become bywords among Americans—Victoriano Huerta, Emiliano Zapata, Pancho Villa.

This tragedy brought civil war of the worst sort. It ruined Mexico. It killed off something like a quarter of a million of her population. And it got nobody anywhere.

Venustiano Carranza, in the north, disavowed Huerta, enlisted the aid of Villa, sent southward Alvaro Obregón, an able general, to try conclusions with Huerta. Obregón chased away Huerta; he smashed Villa, when the latter opposed him; he lived to see Zapata and Carranza murdered; and he was himself assassinated at the height of his power.

Into this terrible era falls the American bombardment of Vera Cruz and the dispatch of American troops under Pershing into Mexico, to catch Pancho Villa, whose audacity had finally led him to raid a town in New Mexico. Pershing didn't catch Villa, but that didn't matter much, for Villa survived the expedition against him only a short time.

The régime of Plutarco Elías Calles, whom Obregón had put in shortly before he was murdered, was characterized by a determined attack on the Catholic Church, which split Mexico wide open. Side by side with the anti-church movement went ambitious attempts at sweeping social reforms. To these were added, under President Lázaro Cárdenas, who succeeded Calles in 1934, and is still on the job, a big drive against foreign oil interests in Mexico, especially American. This has proved a source of acute embarrassment to President Roosevelt, Secretary of State Hull, and everybody else interested in the success of our new Good Neighbor Policy toward Latin America.

During the Lima Conference last Winter, Cárdenas, with pointed unfriendliness toward us, started selling expropriated American oil to German interests. Roosevelt and Hull, bent on creating good will at Lima—and sufficiently bothered there by Argentine intransigence—decided to pussy-foot on Mexico. In doing so, they certainly cut the ground from under the feet of those Latin Americans who love to harp on our high-handedness in dealing with our neighbors. Unfortunately, however, their moderation did not keep Bolivia from imitating Cárdenas' methods—and (at the present writing) Chile seems to be weighing the pros and cons of doing likewise.

*　　*　　*

COLOMBIA has always paid high honor to things of the spirit. She has produced excellent writers. Colombians claim to speak the best Spanish in the world. They have occasionally elected a man President primarily because he was a poet. In fact, their respect for poetry is only exceeded by their facility in manufacturing it. To thousands of Colombians, falling off a log is more difficult than writing a poem. Yet, in

spite of this, they have not been able to escape political turmoil.

Something like thirty fratricidal wars have stained their
history since they emerged from Spanish rule.

Colombia (originally New Granada) broke away, in 1830,
from the union with Venezuela and Ecuador which Simon
Bolívar dreamed would be the nucleus of Latin American
solidarity. Her first leaders, Santander and Obando, both of
whom had fought under Bolívar, did good work, as did some
of their successors, in trying to build up their country. Yet,
only a comparatively short time ago, it was again rent by a
terrible civil war, which killed off tens of thousands of
Colombians.

In 1903, Panama seceded from Colombia, was promptly
recognized by the United States as a republic, and, with equal
promptness, leased to us the strip of land through which the
Panama Canal now cuts. That move on our part ("I took the
Canal Zone" boasted Teddy Roosevelt) outraged Colombians,
also numerous highly articulate people throughout Latin
America. These individuals still make wry faces when they
think how the Panama Canal was born. But time is blurring
their resentment. Maybe the Good Neighbor Policy will ob-
literate it altogether.

Colombia's most recent record has been excellent. Competent observers think that democracy has as good a chance
there as anywhere in Spanish America. The potential wealth
of that land of poets is a poem in itself.

* * *

PANAMA, being inhabited by Latin Americans, thinks, now
and then, that it is a long time between revolutions. But revolutionary dreams among the Panamanians are usually crushed

by the stern glance and upraised forefinger of that severest of duennas, the American administration of the Panama Canal Zone. In the agreement between the United States and the Republic of Panama there is a clause which allows us to intervene in case of disorder. And ever since the days of Theodore Roosevelt, we have not allowed the Republic of Panama to forget that clause.

Nevertheless, just to keep in practise, Panamanians staged a bloodless revolt only a few years ago, while Uncle Sam, for special reasons, looked the other way.

Aside from a certain amount of friction, Panama and the United States get along remarkably well. And the Canal is an immense source of pride to the little country.

* * *

VENEZUELA, native land of Simon Bolívar, liberated by him along with New Granada, Ecuador and Peru, must have been in his thoughts as much as any of those other countries when he uttered his despairing words, "I have plowed in the sea!" Just before his death, the Venezuelans had exiled him; and could he have continued to watch them from his grave, he would have seen them hurtle from one sanguinary conflict into another, bringing to naught all his dreams.

Though the Venezuelans have had twenty constitutions, they have scarcely thought twice about shaping their actions constitutionally. "A constitution, to us Venezuelans," a disillusioned citizen of that country once remarked, "is just a nice document to be kept in a nice glass case."

They have also bestowed upon themselves about fifty civil wars, big, medium and small. In the course of these, the Venezuelan comrades of Bolívar in the War of Independence against Spain—Páez, the Centaur; Mariño, Monagas—gradually gave place to new generations of hard-fisted soldiers.

Antonio Guzmán Blanco—handsome, picturesque, able, vain and unscrupulous—became dictator in 1870. He stayed dictator for eighteen years. To him goes the credit—or dis-credit—of managing to live the life of Reilly in Paris, while keeping a country thousands of miles away under absolute control. On several occasions, feeling bored with life in Vene-zuela, he installed a puppet president, wished upon himself pleasant and lucrative diplomatic jobs across the ocean, lived in Europe (usually in a magnificent house near the Arc de l'Étoile, in Paris) and sent peremptory cables to Venezuela whenever he needed money, to the great detriment of the Venezuelan Treasury.

Finally, one of the puppets could stand it no longer.

"Send me dough!" cabled Guzmán.

"To hell I will!" replied the "President." And he proceeded to stage a bloodless revolt, which made him president in reality, and he caused to be pulled down a lot of statues which "The Illustrious American" (the dictator's pet name for him-self) had erected in his own honor. So dazed was Guzmán Blanco by his puppet's obstreperous actions that he died years later in Paris, without ever knowing exactly what had hit him.

After four quiet years, Venezuela blew up again when the roughneck Joaquin Crespo landed himself in the presidential chair, after a successful revolution, which, among other things, sent my father into exile—hence a swift kick to Crespo's memory!

In 1895, during Crespo's tenure of office, Venezuela's long-standing dispute with Great Britain, concerning the boundary between her territory and British Guiana, got so serious that it moved President Grover Cleveland of the United States to send what amounted to an ultimatum to the British, warning them to watch their step.

Never before had there been such unequivocal assertion of the Monroe Doctrine, Magna Charta of the "America-for-the-Americans" idea, which, proclaimed by President James Monroe in 1823, had been the backbone ever since of American policy toward Latin America. For a while it looked as if Cleveland's bombshell might provoke John Bull to war. But he chose peace. The dispute with Venezuela was adjusted by negotiation.

All that Crespo did in the dictatorial line was presently dimmed by Cipriano Castro (1899-1908) and eclipsed by Juan Vicente Gómez. The latter looked for a while as if he was going to beat Porfirio Díaz's all-time high of thirty-five years of dictatorship. But, when he died in 1935, he had ruled only twenty-seven years.

Castro, Gómez's predecessor, aside from spectacular feats in battle-winning, brandy-drinking and woman-chasing, distinguished himself by getting into a row with Britain, Germany and the United States, which almost cost him his shirt. He survived it, however—his shirt was fated to fall to Juan Vicente Gómez. When Castro went to Europe for a surgical operation, Gómez, whom he had left in charge, calmly grabbed Castro's job, and made it perfectly clear to the incensed Cipriano that if he ever landed in Venezuela he would never get far beyond the landing spot.

Castro stayed away. He died years later in Puerto Rico, under the protection of the United States, which he had defied in the days of his dubious glory.

Gómez disappointed hosts of enemies by dying peaceably in his bed, surrounded by squads of weeping concubines and bastards. They soon had to dry their tears and sprint for the nearest seaport, with thousands of the dead dictator's foes close at their heels.

Gómez certainly kept order in Venezuela, and it was during his reign that the great Venezuelan oil wells, which have brought unparalleled prosperity to the country—for much of which he got credit—were discovered. But he was shockingly cruel, selfish, and a prize nest-featherer—the fortune which he amassed made Guzmán Blanco look like a piker.

Under López Contreras, a man of much moderation, whose aim seems to be to live without enemies, Venezuela has so far refrained from returning to pre-Gómez political turbulence. American influence, largely oil-born, is growing in the country by leaps and bounds—which, let us hope, is a good augury for peaceful years to come.

*   *   *

CENTRAL AMERICA, with the shining exception of Costa Rica, that most peaceable and most democratic of all Latin American countries, has had a record of bloodshed, political turmoil and financial chaos that is almost incredible. From 1821, when the Central Americans broke loose from Spain without a struggle, internecine and international fighting have killed thousands of the natives, and left desolation in their wake.

The list of dictators who have ruled over Guatemala, Nicaragua, Honduras and El Salvador is imposing. In Guatemala, Barrios ruled twelve years, Carrera twenty-one, Estrada Cabrera twenty-two. And Zelaya, probably the worst of the lot, wished himself on Nicaragua for sixteen years.

One of the consequences of Zelaya's rule was American intervention in Nicaragua, about which Latin American foes of "los Yanquis" still grow acidly eloquent on slight provo-

cation. Following Zelaya's resignation in 1909, the first
American Marines landed on Nicaraguan soil. This action
resulted in the stationing of a guard of one hundred Marines
at our legation at Managua, the Nicaraguan capital. It was not
withdrawn until 1925.

Withdrawal precipitated such an infernal row that the
president requested us to intervene again. This time we sent
no mere legation guards; United States troops were pumped
into disorderly Nicaragua in such numbers that in 1928 they
reached a total of nearly 6,000. For three years, during this
American occupation, the American troops kept up a running
fight against General Sandino, whom most Americans (in
their infrequent thoughts about him) dismiss as a bandit and
enormous numbers of Latin Americans enshrine as a hero.

In 1933, the last United States Marines sailed for home.
There have been a number of other American interventions
in the other Central American republics, but none of them
reached the importance, nor ruffled Latin American sensibilities to such a painful extent, as the one in Nicaragua.

Of late years, El Salvador, Guatemala, Honduras and Nicaragua have been doing better—with little Costa Rica looking
on, in superior aloofness, from the side lines. Once, soon after
the Spaniards had been chased away, she tried union with
them. Once was enough.

*   *   *

HAITI, the Black Republic—the great majority of its three
million inhabitants are wholly or partly Negro—was recognized by Spain as a French colony in 1697, having developed
from scattered settlements of Frenchmen who used to supply
meat to the pirates whose ships put into Haitian inlets. For a
century, the colony, called then Saint-Domingue, rolled in

riches, derived from big exports of sugar and other products to Europe; but the enjoyment of prosperity was tempered, for resident whites, by the menace of revolt among the hundreds of thousands of slaves, pure Africans or of African descent, who worked Haitian plantations.

Not only prosperity but every semblance of civilization was swept away when, as a result of the French Revolution, the blacks revolted. They and the whites fought each other for years, amid horrors of torture, devastation and massacre hardly to be paralleled in all history. Out of this hideous welter, the Negro Toussaint l'Ouverture climbed to supreme power. He held under his rule, over a short period, both Haiti and the other two-thirds of the island, comprising the Spanish colony of Santo Domingo.

In 1802, Napoleon decided to crush Toussaint. French troops, under Leclerc, compelled the Negro leader, together with his cruel confederates, Christophe and Dessalines, to surrender. Toussaint was subsequently thrown into prison, where he died.

Christophe and Dessalines soon rose against the French. They initiated warfare as horrible as what had gone before. Eventually British intervention drove the French from Haiti.

Dessalines, having proclaimed himself emperor in 1804, inaugurated another reign of terror and horror, filled with dreadful massacres of whites. After he was killed, Christophe proclaimed himself King Henry I of Northern Haiti. He built a palace of barbaric magnificence and a stupendous citadel, on top of a steep hill, the ruins of which are to this day stared at in amazement by American tourists.

Christophe killed himself in 1820. Shortly before, he had been succeeded by Pétion, a better ruler, who befriended

Simon Bolívar, then undergoing one of his various periods of exile in the West Indies. Pétion was succeeded by Boyer, who ruled over the entire island for nearly a quarter of a century. After he was ousted, the Santo Domingans achieved freedom from Haiti and formed the Dominican Republic in 1844.

From that time onward, Haiti had decades of alternating bloody dictatorships, punctuated by almost continuous fighting. Haiti's presidents (to use a name for her black dictators which was richly undeserved) were lucky if they got out of the presidency without being kicked out. Two of them were murdered. One, Soulouque, a Negro like the rest of them, imitated Dessalines and Christophe by crowning himself emperor.

Again and again the situation got so unendurable that foreign nations, including the United States, interfered. In 1915, after the hideous murder of President Sam by a bloodthirsty mob, Admiral Caperton, of the United States Navy, landed marines from his ships on Haitian territory. Thus began that active American intervention in Haiti which brought little if any joy to any North American and much suspicion of American incentives, coupled with violent diatribes against aggressive Yankee foreign policy, from South Americans.

American troops stayed in Haiti for nineteen years. The occupation had its brutal side, like most military administrations, but it certainly cleaned up the country.

It ended in 1934. Some people in Latin America think we were not only justified in our military measures but wise in the use of our power over the Haitians. Others, though, have never ceased to blame us for doing what we did. It will take a lot of Good Neighbor Policy to make them change their minds.

* * *

NEAR NEIGHBORS

The Dominican Republic can at least maintain that, bad though its history has been, that of its next-door neighbor, Haiti, has been worse.

Events leading up to American intervention in the early part of this century are utterly confused, almost completely unprovided with a thread to bind them together. After domination by Spaniards, Haitians, Frenchmen, and Spaniards again— Santo Domingo was actually a Spanish colony as late as the time of our Civil War—the country got into such a state of anarchy as an independent "republic" that financial ruin necessitated the appointment, in 1904, of a United States official, empowered to take over the customs receipts of one of the principal Dominican ports. This power was extended, the next year, to the collection, by American representatives, of all Dominican customs duties.

One might have expected that this would have acted as a warning to the natives of what might be in store for them if they did not pull themselves together. But it had no such effect. Affairs got into such a mess that, in 1916, when Woodrow Wilson was President, American troops landed on Dominican soil. They stayed eight years. As in similar occupations elsewhere, rough tactics, seemingly inseparable from military rule, were offset by the absolutely unprecedented stability brought to the occupied country.

After our withdrawal, General Trujillo, head of the Dominican army, assumed the presidency. In 1934 he began his second term as autocrat of the country.

Every day he gets the usual mixture of adulation from his admirers and execration from his foes. Two happenings during his dictatorship stick in one's memory—his changing of the name of the ancient city of Santo Domingo to Ciudad

Trujillo, and the awful massacre, by Dominican soldiers, of entire batches (some say the total ran into the thousands) of Haitian laborers, who had crossed the Haitian-Dominican frontier in search of employment.

* * *

In the foregoing, I realize, there is an awful lot about fighting. But no chronicler of Latin America can dodge it. Revolutionary outbreaks, it must be remembered in extenuation, have been unknown in some southern republics for years; and, in others, when they still occur they tend to be short, sharp coups d'état, over almost immediately, instead of the long and bloody conflicts that have caused misery and disruption in the past.

Foreigners should also remember that, revolution or no revolution, daily life in Latin America pursues superficially an unruffled course, full of amenity and laughter and grace. Family life of genuine depth and singular attractiveness remains of dominant importance; and social activity, which has a sparkle hard to duplicate, goes on despite *pronunciamientos* and barrack revolts.

I have seen Venezuelans dancing at afternoon garden parties in Carácas, their capital, serenely indifferent to the crack of the rifles of government soldiers, who were taking pot shots at guerrillas on the mountain slopes surrounding the city.

Better schools are doing a lot to cool hot Latin American blood—though it must be admitted that political turbulence appeals to some students more than sober study. And growing contact with other continents is bringing a new restraint and moderation.

In fact, a paradoxical situation is arising in Latin America. Whereas Europe, which used to reprove Latin Americans for disorder, is getting more disorderly every day, Latin America, the breeding-ground of revolutions, is steadily calming down.

In a street car in Havana I counted, among twenty-four advertising cards, twelve printed in English. Every one of them sang the praises of American products. Of the other dozen, which were in Spanish, two also extolled articles made in the United States.

That is Cuba.

Americans feel less like foreigners there than anywhere else in Latin America. Foreigners they undoubtedly are, no matter what they do or say—alien the Cubans remain, no matter what the circumstances—but never to the degree that we and the native-born differ in Mexico and Lima, in Bogotá and Rio and Buenos Aires.

Nowhere in Latin America do those North and South Poles of character and mentality and outlook on life, the North American and the South American, get so close to each other as they do in Havana. Nowhere else do they find so much common ground and rub each other so little the wrong way. If, by some miracle, one of our cities should be transformed overnight into a Latin city, without losing its essential Americanism, it would resemble Paris a little, Buenos Aires a little more, Havana a lot.

For this there are several reasons. Among them the accident of geography doubtless deserves first place.

Though Cuba, unlike Mexico, has no common frontier with the United States, the Cubans are much nearer to us than the Mexicans. Though two hundred miles of blue water separate their island from the nearest point in Florida, there is no comparison between the essential alien-ness to us of the average Mexican and that of the average Cuban. The latter scarcely thinks of the narrow strip of ocean between his country and the United States as a dividing line at all. Cuba, moreover, is only 1,200 miles from New York, and Havana, Cuba's metropolis, is nearer our other great centers of population—Chicago and Philadelphia, Detroit and St. Louis and Boston—than is Mexico City.

Another important reason for the closeness of Cuba to the United States is that, economically, she is largely dependent on us for her very existence.

For generations we have taken the major portion of the Cuban sugar crop, which eclipses every other Cuban product as an article of export. Many American millions are invested in Cuban sugar, and many Americans in the sugar business live in Cuba for years on end—both of which facts contribute materially to our influence there and to the spread of American customs in the Cuban republic.

There is also a cultural factor: the proximity of Cuba to the United States, combined with the interlocking of Cuban and American business interests, have long made it customary for Cuban parents to send their children to be educated in our schools. As a result of this, an increasing number of young Cubans, boys and girls, has been returning to their homes year after year, imbued with the American slant on people and things. These youngsters think American thoughts, talk American baseball slang. They are impatient of old traditions emanating from a bygone day in Cuba, of which they have no knowledge, with which they feel no sympathy.

This may have its unfortunate side. Ruthless obliteration of tradition, some of it full of beauty and grace and the fragrance of the past, does not necessarily bring in its wake something better—or even just as good. But that is not the point: the point is that the influence of the United States, excellent, good, fair and indifferent, is steadily rising in Cuba. And those Cubans who object to it are being left more and more helpless to combat and overcome it.

In addition to the above reasons for American penetration of Cuba—a penetration unequaled so far for depth and durability in all the rest of Latin America—there is the political factor. This makes it practically impossible for a Cuban Government openly and lastingly hostile to Washington to exist in Cuba for any length of time, and, conversely, it imposes upon each succeeding Cuban administration, without actual employment of force on our part, the necessity of at least a superficial show of pro-Americanism. This is calculated, in the long run, to exert a weakening influence on even the most recalcitrant anti-Americanism among Cubans, and to help, proportionately, the onward march of our influence.

These four factors find valuable and growing cooperation from American tourists in Cuba.

Pouring into Havana in ever-increasing numbers, literally swamping the center of the city on days when several cruise ships from New York are in port, they serve, every one of them, as messengers of Americanism. They are a peaceful, unarmed army of invasion, which leaves behind it a tinge of northern twists of phrase and turns of ideas such as no armed body of invading soldiers, enforcing the orders of a foreign government, could ever hope to spread.

The American tourist in Paris remains always alien; in fact, he remains so in London, though he often has English blood in his veins and English words on his tongue. But in Havana, for some curious reason, he seems to "belong." Around him may be yellowing old buildings, alive with the spirit of Spain, and people jabbering Spanish amid most un-Anglo-Saxon excitement, yet the tourist from Ohio and Vermont and Wisconsin seems as much a part of the picture as the Cuban sugar planters, in their Panama hats, and the swarthy, sandaled vendors of tropical delicacies.

It may be contended that an army of American tourists, however large, which only sees Havana and practically never anything else in Cuba, cannot exert any deep influence on the country; but one must not forget that, since Havana, the preponderant factor in the shaping of Cuban thought, is growing steadily more American, what with tourists and other Americanizing influences, it must naturally be spreading Americanism all over the island.

So much for the five factors making for Americanism in Cuba which most readily occur to the analyst of present-day Cuban conditions. But there is a sixth, an important one, which must not be forgotten: the feeling of gratitude among Cubans for our help in their war of independence against Spain. Cynics say that this feeling exists only in the breasts of members of the older generation, and not in as many of those as one might expect—that the younger Cubans are as indifferent to memories of the battles of Santiago and San Juan Hill as they are to all the grace and beauty and fragrance implicit in the old Spanish traditions which they scornfully ignore and despise. This, however, many an American visitor finds it hard to believe; and many an appreciative word which he hears from Cubans, old, middle-aged and young, about Theodore Roosevelt and Admiral Sampson and Leonard Wood, confirms him in his belief that memories of 1898 are as imperishable in the hearts of the Cuban nation as are ours of Lafayette and Rochambeau.

[273]

Yes, Americans are less alien to the Cubans than any other Latin American nation. Other parts of Latin America are adopting, more and more, a superficial resemblance to our country, a skin-deep appreciation and application of our ways to their own daily lives. But it remains skin-deep.

There is something in the Latin American temperament which, except in Cuba, still successfully resists American infiltration. Despite American moving pictures and machinery and tourists and gadgets of every description it remains, first, last and all the time, un-American. Not so in Cuba. There, and there only, Americans have broken down the first line of spiritual resistance against them. What the American visitor to Cuba sees arising on every side, and growing year by year, is not Americanization. It is Americanism.

*　　*　　*

Cuba, like most of the rest of Latin America, proclaimed allegiance in 1809 to Ferdinand VII of Spain, and refused to recognize Joseph Bonaparte, placed on the Spanish throne by his brother, Napoleon, in Ferdinand's place. But unlike the rest of their Spanish American kin, the Cubans did not, as their next step, stage a war of independence. The Spaniards were too strong on the island. Surrounded from the twenties of last century onward by independent republics, Cuba remained until almost the very end of that century, under the Spanish flag, sharing with Puerto Rico the anomalous distinction (not at all relished by either Cubans or Puerto Ricans) of being the last bulwark of Spanish authority in the New World.

Even stubborn Spain, after the jolts she had received on the American mainland, realized that she must be more liberal toward her Cuban subjects, if she was to retain her hold over them. But reforms, reluctantly granted on paper, became dead letters in practice. The old abuses, which had flourished so luxuriantly in the rest of Spanish America, persisted.

The craving grew among Cubans for freedom. In 1850, Narciso López, a Venezuelan, who had risen to prominence in Spanish military service, landed a small force, assembled in New Orleans, on Cuban soil. Failing in this first attempt, he returned to the United States and again led an expedition to Cuba, but was captured and executed.

That was the spark. Four years later it was a flame. Céspedes, whose name still thrills every Cuban, rose against the Spaniards in 1855, thus initiating the terrible Ten Years' War. Accompanied at every step by ardent North American sympathy, joined by men whose names later rang through the United States, Céspedes fought bravely until he was killed in 1873.

Estrada Palma stepped into his shoes. Máximo Gómez, who was to live to be the Grand Old Man of Cuba's fighters for freedom, skilfully trained battalions of patriots, resolutely led them to victory, and kept up their spirits in defeat, ably seconded by that other legendary figure of Cuban warfare, Antonio Maceo.

But Spain's soldiers, though badly organized and ill-treated, fought with Spanish valor. Five years after the death of Céspedes, the Cuban patriots were done for. In 1878 they signed the Treaty of Zanjón, confirming on their island that Spanish rule which they had hoped to crush.

Their defeat, however, was only temporary. Máximo Gómez was still alive. So was Antonio Maceo. To that indomitable pair was now added another quite as fiery, José Martí. After a long exile, much of which was passed in New York, Martí, in April, 1895, landed on his native island. He was promptly joined by Gómez and Maceo, who had long been in readiness for his coming. The war destined to bring at last to Cuba her long-coveted independence had begun.

It dragged along, steeped in horror. Under Weyler, called "the butcher," the Spaniards countered every Cuban blow. Weyler actually built a regular barrier across the island, the famous Trocha, cutting off districts where the patriots were strong from others where Spaniards were dominant. Bloody battles followed each other closely. Sugar estates were burned. Ruin and starvation reigned. In 1898, Maceo was killed, a terrible blow to the Cubans. But salvation was at hand.

Americans had followed the cruel conflict amid a rising tide of pro-Cuban sympathy. This culminated, after the mysterious blowing up of the U. S. battleship *Maine* in Havana harbor, in an irresistible demand for war against Spain.

An American army landed on Cuban soil. There was sharp fighting. Theodore Roosevelt, theatrically leading the "Rough Riders" to the conquest of Spanish positions outside Santiago, paved the way for his seven spectacular years in the White House. Leonard Wood, preserving a calm that was in refreshing contrast to prevailing hysterics, prepared in war for brilliant achievement in peace.

Finally, the American army in Cuba occupied Santiago. On the sea, American victory came with dramatic swiftness. After Dewey, out in the Philippines, had disposed of one Spanish fleet, Sampson and Schley, operating off Santiago, crushed another, in the decisive victory of the war. This battle cost the United States the life of one man—he died of heart disease, brought on by excitement.

Peace soon followed. Puerto Rico became a part of the United States, Cuba a sort of American protectorate. The red-and-yellow banner of Spain—*la bandera de sangre y oro*—

symbolical, to thousands of Latin American patriots, of the blood Spain had always spilled and of the gold which she had always coveted—disappeared, after a full four hundred years, from the American Continent.

Belying a certain amount of suspicion among Latin Americans as to the purity of American motives, the United States did not annex Cuba. For three years Americans ruled there wisely and well, doing away with corruption, conquering yellow fever and otherwise acquitting themselves meritoriously. In 1902, General Leonard Wood, head of the American administration, handed over the conduct of affairs to Señor Estrada Palma. But the United States kept a string attached to the island which it had freed, the celebrated Platt Amendment, which authorized American intervention in Cuba under certain circumstances and which was not abrogated until our present-day Good Neighbor Policy had got under full sail.

Soon there was a rumpus in Cuba of the typical South American sort, which necessitated a trip to Havana by portly and conciliatory William Howard Taft. He found Cuban affairs so tangled that, in 1906, his friend Teddy Roosevelt, who had for some time past been established in the White House, appointed him provisional governor of the island. This first return of the Americans to Cuba (whether the Platt Amendment justified it and others after it has been a subject of furious debate) lasted until 1909. Then we again stepped out, this time in favor of President-elect José Miguel Gómez—again getting the laugh on worriers about "Yankee Imperialism," who had again started wringing their hands all the way from the Rio Grande to Cape Horn.

After years of comparative quiet, an era characterized by a Cugar sugar boom under dictator Machado which brought fantastic prosperity, a financial crash wiped away that prosperity almost overnight.

Things got black. It looked as if we would have to intervene again. But there was now strong opposition in Washington to such action. The Good Neighbor Policy, after having been carefully tended and watered, was about to blossom. It ill-behooved Uncle Sam to do anything that might enable anti-Americans in the southern republics to denounce the budding new policy as mere hypocritical camouflage of imperialistic designs. So Sumner Welles, whose zeal in Cuba and elsewhere in Latin America had brought him to the post of Assistant Secretary of State, managed to patch things up peacefully.

That same year the Cuban army turned against Machado. He was forced to flee for his life. Fulgencio Batista, a sergeant, seized the government. Ever since, though there have been several Cuban presidents, they have exercised no real authority. Batista is boss of Cuba.

He keeps order by frankly militaristic methods. When I was on the island recently, I saw his home, a pleasant villa surrounded by a military garden city, entirely inhabited by officers and soldiers, and provided with clubhouses, attractive bungalow-like barracks and extensive recreation grounds. There the ex-sergeant (he is now a colonel), supreme ruler of Cuba, lives with bayonets all around him, like an uneasy Roman emperor in a hollow square of Praetorian Guards.

Batista is working out the salvation of Cuba—that is, his friends say he is. His enemies think otherwise. Like all Cuban leaders, he is faced with a terrible task, that of governing a people who, as one commentator has put it, "are blessed with a joyous sensibility to those aspirations of life which have no market value."

So far, he has got away with it, backed by Washington, to which city he recently paid a visit marked by flattering cordiality on the part of our government officials, from President Roosevelt down.

* * *

Cuba is in the iron grip of a dictator. He is not Colonel Fulgencio Batista. Nor any other Cuban. Nor any foreign resident of the island. Nor any human being anywhere. The name of Cuba's dictator is Sugar.

On whether the Cuban sugar situation is good or bad depends whether the Cuban republic is prosperous or impoverished. Cuba is a one crop, one market country. Her sugar production eclipses everything else that she raises; and the United States towers over all other buyers of Cuban sugar. Sugar and Uncle Sam—those are the twin foundations of the entire economic structure of Cuba.

And just now the Cubans are worried over sugar and discontented with Uncle Sam.

They do not like the downward curve in the price of sugar. Very few of them expect a return of the boom years, the "dance of the millions," when a rain of gold descended on Cuba, bringing unprecedented wealth. But they do want a stabilization of the price of sugar at the point, at least, where it was in 1937.

That gave Cuban sugar growers a bare margin of profit. The 1937 price of Cuban sugar, in the American market was 2.41 cents per pound, f.o.b. Cuban ports. Last year it fell to 1.93. By last February it had slid down to 1.80 cents per pound. Last summer it was still about that. The corresponding figures, for the combined American and world markets, were 1.17 cents per pound in 1937, 1.03 in 1938, 1.13 for the first two months of 1939.

That means that Cuba is still faced with the prospect of selling two-thirds of her sugar crop, the average taken by us, to the United States, and one-third to other countries, at a figure below 2 cents per pound, which, to many Cubans, does not represent a sufficient profit. Therefore, as is always the case when the clouds gather, some Cuban sugar men have been wildly clamoring that Uncle Sam do something about it. As a particularly eloquent argument, they point out that Cuba's purchases of American products, always large, increase invariably in direct sympathy with the sugar situation, having reached the staggering total of $500,000,000 in 1920, the banner year of the Cuban sugar boom, and dropped to a miserable $23,000,000 in 1932, Cuban sugar's blackest twelve-month.

But doing something for Cuban sugar interests is no easy matter for Uncle Sam. He also has to consider those competitors of the Cubans, the beet and cane sugar producers of the continental United States, and the cane growers of Puerto Rico, Hawaii and the Philippines, who constantly grow more important and more clamorous. As a result of this dual necessity, he tries, by the application, with variations, of our sugar quota system—which allots a certain share of the total sugar consumption in the United States to Cuba and other shares to her competitors—to please everybody and seldom succeeds in pleasing anybody. And some of Cuba's sugar growers, unable to find redress in a world market which, compared with past years, is restricted, are redoubling their insistent demands for concessions from us, to facilitate the sale of their sugar. The alternative, they darkly hint, may be another crisis on their island, like that of 1932, which may again bring ruin and revolution in its wake.

The story of sugar in Cuba makes thrilling reading. As one gets deeper and deeper into the mass of figures, at first sight dry as dust, which tell that story, they gradually take on the color and movement and surge of drama, the capacity to grip and disconcert and amaze. Cuba's whole economic development, the inner history of her political upheavals, the rise and fall of her statesmen, her past, her present, and her future, are all inextricably bound up with that one short word, sugar.

Through the fourteen years from 1900 to 1913 inclusive, the era just before the World War, the average price of Cuban sugar in the American market—then, as now, dominant in Cuban economics—was 2.4 cents per pound. The war brought a sensational upward trend. It culminated, in 1919, in a price of 4.8 cents, double the average pre-war figure. This was due to the great demand for sugar caused by the conflict, the disappearance from production of many of the important beet areas of Europe, and the big wave of speculation which set in.

Yet all this was only a weak foretaste of the boom that was soon to sweep over Cuba—bringing at first, a flood of riches, and later, a flood of bitter brief and vain regret.

In 1919, the price of Cuban sugar in New York climbed to 6.6 cents a pound, eclipsing the World War average. Then the next year, it soared to the incredible, unheard-of top quotation of 11.3 cents, much more than double the sensational World War rate.

Unbounded joy came to Cuba. Cuban sugar interests expanded their operations by leaps and bounds. New tracts of land were planted with sugar; existing mills put in costly new machinery; new mills sprang up. In New York and Paris,

Palm Beach and Monte Carlo, Cuban sugar millionaires scattered dollars in crazy generosity. And in thatched Cuban villages, clustering around sugar mills which were grinding cane to their uttermost capacity, dusky rural musicians twanged their instruments with a new vigor, while the gatherers of the precious crop, in laughing, whirling thousands, danced their native "rumba" with new zest and abandon. The mirage of "permanent prosperity" dazzled the Cuban nation.

Then came the crash.

With an abruptness that left Cubans pale and gasping, the price of sugar dropped in New York from that all-time 1920 high to 3⅓ cents per pound—less than one-third the record price. The bottom had fallen out of the sugar market. Fabulous riches decreased, shrank, vanished. Death came to Cuba's new-born joy; and following still another drop in price, incipient despair gripped the island.

In 1923 and 1924 a ray of light struggled to pierce the gloom, for prices rose deceptively. Soon, however, they tobogganed again.

The New York average price for Cuban sugar, in the five years 1925-29 inclusive, was 2½ cents, only a little over one-fifth of the 1920 maximum. And that heralded another dismal slide—to 1.47 cents in 1930, to 1.33 in 1931, and then, the crowning deathblow, to *nine-tenths of one cent*, in Cuba's year of catastrophe, 1932.

With that year's collapse, President Machado, only a short time before Cuba's powerful dictator, was swept out of office into ignominious exile. The sugar industry, geared to the boom years, stubbornly continued to grind crops far beyond the capacity of the American and world markets to absorb. The whole structure of Cuba sagged and tottered and swayed. To appreciate fully the shattering nature of the blow which it had received, one must consider, along with the rise and fall of the market price of Cuban sugar, the figures covering the island's total yearly sugar production and its total value over those fateful years.

In the period just preceding the World War, the Cuban sugar crop stood at about 2,600,000 tons yearly. As the war progressed, this production, spurred by spectacular rises in price, jumped upward until, by 1918, it had reached 4,000,000 tons.

Then the "dance of the millions," whirling into its delirious stride, drove the Cuban sugar output to the dizzy pinnacle of 5,000,000 tons for 1920.

When the crash came the next year, production did not fall at once commensurately with the market price of sugar. Obstinately hoping for better days, producers grimly continued to grind amounts of sugar which the market as obstinately refused to absorb. The total Cuban sugar crop for 1925-29—following a small recession immediately after the 1921 collapse—rose again to the top 5,000,000 ton figure.

But no amount of optimism among the sugar growers could check the onward march of crisis; they were forced to pull in their horns, with the result that the crop slid steadily downward. Finally, by 1932—the black year—it had been reduced to 2,000,000 tons, less than one-half the boom total. Since then it has gradually picked up until, in 1938, it was again at the 3,000,000 ton mark.

During those years of fabulous wealth and dire collapse the value of Cuba's sugar output also went through spectacular vicissitudes. The average yearly gross income of the Cuban sugar industry, derived from raw and refined sugar and sugar by-products, for the pre-war period 1910-14, was $119,000,000. For the World War period (1914-19) it was

$352,000,000, nearly three times as much. Then, in the boom year 1920, it rose to the record all-time high of $774,000,000; and for the five-year period 1920-24, it averaged $426,000,000.

The first years of the slump (1925-29) brought it to an average of $267,000,000 yearly and the ensuing period of collapse sent it down to the all-time low of $91,000,000 annually, little better than one-fifth of the yearly average of the boom period.

Side by side with these alternations of rise and fall in Cuban sugar fortunes, the United States has operated a long series of expedients for keeping Cuban sugar interests from howling, while at the same time, preventing competing interests in the United States proper, together with those in Puerto Rico, Hawaii and the Philippines, from too frequent and tempestuous outbursts of rage at alleged preferential treatment of the Cubans. These culminated a few years ago in the present sugar quota system, whereby Cuba is allowed a share in our total sugar consumption running, roughly, to two-thirds her annual crop.

Discontented Cubans eagerly scan the horizon for remedies. But what they find there is little calculated to cause encouragement.

FORTY-ONE years ago, when the Spanish American War was on, and people in our eastern states half expected to be bombarded at any moment by warships sent by Spain to defend her last remaining possessions in the New World, the United States battleship *Oregon*, one of the most formidable units of our navy, received imperative orders to rush at top speed from her station in the Pacific and reinforce her comrades of the Atlantic.

There was no Panama Canal then.

With funnels belching black smoke, with throbbing engines and loaded cannon and decks cleared for battle, the *Oregon* sped down the western coast of South America, rounded Cape Horn, pounded up South America's other shore, a full 13,000 miles, while the United States caught its breath and hoped and waited.

The *Oregon* got there.

After sixty-eight days of steaming, she reinforced our Atlantic fleet in time to render splendid service at the decisive defeat of the Spaniards off Santiago—while the American nation uttered deep prayers of thanksgiving. Had the Spaniards been stronger, had their leadership been bolder, had some mishap delayed the *Oregon*, the tale might have been tragically different. With part of our fleet in the Pacific, the other in the Atlantic, and those 13,000 miles of salt water between them, the consequences might have been serious.

But as matters now stand, no successor of the doughty

Oregon need circle Cape Horn to join the rest of our navy. Today we have the Panama Canal.

That peerless prince of strategic waterways makes it possible for any warship of the United States in the Pacific to join any in the Atlantic—or vice versa—within a fortnight; for the 13,000 miles of 1898 have been cut by the Canal to a mere 5,000. Within the short space of two days the entire American navy can pass through the Canal and deploy, in full battle strength, against a foe menacing us either from the Orient or from Europe.

That is why the Panama Canal is hailed by strategists as the most valuable example in all history of "interior lines" for the naval defense of a nation. That is why military and naval experts are unanimous in deeming it the keystone of our whole national defensive system. That is why, in President Roosevelt's gigantic program for assuring our national defense, many millions of dollars have been earmarked to strengthen the existing protection of the Panama Canal Zone and provide new and stronger protection, at the earliest possible moment.

The economic importance of the Canal may be inferred from the fact that it carries almost as much tonnage as the Suez. Up to July, 1937, gross receipts for tolls had amounted to $406,215,948. During the fiscal year 1936-37 more than 5,300 vessels used the Canal. East-west traffic included shipments of manufactured iron and steel, scrap metal, oil, paper, cotton, various metals; traffic from west to east was chiefly in oil, lumber, ore, sugar, nitrates and wheat.

*   *   *

Our steamer goes her way cautiously between two long breakwaters jutting out from shores thick with tropical vegetation. Passengers line the rail in scores—those who have never been to the Canal Zone before, eager and expectant; those who know Panama, pointing out, with lordly superiority, the first landmarks emerging ahead—glibly rattling off statistics involving millions of dollars and millions of cubic feet of earth and water. Off the port bow of the ship appear those twin towns lifted to prosperity and importance by the Panama Canal: Colon—hybrid, raffish—and Cristobal—neat, modern.

Everything has a look of age and permanence. As you peer to port and starboard, you can scarcely believe that it is a little over thirty years since the project for connecting the Atlantic and Pacific Oceans, by building a canal across the Isthmus of Panama, emerged, once for all, from the land of dreams into the realm of reality.

It had been relegated to dreamland by the failure of the French company headed by Ferdinand de Lesseps, builder of the Suez Canal, to dig an American counterpart of the Suez waterway. Work was begun on the Panama Canal by the French in 1882, only to come to a standstill in 1888. The intervening years witnessed an orgy of extravagance and mismanagement, an epic of toil and courage, a tragedy of disease and death. In 1904, the United States, having bought out the French company, signed a treaty with the new-born Republic of Panama, relating to the construction of the Canal. In 1905, the Isthmian Canal Commission was formed, and the plans of the commission's engineers for a lock canal across the Isthmus were approved on February 5th, 1906.

In June, 1906, that approval was confirmed. In November, President Theodore Roosevelt—who had smiled benevolently on the revolution which severed Panama from Colombia and made it possible for Americans to build the Canal—paid his famous visit to the Isthmus. One month later bids were opened for the actual construction work.

For eight years after that the Isthmus of Panama rang with a hellish symphony of sound—rattle of steam shovels, shrieks of steam whistles, chug of locomotives, shouts of command in lurid English, grunts of acquiescence or growls of protest from thousands of workers in a dozen tongues, pounding of drill machinery, roar of dynamite explosions. And while Goethals and his army of helpers dug, Gorgas wielded a weapon the lack of which had helped bring disaster to the French: the power to vanquish yellow fever and malaria. Protected from the attacks of insects bearing these deadly diseases, the polyglot cohorts of Goethals labored with irresistible perseverance. They defied heart-breaking obstacles arrayed against them by jealous nature in the form of gigantic landslides, which choked the route through which the waters of their canal were to flow.

At last, in 1913, President Woodrow Wilson pressed a button in Washington. The electric impulse ignited tons of dynamite, placed along the Gamboa Dam on the Isthmus of Panama, 2,000 miles away. That dam through four years had blocked the flow of the Chagres river, enabling Goethals's busy workers to dig the Culebra (now Gaillard) Cut, their most stupendous achievement.

Amid wild cheering from thousands of men, granted a holiday by their bosses, the dam went up with a terrific roar, and the waters of the Chagres, foaming with rage after their long imprisonment, poured into the Cut, filled it, and—the Panama Canal was born! In 1914, twenty-five years ago this year, it was opened to commercial traffic.

Only twenty-five years! That seems incredible to those who see the Canal as it is today. They rub their eyes skeptically when confronted with the huge docks and the busy shipping of Cristobal and Colon; with the broad, man-made waterway, stretching inland through primeval jungle which is the Atlantic entrance of the Canal.

Wonder and skepticism are intensified when you strike out into the interior of the Isthmus and become really acquainted with that most renowned of artificial waterways, which—as some poetic person remarked, "divides the Continent to unite the world." (Another, less poetic, after contemplating its huge gates and tremendous steel-walled locks and general air of overpowering efficiency and massiveness, chuckled: "So endearing, engineering!")

*　　*　　*

The Panama Canal is so solid that it seems to have merged into scenery enclosing it; to have become, in the brief space of less than two decades, flesh and bone of the jungle which it has rent asunder.

At Gatun, the steel gates of the double locks, their massive concrete walls, the lofty electric light posts and powerful towing engines seem as much a part of the landscape as the green fringes of shore, stretching away into the distance toward the regions of mystery that lie between the Canal and Colombia, on the one side, and between it and Costa Rica, on the other. And as if to warn off nature from too close encroachment on the works of man, from lingering hopes that she may reassert undisputed sway on the Isthmus and reclaim for the jungle tomorrow what belonged to the jungle yesterday, there is, perched impudently on top of the gigantic Gatun Dam, *a golf links!* Clubhouse and lockers, greens and flags and players in sport clothes, within sight of forests where half-clad natives still live, of waters on whose banks alligators still sun themselves. You cannot help feeling, in contemplating the golf links at Gatun, that natives and alligators and nature herself must take every cry of "Fore" as a personal insult.

How nature has been forced to play second fiddle to man on the Isthmus of Panama is nowhere better shown than at Gatun Lake, just beyond the great Gatun Locks, as you go along the Canal from Atlantic to Pacific.

Nature made no lake at Gatun. Before the American blasters and shovelers came, the Chagres river flowed along what is now the bed of the lake, feeling its way, as it had done since prehistoric days, from the jungle hiding its source to its mouth on the Atlantic shore of the Isthmus. But the Americans built the temporary Gamboa Dam across one section of the Chagres and the permanent Gatun Dam across another. Then, when the former was blown up, the Chagres, instead of flowing Atlantic-ward as it had done all through its existence, filled up the Culebra Cut, in one direction, and in the other, finding its progress arrested by the Gatun Dam, poured its waters into a basin, thus forming—exactly as the American engineers had planned—a great lake, which now supplies the Panama Canal with water.

Dotted over the surface of this lake, silent evidences of nature's defeat, are the tops of trees, all that is to be seen of the forest which covered the basin of land before the Chagres submerged it. Already the trees are dead; they stand, shorn of every leaf, in shallow Gatun Lake.

* * *

At the end of Gatun Lake nearest the Pacific is the part of the Panama Canal which is probably most familiar in name to everyone who has followed, even cursorily, the building and operation of the renowned waterway. Its official name is now Gaillard Cut, in honor of the American engineer, active in its construction, who paid with his life for his labors. On the right bank, as you thread your way toward the Pacific, is a memorial tablet to Gaillard. Yet, in spite of official action and commemorative tablet, the name "Culebra"—meaning "snake" in Spanish—still stubbornly clings to the cut.

As you glide through it today in the American Government steamboat, there is little to recall the banks, gashed deep by machinery, and the mammoth ditch, empty of water and swarming with workmen, which, thirty years ago, were the sum total of Culebra. Except on some rocky surfaces, the banks are fringed with vegetation; and the ditch is filled to a depth of forty-five feet by the placid, currentless water deflected from the Chagres river to serve the purposes of man. The landslides which brought sudden death to many diggers and temporary discomfiture to their chiefs have left only superficial traces of their devastating progress.

All is peaceful. On the big steamers, moving slowly from Atlantic to Pacific, or Pacific to Atlantic, sailors lean on the rail, lazily eyeing you as you glide lazily past in the little government steamboat. The lecturer aboard that steamboat, pressing megaphone to mouth, pours out volleys of information at machine-gun speed, spraying his hearers with a deadly hail of statistics. Big and little steamboats, tourists and lecturers, earnest ladies taking notes—that is the Panama Canal of today.

* * *

Beyond Gaillard Cut are the Pedro Miguel Locks and the Miraflores Locks, now as much a part of the Isthmian picture as their giant kinsfolk at Gatun. And beyond them you come to Balboa, an American Spotless Town set in the midst of tropical landscape. Spick and span bungalows, motor cars speeding over the perfect pavement of shady boulevards, soldiers in the uniform of Uncle Sam sitting before barracks built with every regard for up-to-date comfort and sanitation —a fit place, this Balboa, for rubbing your eyes in amazement and asking once more whether it is not all a mirage. And beyond Balboa is Ancon, another bit of the United States; and beyond Ancon—fortunately for those already half believing in the mirage—is Panama City.

For Panama City is still, to some extent, what you expect a Latin American city to be. To be sure, association with French and American canal builders during the last half century has rubbed away much of its Spanish coating and given it a cosmopolitan veneer. Enough is left, however, to make the visitor dismiss the idea that what he has just seen is sheer dream stuff. Looking at Panama's venerable cathedral, a typical church of Spanish colonial days, he reflects: "After all, I am a couple of thousand miles south of New York."

But the place where he really forgets for a moment Canal and Canal Zone, engineering and statistics and the whole twentieth century, is Old Panama. Around Old Panama there is a magic in the air; he who breathes it drinks a potion of forgetfulness which closes his eyes to the present.

Old Panama, hugging the Pacific shore, is today but a mournful confusion of ruins. The shell of a monastery, a gaunt tower rising out of the jungle, remnants of walls, the broken arch of a bridge—these are all that remains of the splendid Spanish city, where the gold and silver of Peru were landed from treasure ships, loaded on the backs of mules, and sent along old trails threading the Isthmus to the Atlantic shore, there to be loaded onto other treasure ships and added —unless Drake or some other freebooter intercepted them—

to the vast wealth of the Spanish King.

Mute though they are, the melancholy ruins of Old Panama tell eloquently of the most audacious exploit in the whole history of buccaneering: the capture and ruthless sacking of the city by Henry Morgan and his army of desperate pirates, drawn to his banner by the one thing they had in common, the lust for Spanish treasure. Once they had scaled the walls of Old Panama, that lust was gorged to satiety. Morgan's men cut down the last Spaniards with fight still in them, smashed their way into mansion and church and monastery, and loaded down with gold, silver and jewels, toiled back over the Spanish trails to where their pirate galleys lay anchored on the Atlantic shore.

Old Panama never raised its head after Morgan's visit. Those of its inhabitants who survived never tried to build anew the homes to which the pirates had set the torch; they preferred to rear another city, better fortified against enemies, a few miles from the scene of their discomfiture and impoverishment. That new settlement has come to be what we now know as Panama City.

Returning thither after wandering through Old Panama, thoughts of the past are dashed abruptly from your mind. You are in a motor car; you drive past a race-course, between rows of brightly painted villas; eventually, you are disputing the right of way with a twentieth century trolley car.

*   *   *

On the Isthmus of Panama the atmosphere is American and pushing and triumphant. "We Americans built the Panama Canal!"—"We Americans defeated yellow fever and malaria!" —"We Americans dug the Culebra Cut and created Gatun Lake and harnessed the Chagres river!" Thus it goes, with unending variations—the American Song of Success. At times it becomes monotonous to the visitor. The best thing he can do at such times is to hire himself a steam launch and steer inland from Colon, not toward the mouth of the American canal but to that of another waterway, to the eastward.

It is a silent, melancholy waterway. Its banks are jungle. Half-sunk in the mud are rusty boats, abandoned and rotting away. Half-hidden in the underbrush on each side are machines red with rust, flung there long ago when they had become useless. Tumble-down shanties made of planks and oil cans, line the shore; Negroes and Indians gaze curiously from them at the chugging launch.

Everywhere is a soft and melancholy beauty. Here is not even the faintest echo of that Song of Success which resounds along the Panama Canal, from Cristobal to Gatun, from Gatun to Pedro Miguel to Balboa, to Panama.

For this abandoned waterway is the old French canal. Begun with high hopes by de Lesseps, builder of the Suez Canal, and his comrades, it was destined never to be completed. After some miles had been dug, the French canal company, beset by a storm of ugly accusations, crashed into bankruptcy. Its vessels and machines were left to decay. And the waterway which was to form part of the great Atlantic-Pacific canal became a mere intruder into the jungle solitude which those who dug it hoped that it would conquer. Only a small part of the French canal was found usable by the Americans when they came to Panama and started to build their canal. The rest is that waterway of beauty and silence and sadness which cuts through the jungle from Cristobal, that American-created town, toward Gatun, that American-created lake.

*   *   *

SO ENDEARING, ENGINEERING

From the handsome railroad station of Panama a train of cars just like those in the United States, behind an engine which would be quite at home in an American roundhouse, rushes you back across the Isthmus. To your left you catch glimpses of the Canal; of great steamers being raised or lowered in its huge locks. To your right, somewhere behind the belt of forest stretching away to distant mountains, is the mule track over which the Spaniards hauled their treasure, over which cut-throat Henry Morgan came to wrest it from them in furious battle. And somewhere out there is that "peak in Darien" whence Vasco Nuñez de Balboa, first man of European blood to see the Pacific, gazed, silent, on its vast expanse of shimmering water.

Only four hundred years ago! Surely many more years separate you from those mythical times. For you stand in the railroad station at Colon, and over there beside the great dock, the steamer which brought you to the Isthmus is giving out deep notes of impatience. Less than three hundred years since Henry Morgan sacked Panama. Only a few more than one hundred since the flag of Spain vanished from the Isthmus. And since the men of de Lesseps first gashed its soil with their shovels, hoping to sunder it and force it to give passage to the canal of their dreams, less than sixty years! Impossible!

*　　*　　*

It takes about eight hours to "transit" the Canal—as they say in the Canal Zone—and the trip still produces certain old impressions of other years, when the threat of war was not so present in men's minds. One is still struck breathless by the precision with which locks are opened and closed, filled with water and emptied of it; by the matter-of-fact casualness with which the little electric engines alongside the ship tow it away from one ocean and toward the other.

There is no shouting. No arms are waved frantically. No arrogant words of command are bellowed. Nobody swears. Negro workmen—so prone, elsewhere, to volubility and excitement—move, with scarcely a sound, about their tasks. At the lock side, white foremen, cigarettes in mouths, stand apparently unconcerned.

Yet there's never a hitch. A whistle now and then—the buzzing of an electric bell—a man, perched high up in a nearby building, speaking quietly through a telephone. That's all. Two or three curt gestures, and your ship slides out from behind the massive gate of Gatun Locks and starts over the calm expanse of Gatun Lake.

Another impression remains as striking today as when the Canal was younger: the unbelievable proximity of the jungle.

Here we have the last word in engineering progress, processions of engineering miracles, acres of gleaming machinery, up-to-the-minute structures for housing the thousands of men who operate that machinery—steel and steel and still more steel—yet some hundreds of yards away the jungle glowers, a jungle so dense that one almost expects lions to roar from its depths as one's ship is towed past, and tigers to slink from primeval fastnesses to make a meal of intruding man.

It would seem so appropriate to see pretty villas bordering the Canal on each side; to follow with the eye macadamized highways, winding up the hills that encircle it; to contemplate nice little towns, with neat sidewalks and filling stations, clinging to the slopes. Instead of all this—nature, untrodden and untamed, jungle untouched and sinister.

Those old impressions still persist—but there is now a new one: the impression of almost complete invisibility shrouding the thousands of soldiers, the scores of cannon and planes

marshaled all around, to watch over this great strategic inter-
oceanic thoroughfare.

From one end of it to the other even the most unimagina-
tive tourist is conscious that big guns are wickedly pointing
at him from emplacements out there in the jungle; that, at a
sharp signal, clouds of warplanes would swoop over him in
deadly readiness.

But where are they?

Posted at key points throughout the Canal Zone are thousands of men of the United States army. Watching over its
approaches are swift naval vessels; parked about its airdromes
are many bombers and pursuit planes. Fronting its entrances
are strong forts. But for all the tourist sees of them, they
might as well not be there at all.

When I "transited" the Canal a few months ago there was
a group of khaki-clothed United States soldiers, with their
rifles stacked in front of them, standing informally before one
of the buildings beside the Gatun Locks. And at Pedro
Miguel Lock, a bit beyond, another squad, about ten in all,
nonchalantly gave our ship the once over—and they didn't
even have rifles!

Otherwise—just the Stars and Stripes flying over barracks,
veranda-enclosed, like huge bungalows—a military truck now
and then, jolting along, with three or four soldiers clinging,
like brown barnacles, to its sides—and the ever-present feeling
that, despite all this casualness and invisibility, military eyes
are watching everywhere, military brains ceaselessly sizing
you up. It gives a visitor from the United States a pleasant
sense of security—a good thing, he reflects, that this most
vital link in the defense of his country is being operated and
guarded with so little noise and so much efficiency.

Experts practically exclude the possibility of a naval attack on the Panama Canal. Even assuming that an enemy fleet could put the United States navy entirely out of action—certainly a bold assumption!—the consensus is that the big coast-guard guns at the Canal entrances could annihilate all enemy ships coming within their range. So deadly would be the fire which they would concentrate on any enemy warship standing in to shore that the latter would be compelled to remain to seaward at such a distance as to preclude the possibility of bombardment of the Canal's defenses.

But when it comes to other possible methods of hostile attack, there is no such feeling of assurance among those whose job it is to guard the Panama Canal. As major war-time dangers they list these:

1. Attack from the air.
2. Attack from the land.
3. Attack by means of sabotaging tactics.

Aerial attack is generally held to be the greatest of all perils.

Military and naval experts envisage the possibility that a situation might arise in a war between the United States and a hostile alliance—say, Japan, Germany and Italy—which would necessitate concentration of our full naval fighting force in the Atlantic to meet attack from Europe. This would make it possible for Japan to strike a sudden blow from the air against the Panama Canal, either from air bases secretly provided on land, or from an aircraft carrier stationed out in the Pacific.

There is only a remote chance of such a contingency, of course; but true to their habit of resolutely facing the worst, experts in the Panama Canal Zone insist on taking this possibility into account. After all, they point out, Germans (and Japanese) are showing great activity nowadays in Latin and

Central America, and that activity, though primarily commercial at present, might easily be transformed into openly hostile moves against us, in the event of war.

Another possible land base for aerial attack on the Canal would be the Galapagos Islands in the Pacific, not far from Panama. The best way to eliminate the threat from these, some think, is for the United States to buy or lease the Galapagos group from Ecuador.

In the immediate vicinity of the Panama Canal those entrusted with its defense particularly want new strategic roads in order to facilitate anti-aircraft measures. Existing roads, it was held, when I was last there, were inadequate. There was also need it was felt, of improved methods of anti-aircraft fire control, etc. Already good work was under way to correct deficiencies; but when questioned concerning the exact nature of these, those in the know shut up like clams.

As for defense against land attack, some Canal Zone authorities maintain that—supposing the entire American war fleet in a war against Germany, Italy and Japan, were concentrated in the Atlantic—the Japanese might conceivably (at enormous risk to themselves, of course) land a considerable force at some point on the Pacific side of the Isthmus of Panama. From this as a base they might initiate offensive operations against the Canal. To frustrate such moves, one American school of thought (especially vocal in the Canal Zone) advocates heavy reinforcement of the present garrison there. Some call for a total garrison, including increased air forces and contingents of other arms, of 30,000.

Better means of communication also figure prominently in their calculations. They want a real military road—straight, wide, hard-surfaced, capable of defying all weathers—connecting the Canal Zone with the immediately adjoining stretch of Pacific shore, which includes excellent beaches and sheltered inlets where hostile troops could be landed.

Most experts agree that the Atlantic approaches of the Panama Canal present little chance to an enemy of successful attack. First, the outlying defenses of the Canal on that side—notably our base at Guantanamo, Cuba, and the narrow sea passages from Europe skirting Puerto Rico (now a full-fledged military zone) and the Virgin Islands—would be far easier to watch and defend than the Canal's approaches on the Pacific side. Second, even if a hostile force succeeded in landing on the Caribbean shore of the Isthmus, it would have to toil forward over terribly difficult country before it could reach the Canal. Nevertheless, some military men strenuously champion hard-surfacing and general improvement of existing coastwise trails in this region, on both sides of the Caribbean entrance to the Panama Canal, in order to make them usable even in the worst part of the Isthmian rainy season.

Lastly, as to sabotage:

Even the most confident experts here do not expect invulnerability for the Canal—against sabotage or anything else. In spite even of the best precautions, they realize desperate enemies might conceivably wreak havoc in the locks.

One possibility would be for a group of hostile daredevils to take into the Canal an ordinary freighter, apparently harmless but in reality equipped with special mine-laying apparatus, and plant, at various points in the locks, a string of mines which might later explode with devastating consequences. Another would be for a crew of desperate foes of ours to blow up a similar freighter inside one of the locks, thus effectively blocking all traffic over a period that might be decisive in a war.

Most effective as a way to combat such contingencies in

time of peace, would be to halt every ship, no matter what her flag or character, seeking to pass through the Canal, and instead of merely subjecting her to a somewhat cursory inspection as is now customary, to force her to dock and unload every bit of her cargo for minute official examination. Were that done, no mine-laying apparatus or bombs could possibly be sneaked into the locks. But such drastic procedure before a war was on, it is realized, would cause a storm of protest from shippers, even in a period of strained international relations.

If the projected additional locks for the Panama Canal are constructed it is a foregone conclusion that they will embody a number of improvements—most valuable from the standpoint of defense against aerial and other forms of attack—with which the existing locks are unprovided. This lack is because it was impossible for the builders of thirty and more years ago to envisage the deadliness which warplanes have developed as instruments of destruction. In the Canal Zone most details for publication concerning what is being done are politely but firmly refused; it may be stated, however, that one improvement would be the concealment underground of parts of the machinery for opening and shutting the new locks corresponding to machinery in the existing locks which is dangerously exposed.

When an outsider hears Canal Zone bigwigs indulge in gloomy talk of possible hostile depredations from the air, of possible landings of enemy soldiers perilously close to the waterway which is the core of our national defense, of "suicide squads" of our enemies dynamiting themselves to eternity in the canal locks but leaving those locks shattered and useless, he is constantly tempted to smile incredulously and accuse such killjoys of calamity-howling. But they don't care. They refuse to budge an inch from their dire theories.

One of them, whose assumptions of such dreadful possibilities I frankly questioned, came right back at me with the categorical statement that some of our own naval flyers, during maneuvers over the Canal in which they were confronted theoretically with opposition, succeeded, nevertheless, in making swooping dives to a position overhead so close to the locks that, had they been engaged in actual warfare, they would have been able to wreak terrible havoc with bombs. He also declared that recently some of our Canal Zone aviators, flying at a height of 18,000 feet, and using as a target an outline on the ground below them closely resembling, in size and general contour, one of the great locks of the Panama Canal, made a score of 50 per cent in their attempts to bomb this target—in other words, *they hit it every other time.*

"Now call me a calamity-howler," he concluded triumphantly.

No—over-confidence is most emphatically not conspicuous just now among those upon whom would devolve the wartime defense of the Panama Canal.

In the Canal Zone one meets on all sides quiet, tight-lipped vigilance, grim acceptance of threatening perils coupled with equally grim determination to meet and overcome them. But nowhere is there empty bragging; nowhere are the official sentries guarding this thin stretch of water, kernel and core and nerve-center of our national defense, nodding at their posts; nowhere is there any blind under-estimation of possible foes. And that, in these days when war clouds are steadily spreading and steadily growing blacker on the international horizon, is a most comforting thought.

MARK TWAIN once said that everybody talked about the
weather, but nobody did anything about it. Today, everybody talks about the Good Neighbor Policy, but nobody
knows anything about it. What, nobody? Well, almost nobody. Take, for instance, me. I returned recently from an
extensive tour of the Latin American republics, at which that
policy is aimed, simply bursting with lore about it, brimming
with desire to lead people into the light concerning it.

"What," inquired a friend coldly, "is the Good Neighbor
Policy? What has it accomplished?"

There was my chance!

Leaning forward eagerly, I talked, without pause for rest
or refreshment, throughout an unbelievable number of minutes. When I finally came to a stop, he inquired frigidly:

"What is the Good Neighbor Policy? What has it accomplished?"

I was about to start all over again, but he checked me.

"You speak," he told me icily, "but you say nothing."

"In your statements there is a dearth," he added glacially,
"of brass tacks."

He took his hat. He took his leave. And I took the next
train for Washington.

There I found the atmosphere impregnated with a strong
odor of Good Neighbor Policy. One got a feeling everywhere that Cordell Hull was close at hand, striding up and
down, muttering: "I *will* think about Brazil! I will *not* think

about Mexico!" One expected, at any moment, to have Assistant Secretary of State Sumner Welles, Mr. Hull's most active Good Neighborite collaborator, suddenly buttonhole one and begin to chant the names of all twenty of the Latin American republics, together with their areas, populations, principal articles of export and comparative degrees of Good Neighborliness. One dreamed at night of squads of clerks, over at the Export-Import Bank, wrapping up packages of greenbacks and tucking into them neat cards reading, "To dear Brazil, from Franklin," or "To a good little Nicaraguan dictator, many happy returns of the dough, Cordell."

But there was no time to lose. Equipping myself with a reliable compass (in case I got lost in unexplored reaches of State Department or Department of Commerce corridors), I set out on my quest for an answer to the questions of my gloomy and glacial friend.

Preliminary research soon disclosed that President Roosevelt himself deserves the credit of having launched the phrase "Good Neighbor Policy" as a description of the new attitude toward Latin America which he is seeking to make typical of his administration. He used it first in his 1933 inaugural speech, when he dedicated the American nation to "the policy of the Good Neighbor—the neighbor who resolutely respects himself, and because he does so, respects the rights of others—the neighbor who respects his obligations and respects the sanctity of his agreements in and with a world of neighbors."

Later, after the new policy was well under way, Sumner Welles, who had by this time made himself Head Trumpet-Blower and Drum-Pounder-in-Chief of Good Neighborliness, further defined the new orientation as follows:

"Our new policy of the Good Neighbor has been predicated upon the belief of this government that there should exist an inter-American political relationship based on a recognition of *actual and not theoretical equality* between the American republics; on a complete forbearance from interference by any one republic in the domestic concerns of any other; on economic cooperation; and finally, on the common realization that, in the world at large, all of the American republics confront the same international problems, and that, in their relations with non-American powers, the welfare and security of any one of them cannot be a matter of indifference to the others."

He added that to attain these objectives, acts and not words were required.

Well, Acts-not-Words has been no mere empty window-dressing slogan.

In October, 1933, only a few months after President Roosevelt's official inauguration of the Good Neighbor idea, President Arias of the Republic of Panama, visited Washington and arranged a *friendly agreement* doing away with certain points of friction between his country and ours.

A couple of months later came the Seventh Pan-American Conference at Montevideo. Our delegation to that conference was headed by Cordell Hull in person, this being the first time that a Secretary of State of this country had ever been a delegate to any inter-American talk-fest.

"The atmosphere was very bad when the Conference started," he told me at Montevideo. "Some of the South Americans who were delegates to it, accustomed to use an anti-American attitude for political purposes, were reserved and suspicious. I adopted a method of calling informally on them. I would simply let them know by telephone that I was coming to see them. If they were busy, I saw someone else at their offices; if not, I saw them personally. Soon a free-and-easy spirit was established; why, I talked with one of them while he was in his bath!—there is nothing like getting to know foreign statesmen. And they began to come and see me in the same informal manner. As a consequence, before the end of the conference, there was an enormous improvement in the atmosphere."

To the amazement of skeptical Latin Americans, still mindful of the days of "Manifest Destiny" and "Dollar Diplomacy" and "The Big Stick," Secretary Hull, acting for the United States, signed at Montevideo a "Convention on the Rights and Duties of States, which laid down the fundamental principle that *no State has the right to intervene in the internal or external affairs of another*." That was certainly a different tune from the one that Teddy Roosevelt used to play!

In further pursuit of Acts-not-Words, an *Export-Import Bank* was created at Washington, in February, 1934, little more than a month after the close of the Montevideo Conference, for the purpose of helping to finance and facilitate exports and imports and the exchange of commodities between the United States and foreign countries—particularly Latin America. Since its foundation the Export-Import Bank has got itself talked about a lot. Some like it. Some don't. Senator Borah thinks it too lavish with Uncle Sam's money. Enthusiastic Good Neighborites think it not lavish enough.

Those three opening achievements were mere appetizers. Good Neighborites next proceeded to get down to brass tacks of the brassiest and tackiest sort, viz.:

Shortly after the creation of the Export-Import Bank, they took a step which made many anti-Americans to the south of us jump up, as if they had sat down on a mobilized porcupine, by engineering the conclusion of a new treaty, on May 29, 1934, between the United States and Cuba which *expressly abrogated the previous treaty, made in 1905, which had included the noted and notorious Platt Amendment*, by which the Cubans had acknowledged the right of the United States to intervene in Cuba in certain emergencies of a political nature. That amendment—though much might be (and has been) adduced in its favor—was ever since its birth a most pestiferous thorn in the side of our relations with Latin America. In the minds of thousands of Latin Americans, the Good Neighbor Policy did not pass from dreamland into reality until the day on which the Platt Amendment was kicked downstairs.

Less than three months later, another shattering blow was landed by Washington on obstinate South American believers in the theory that the word Roosevelt must necessarily mean the same thing, irrespective of whether it was preceded by Theodore or Franklin. *Our Marines, who had been occupying Haiti since 1915, were withdrawn to the last man*, and the conduct of Haitian affairs left entirely to the Haitians. That took away a vast amount of ammunition from our critics in Latin America and correspondingly elated the Good Neighborites.

Meanwhile, there had been active work behind the scenes for the conclusion of trade agreements, of a mutually beneficial kind, between ourselves and our neighbors. This resulted, within three weeks after the last United States Marine had waved good-by to the receding shores of Haiti, in the conclusion of *the first of these agreements, with Cuba*, in September, 1934. This was followed, during the ensuing two

years, by *six similar agreements*, all mutually beneficial to
the signers, between the United States and:

> Haiti
> Brazil
> Honduras
> Colombia
> Guatemala
> Nicaragua

With these dozen items as evidence that their Good Neighbor protestations really meant something, President Roosevelt and Secretary Hull sailed away, in December, 1936, to attend the Inter-American Conference for the Maintenance of Peace, at Buenos Aires. Since 1933, the year of the Good Neighbor Policy's birth, a marked change had begun to be apparent in inter-American relations. In the southern republics of our hemisphere the theory that Uncle Sam was no better than a Big Bad Wolf was losing ground. And it has continued to do so in the years since 1936—to the intense gratification of Good Neighborites in general and Cordell Hull in particular.

"Before Montevideo," he told me in Washington recently, "I was rawhided by the press of Latin America in the most malignant manner. Papers down there said, 'Here is the big bully (the United States) looking from the Rio Grande to Cape Horn again, seeing whom he can insult and whom he can plunder.'"

But, at Buenos Aires, there was much less of that sort of thing. The conference there resulted in the signing of a number of agreements, culminating in a *Declaration of Principles of Inter-American Solidarity and Cooperation*, which, after some high-flown language of extreme friendliness toward every nation on this Continent, wound up thus:

"The Inter-American Conference for the Maintenance of Peace DECLARES:
That the following principles are accepted by the international American community:
  (a) Proscription of territorial conquest, and that, in consequence, no acquisition made through violence shall be recognized;
  (b) Intervention by one State in the internal or external affairs of another State is condemned;
  (c) Forcible collection of pecuniary debts is illegal; and
  (d) Any difference or dispute between the American nations, whatever its nature or origin, shall be settled by the methods of conciliation, or full arbitration, or through operation of international justice."

After Buenos Aires, the Good Neighborites continued to shout "Acts-not-Words." Their persistent clamor resulted, in May, 1938, in the creation, at Washington, of an *Inter-Departmental Committee on Cooperation with the American Republics*. In this Committee the following thirteen governmental departments and agencies are represented:

The Departments of State, Treasury, Interior, Agriculture, Commerce, and Labor; the Library of Congress; the Smithsonian Institution; the Federal Communications Commission; the United States Maritime Commission; the Export-Import Bank; the National Emergency Council; and the Civil Aeronautics Authority.

Since its creation, the Committee has taken up a total of seventy-four separate proposals, all tending to the betterment of relations between the United States and the twenty republics of Latin America.

Next in order came the establishment, in the summer of 1938, at the Department of State, of a *Division of Cultural Relations*, to have general charge of official international activities such as exchange of professors, teachers and students; cooperation in music, art, literature, etc.; distribution of libraries of works representative of the United States, and translations thereof; participation, by the United States Government, in international expositions; international radio broadcasts, etc., etc.

That same summer saw also the signing, with the blessing of our State Department, of a *contract between the Haitian Government and a big American engineering company*, for an ambitious program of public works in Haiti, including roads, bridges, wharves, drainage canals, irrigation projects, and schemes of agricultural development, involving, all told, the expenditure of $5,000,000. The engineering company made an arrangement with the Export-Import Bank whereby the bank agreed to discount notes given by the Haitian Government in payment for work performed and materials furnished. It was also agreed that necessary construction materials and equipment not already ordered by Haiti, or produced in that country, must be purchased in the United States and transported, if possible, in American vessels.

During that same month, owing largely to the efforts of the United States Government, *Bolivia and Paraguay signed a treaty putting an end to the protracted, bloody and futile Chaco War.*

That most devoutly-to-be-wished consummation was followed, in the summer of 1938, by the creation, at the Department of State, of a *Division of International Communications*, to be charged with the elaboration and carrying into effect of comprehensive and coordinated programs of international aviation, radio, motion pictures, telegraph, cable and shipping; with assisting in the preparation and interpretation of treaties in this field; with the drafting or reviewing of all correspondence with foreign governments and their missions in this country, American diplomatic and consular officers, government departments, and all other correspondence pertaining to international communications and activities; with maintenance of liaison with other government departments and agencies in matters pertaining to international communications; and with collaboration with foreign missions in Washington. This new Division was established with the special view of improving United States-Latin American relations in the interests of the Good Neighbor Policy.

In addition to all this, that policy was the motive power behind the conclusion, in 1938, of additional trade agreements (bringing the total thereof to nine) between the United States and two more Latin American neighbors: El Salvador and Costa Rica.

Stuffing into his satchel the records of all these Good Neighborly achievements, that courtly and indefatigable Tennessean, Cordell Hull, proceeded again to South America, in December, 1938, for the third time in five years, to head the United States delegation to the Eighth Pan-American Conference at Lima, Peru.

Since the Montevideo and Buenos Aires meetings, Hitler's Germany had become ominously aggressive, so much so that Good Neighborites of the more pugnacious sort felt that teeth must be put into the Good Neighbor Policy if it was to be of any use to anybody. While not abandoning its essentially peaceful character, Mr. Hull pointed out at Lima, to the rest of the delegates from the American republics assembled there, the urgent necessity for such a major dental operation.

But he struck a snag.

Argentina wanted as little done at Lima as possible. At times it looked as if the Conference would blow up in general recrimination and complete failure—which would have been a source of immense satisfaction to German and Italian totalitarians, malevolently watching it from across the Atlantic.

But Mr. Hull obstinately plugged along—he told me later that he hardly got any sleep over a stretch of something like ten days and nights—until he finally succeeded in having the Argentine and all of the other delegations present sign the so-called *Declaration of Lima*—which, if not exactly bristling with teeth, is, at least, by no means toothless.

Here is its toothiest section:

"CONSIDERING:
"That the peoples of America have achieved spiritual unity through the similarity of their republican institutions, their unshakable will for peace, their profound sentiment of humanity and tolerance, and through their absolute adherence to the principles of international law, of the equal sovereignty of States and of individual liberty without religious or racial prejudices;

"The Governments of the American States
"DECLARE:
"First. That they reaffirm their continental solidarity and their purpose to collaborate in the maintenance of the principles upon which the said solidarity is based.

"Second. That, faithful to the above-mentioned principles and to their absolute sovereignty, they reaffirm their decision to maintain them and to defend them against all foreign intervention or activity that may threaten them."

That document may not be all that Franklin Roosevelt and Cordell Hull, Good Neighborite-in-Chief and Chief-of-Staff, respectively, of the Good Neighbor Policy, had meant it to be, but it certainly was better than nothing. The very fact that to it were appended the signatures of delegates representing every one of the twenty-one American republics was, in itself, striking proof of the steady development of inter-American solidarity. Pocketing it, Mr. Hull stepped up the gangplank of his homeward-bound ship, with (officially) an enormous number of low bows and high compliments to all his Latin American colleagues, and (unofficially) a shake of the fist, accompanied by a couple of sizzling Tennessean oaths, in the general geographical direction of Argentina.

After his return to Washington, the Export-Import Bank, Santa Claus of Good Neighborliness for whom the Good Neighbor Policy is summed up in the words "Say it With Dollars," again stepped in. In the first half of 1939, pursuant to instructions from the State Department, *it pressed bags of dollars in the form of credits, on Brazil, Nicaragua and Paraguay.*

The procedure, in each case, was charming in its simplicity:

One after the other, Senhor Oswaldo Aranha, Foreign Minister of Brazil, General Anastasio Somoza, dictator of Nicaragua, and General José Félix Estigarribia, President-elect of Paraguay, arrived in Washington, made a deep Latin bow in front of President Roosevelt and Secretary Hull, and did a stately dance, so to speak, chanting things like "Renewing my expressions of appreciation of your government, believe me your sincere friend" and "I avail myself of this opportunity to renew to Your Excellency the expression of my personal gratitude." To these, President Roosevelt and Secretary Hull, without an instant's hesitation, replied, "I extend, Excellency, the assurances of my highest and most distinguished consideration," etc., etc. And each time, after the exchange of a few such beautiful inter-American bouquets, the President of the Export-Import Bank stepped forward, did a nice solo pirouette, and whispered in the ear of each of the visitors from the south something to this effect:

"The money for you is at the bank. Please come around and fetch it away."

Similar polite international get-together ballet steps, recalling, in their courtly formality, the measures of old-fashioned minuets, are scheduled, for the near future, between Mr. Roosevelt, Mr. Hull and President Pierson of the Export-Import Bank, on the one side, and on the other, picked governmental dancers from Cuba, Chile and Ecuador.

As a further feather in the cap of the Good Neighbor Policy, a *trade agreement with Ecuador*, tenth in the series of such agreements, was concluded last May.

Still another item was added to the lengthening list of achievements of the Good Neighborites by the putting into effect of an official authorization—passed, after amendments, by Congress, in May, 1938—enabling the United States Government to lend to the governments of other American republics, at their request, the *services of technical experts* and other employees possessing special qualifications. As a consequence of this authorization, American experts in highway engineering, immigration procedure, agriculture, library administration, etc., have been dispatched to a number of countries in Latin America.

Furthermore, our government has been busy sending military and naval missions southward. In 1933, only one such was in existence, our naval mission to Brazil. Now, American military missions are stationed in Argentina, Brazil, Colombia and Haiti, and naval missions in Argentina, Brazil, Colombia and Peru. In addition, officers of the United States army have been detailed as military instructors to Nicaragua and Guatemala.

Finally, *United States Military and Naval schools have been opened to students from Latin American countries.* Already, a number of youths have availed themselves of the opportunity to attend these schools, particularly from Argentina, Chile, Colombia, Ecuador, Mexico, Peru and Venezuela.

And that completes, up to the present writing, the record of achievements of Messrs. Roosevelt, Hull, Welles & Co., exporters of inter-American Good Neighborliness. *Twenty-eight—count 'em—twenty-eight.*

As early as the days of the Buenos Aires Conference back in 1936, Sumner Welles was already so enthusiastic about Washington's new official orientation that he put himself on record as believing that "it marked the end of an old chapter in inter-American relations and signalized the beginning of a new effort in the Western Hemisphere." Since saying that he has been making speeches all over the United States, zealously chronicling each successive act of the Good Neighbor Policy and seeking to drive home to his fellow-countrymen its immense significance both as an instrument of inter-American good will and as a source of effective protection for every one of the republics of this hemisphere against potential aggression from overseas.

These speeches constitute a veritable history, step by step, of the Good Neighbor Policy. Mr. Welles, diplomat and propagandist, suave advocate and hard fighter, has been closer

to it, during the six years of its official existence, than anybody, except Cordell Hull. And he has been even more articulate than Mr. Hull in telling all about it.

Here, in much-condensed form, but in his own words, is
the Welles-Description-and-Defense-of-the-Good-Neighbor-
Policy, as dinned by him, up and down the length and breadth
of the land, into the ears of clubs, societies, associations, ban-
quet committees and Chambers of Commerce, from the time
when Good Neighborism was a baby up to the proud conclusion, the other day, of its twenty-eighth achievement:

> "During the decades immediately following upon the
> declaration of their own independence by the majority of
> the American Republics, their struggle to maintain that in-
> dependence, and their endeavor to construct that system
> of democratic and representative government which the
> people of the United States had themselves established were
> viewed *with a genuine and friendly sympathy* by our own
> government and people and not infrequently voiced by
> outstanding American statesmen of that period.
>
> "Thereafter, the United States undertook a policy of
> *aggressive territorial expansion* which may perhaps be said
> to have reached its most extreme form in the War with
> Mexico and to have ended a few years subsequent to the
> War with Spain. It was during that period that there were
> sown seeds of the abiding belief on the part of the peoples
> of Latin America that the United States was dominated by
> imperialistic ambitions.
>
> "With the turn of the century there began to be mani-
> fested what might be termed a *missionary spirit* on the part
> of our own people. Certain of the republics of the Carib-
> bean and of Central America appeared to offer a fertile
> field for the manifestation of this evangelistic spirit. Public
> opinion here seemed to believe that, because we ourselves

had attained a notable degree of advancement in the art of government, our own standards should prove desirable if laid down for the peoples of those adjacent countries, notwithstanding the fact that those standards might be neither adapted to, nor desired by the peoples of those independent nations. Treaty relationships into which we entered, during those early years of the twentieth century, with Cuba, Haiti and the Dominican Republic, and the armed interventions undertaken by the United States in certain of the Caribbean and Central American Republics during that same period, have their origin, I am convinced, in this root cause. That pressure from commercial and financial interests within the United States played its part in the formulation of this policy of domination cannot be denied. The policy so undertaken was, of course, likewise predicated upon the belief that, were the United States itself to refrain from undertaking this type of self-imposed assistance to these weaker nations, when domestic turmoil occurred, some non-American power would intervene, in direct violation of the fundamental principles of the policy of self-preservation of the United States.

"And yet, as one looks back today, what have we as a people gained by that particular manifestation of policy? *I know of no act of intervention undertaken by the United States which has accrued to the benefit of the American people.* We reaped only hostility, suspicion and ill will, and in similar degree, I am unable to find that the people of those countries where such intervention took place gained any benefit other than the temporary advantage which the road construction or the sanitation imposed upon them brought them, for it has been demonstrated by this experience that domestic peace and the utilization of the orderly processes of democratic self-government cannot be imposed from without by an alien people.

[317]

"Finally, it has been brought home to us, during these same years of the twentieth century, in unmistakable terms, that if the people of the United States desire to avail themselves of the continental market for the benefit of their own export trade, or if they desire to reclaim the good will of their southern neighbors, *they will render these objectives impossible of attainment if they persist in their determination to build a tariff wall about the United States*, so high as to make it impossible for the other American republics to sell to the people of the United States.

"It was more than clear in 1933 that, if real progress was to be made in placing inter-American relationships upon that solid foundation of mutual trust, friendship, and understanding which I think today every American citizen believes to be to his own advantage, *the initiative must be undertaken by the United States*. For many years past, in inter-American conferences, the United States delegation found itself suspected by its colleagues of ulterior motives and regarded with open hostility. At Buenos Aires, it found itself an equal among equals and a friend in a gathering of friends.

"The new period before us offers the American democracies, if they stand together, an opportunity unrivaled in its potentialities. I am well aware that certain sensational writers in our own country have claimed that democracy, as we understand it, is held in poor esteem in some of the other American republics. And not infrequently I have also noted an apparent insistence on the part of such writers that the United States ought to do something about it. It is a strange thing that a certain type of professional liberal is always very liberal except in so far as his own point of view is concerned. If there is one thing above all others that the government of the United States today stands for, in its relationship with the other republics of this hemisphere, it is its *utter unwillingness to interfere, directly or indirectly, in the domestic concerns of those nations.* And of one other thing I am equally convinced, and that is, that no matter what certain passing manifestations may indicate, the life of every one of the republics of the Americas is instinct with the spirit of democracy."

Implementation of the Good Neighbor Policy has not been plain sailing. Far from it.

Opponents have rushed at it from all directions. It has made large numbers of people, of all shades of political opinion, sit up and roar with rage. Senator Borah has wrathfully warned its sponsors that they must stop their open-handed spending of good American dollars on possibly bad Latin American objectives. American bondholders with huge sums of money imbedded, apparently beyond hope of recovery, in Latin American investments, continually send clamorous messages to Washington, the gist of which is: "Talk a little less, please, about Good Neighbor messages *to* Latin Americans, and little more, please, about interest payments *from* Latin Americans!"

And the Mexican Government takes oil from Americans and hands it to Germans. And the government of Bolivia hints broadly that it prefers Adolf Hitler to Franklin Roosevelt. And the government of Chile, sitting in profound thought, like that glum statue by Rodin, asks itself: "Shall I go Good Neighbor? Or shall I go Mexican?" And Argentina gives Uncle Sam another dirty look.

But the Good Neighborites, having doggedly negotiated each successive lap so far on their chosen road, refuse to quit in a huff. Far from considering the above-enumerated twenty-eight milestones of the Good Neighbor Policy a sufficient excuse for calling it a day, they are girding themselves for further stunts of the same sort—though Argentines bark and Mexicans bite and bondholders bleat and Borahs bellow.

*   *   *

The old Monroe Doctrine that our fathers and grandfathers knew is dead. From its ashes a new one must arise, built on an entirely different foundation.

Formerly the Monroe Doctrine meant, justly or unjustly, to a large percentage of the people in Latin America, a sort of protectorate of the United States over the rest of the continent.

Actions on our part, like those in Haiti and Nicaragua, caused deep uneasiness throughout Latin America. They strengthened the influence of a school of writers there who never tired of denouncing the predatory aims of the "Colossus of the North," and always saw in our occasional punitive measures against certain neighbors evidence of sinister plans of general domination.

This atmosphere of suspicion has been largely dispelled. The new Monroe Doctrine, already dimly outlined on the international horizon, must be not a protectorate of the United States, but a fifty-fifty partnership between Latin America and the United States.

The people of the Latin American lands are well pleased at the thought that we are willing to come to their aid in case their sovereignty should be threatened by some aggressive European nation; *but they do not want domination by us as the price of our willingness to help them.* Theodore Roosevelt, they like to point out, used to talk about speaking softly and carrying a big stick; it behooves Franklin Roosevelt to speak softly and not carry one. That is the essence of a genuine Good Neighbor Policy, as many intelligent Latin Americans see it—and they do not hesitate to tell North Americans so!

If we resolutely make up our minds, as a nation, to drive forward such a policy to complete success, allowing for the differences between Latin America's twenty component nations and tactfully heeding their individual idiosyncrasies and prejudices, anti-Americanism, in its old virulence, will be doomed to extinction among our southern neighbors. Though some die-hards there will undoubtedly continue to indulge at intervals in outbursts against the "Imperialism" of the United States, and impute to us all sorts of dastardly motives, the fact remains that genuine anti-Americanism will not be able to stand up against genuine Good Neighborliness.

If this administration at Washington, and its successors, do a really good job of spade work, I feel sure that in years to come American visitors to Latin America will feel (as I felt a few months ago in a dozen of the Latin American republics) that sporadic warnings against the "Yankee Peril," and impassioned exhortations to Latin Americans to combat and overcome it, belong to a dying era; that they represent a futile attempt to resuscitate, in its full pristine strength, something which belongs irrevocably to dead yesterdays of misunderstanding.